WAR WITHOUT END
PEACE WITHOUT HOPE

Thirty Years of the Arab-Israeli Conflict

DAVID DOWNING AND GARY HERMAN

NEW ENGLISH LIBRARY
TIMES MIRROR

Printed in Great Britain by Thomson Litho Ltd, East Kilbride,
Scotland
Bound by Hunter & Foulis Ltd, Edinburgh

4500 37681

WAR WITHOUT END
PEACE WITHOUT HOPE

By the same authors

THE DEVIL'S VIRTUOSOS (David Downing)
WOMEN IN CHINA (translated by Gary Herman with Michèle
   Cohen).

CONTENTS

MAPS

This book is dedicated to peace

to the kind of society
in which peace is more than just a dream, and

to the men and women
who will bring that society about.

Men make their own history, but they do not make it just as they please; they do not make it under circumstances chosen by themselves, but under circumstances directly encountered, given and transmitted from the past. The tradition of all the dead generations weighs like a nightmare on the brain of the living.

> (Karl Marx, *The Eighteenth Brumaire of Louis Bonaparte.*)

Young,
Zion was my banner
as the green flag flies
over Arabia.

Older now, I have travelled.
Jerusalem too is a city
and King David, if he lives,
hides in the twisted stone streets
and the Shulamite has grown tired
with the years.

> (Steve Smith, *God's Kaleidoscope*)

ACKNOWLEDGEMENTS

'Death by Water' from *The Waste Land* by T. S. Eliot is reprinted by kind permission of Faber & Faber Ltd and Harcourt Brace Jovanovich Inc. The extract from *The Non-Jewish Jew* by Isaac Deutscher (© Oxford University Press, 1968) is reprinted by kind permission of the Oxford University Press. The extract from *The Politics of Experience* by R. D. Laing (© R. D. Laing, 1967) is reprinted by kind permission of Penguin Books Ltd. The authors acknowledge the Estate of William Plomer for their permission to reprint an extract from 'Father and Son: 1939'.

The photographs in this book are reproduced by permission of the following: Camera Press; Popperfoto; Valerie Wilmer; the Israeli Government; the Egyptian Government; and the Jordanian Government.

The maps were researched by David Downing and drawn by Tom Carter.

The authors would like, finally, to thank their friends Michèle Cohen, Ian Hoare and Janet Scott for their encouragement and help.

Note on Place Names

Where there is no commonly accepted spelling of Arabic and Hebrew names, the authors have consulted *The Times Atlas of the World* (Times Books Ltd) and *The Political Dictionary of the Middle East* (Weidenfeld and Nicolson) for English transliterations of place names and personal names.

Prelude

TWO TOWNS BETWEEN
THE JORDAN AND THE SEA

I

The town of Jericho lies in the Jordan valley a few miles to the east of the thrice Holy City of Jerusalem. On its western flank green hills ascend to Israel's central plateau. In the opposite direction the land sweeps down the surface of the Dead Sea, some 1,300 feet below sea-level. The Dead Sea is a bitter lake, bereft of fauna, surrounded by silence, heat and dry dust. Standing on the ridge of a small hill you observe a barren lunar landscape of salt flats, sand-dunes and tracts of grey dirt. Occasionally the immobile and inhospitable scenery is enlivened by a patch of watered earth and, as you approach Jericho itself, greyness gives way first to brown and then, in a bold reminder of the miracle of life, to a patchwork of brilliant green and gold. Out of the desert the Jordan waters have created a garden.

It is possible that this township of some ten thousand souls was the site of the lost Garden of Eden. Certainly, there on the western wing of the Fertile Crescent – stretching from the Persian Gulf up the Tigris–Euphrates valley and down the Mediterranean's east coast – were to be found the earliest known agricultural settlements in the world. Jericho itself is probably the world's oldest continuously populated town. Archaeological evidence places a grain-growing community there some 8,000 years ago, and some experts argue that the area may have been settled at the very dawn of civilisation 4,000 years before that.

Through the ages the men and women of Jericho have worked and played, suffered and celebrated, buried their dead and raised their children. They have seen kingdoms and empires come and go, they have worshipped the river and the

sun and they have bowed down before the gods of the mighty
and the mightier. They have been governed by the officers and
ideas of the Canaanites, the Babylonians, the Egyptians, the
Syrians, the Israelites, the Judaeans, the Assyrians, the Per-
sians, the Macedonians, the Seleucids, the Arabs, the Mame-
lukes, the Turks and the British. The great warrior Tamurlane
tried to seize the area, as did Napoleon. Jericho belongs to
all of them, which is to say it belongs to none of them but to
the struggling mass of humanity – pagan, Jewish, Muslim or
Christian – who have kept it alive with the sweat of their brows
and the fruits of their labour.

Today Jericho is inhabited by Arabs. They are called
Palestinians, as were their ancestors, 2,000 years ago. But
Palestine itself is a *non*-entity, an eternal province. It is a word
in the passive mood – to be a Palestinian is to be governed, but
never to govern. The Israelis are the rulers now, having seized
Jericho from the Jordanians who seized it from the British.
And it is a salutary reminder of the frailty of empire to walk
through Jericho's streets and see the uncovered earthworks
layered one above the other – a tangible record of the measures
taken by ancient rulers to secure the town they thought was
theirs by right, against invaders who laid claim to equal right.
One layer might be the fabled wall of Jericho which the Bible
tells us was encircled and destroyed by Joshua and his band of
fighting, monotheistic nomads seeking a land to occupy and
govern. But there are other layers, above and below.

Some will seek to justify a formal Israeli annexation of
Jericho by summoning up the spirit of Joshua. They will in-
voke the Old Testament and the record of the ancient Jewish
empire of King David and King Solomon. Zionist thinkers and
strategists have done that for close on a century. They have
argued, quite rightly, that the Jewish religion, its holy books
and rituals, have given the Jews a special identity – no small
part of which is a cherished association with a narrow strip of
land bordering the Eastern Mediterranean. But an association
is not a right, and the Jewish identity does not make Jews a
nation.

The Bible gave the Jews who built modern Israel a unique
sense of continuity with a glorious past, and it gave them a
dream for the future. But the sense of continuity did not itself
confer a right to the realisation of the dream. The Bible is no

title-deed. Like Joshua's people before them, the Zionists had to win their right by conquest over the land and its native population. They came as Jews with a sense of nationhood; they stayed as Israelis with the reality of a nation. But the Promised Land had to be conquered, regardless of the promise.

Israel is but the latest in a long procession of kingdoms, empires and republics that have governed that narrow strip of land. Each one has come to rule by force and has remained as ruler by the threat or exercise of force. This is the Bible's message and the heritage of the ages: that nations are forged in struggle, that governments rule not by god-given authority but by the right of superior force. History records the struggles and the vast parade of rulers and ruled. It is the story of a million Jerichos. And while it is clear that conquest has always been its own ultimate justification, creating the right to govern, it should be just as clear that past victory has never been any guarantee of the future security of governments or rulers. For none rule but by their ability to wield more powerful arms or command greater armies. And the parade goes on.

II

Lydda lies on the eastern edge of the Palestine coastal plain, some fifteen miles south-east of Tel Aviv. Behind the town the hills rise towards the mountain ridge that forms the backbone of Judaea and Samaria, and high on that ridge, further to the south-east, stands the sacred city of Jerusalem.

When the United Nations decreed the partitioning of Palestine in November 1947, Lydda fell within the area allotted to the new Arab state. But the Arabs of Palestine, believing that one does not gratefully accept less than half of one's own land, rejected Partition. Through late 1947 and early 1948, as the British slowly washed their hands of the land and the responsibility, both Jews and Arabs, caught in a spiralling mutual hostility, sought to impose their political and military authority on mutually irreconcilable portions of the Mandate territory.

Lydda was an Arab town then, but to the Jews, fighting as they thought for the interrelated goals of statehood and survival, the racial composition of the town's population mattered little when measured against the military significance of its position. Arab forces in Lydda could control the Tel Aviv–Jerusalem road; only a ten-mile march would bring them to the sea, thus cutting Israel in half. Against such facts the views of those who lived in the dwellings of Lydda were of small importance. For them, as for so many others in the years to come, the decisions would be taken elsewhere. In Tel Aviv or Amman, in Washington, Cairo, Moscow or Damascus.

On the morning of 10 July 1948 the fate of Lydda was decided on a hill a mile or so to the east. There Moshe Kelman, commander of the 3rd Battalion of the Yifthach Brigade, was considering the possibility of capturing the town. The Jordanian Arab Legion was conspicuous by its absence, and so Kelman decided to take the risk. Some hours later, after a few small but bitter struggles, the town was in Israeli hands. The Arab inhabitants were informed that they could stay, as long as they acted peacefully.

‘ The following day one tank and two armoured cars of the Arab Legion rolled hopefully into the town on a reconnaissance mission. Their intention was to determine the local Israeli strength. They did so, and beat a hasty retreat.

The Arab townsfolk, aware of the Legion's arrival but not of its subsequent departure, assumed the town's relief to be imminent. Many took to the streets, killing Israeli soldiers and gleefully mutilating the bodies. The joy was short-lived. Belatedly realising its mistake, most of the mob sought sanctuary in the large and fortified Dahmash mosque. The Israelis pierced the thick walls with a Piat rocket and stormed in to engage the defenders. There was no need. The rocket had already reduced the interior to an Arabesque of blood-soaked Persian carpets and segments of human flesh. The town was brought back under Israeli control. And the inhabitants? ‘The inhabitants must leave for Transjordan within three hours,’ an officer informed the local notables. That afternoon the town's Arab population began the twenty-mile walk to Ramallah and permanent exile.

Lydda was only one town, but its fate was not uncommon. Like most of the tragedies engendered by the Arab–Israeli conflict it rested on an eminently rational series of premises. It is hard to see how any of the various parties involved could have acted otherwise. If Israel was a fact, and if the Arabs refused to accept it as a fact, then an Arab Lydda was a threat to

Israel. An Israeli Lydda, or Lod as it is now named, presupposed the tragedy of exile for the town's Arab inhabitants, a microcosm of the tragedy that has now festered for three decades in the Palestinian refugee camps.

In those camps today, in 1978, the descendants of those who took the long walk to Ramallah still talk of Israel's destruction, still dream of returning to a land most know only from the stories of the old. While the Israeli inhabitants of the prosperous township of Lod periodically vote, in overwhelming majorities, for national governments who talk of little but the struggle for Israel's security. So the vicious circle goes round, through wars without apparent end, through stretches of peace that merely mock the name.

PART ONE

Chapter 1

NEXT YEAR IN JERUSALEM

The War of the Palestine Partition,
November 1947 – March 1949

In enclosed ground resourcefulness is required. (Sun Tzu)

I am certain that the world will judge the Jewish state by
what it shall do with the Arabs. (Chaim Weizmann)

I

On the evening of 29 November 1947 the United Nations
General Assembly voted to partition the British mandate territory of Palestine. This ruling, and the creation of Jewish and
Arab states that it invoked, opened the floodgates on both a
dream and a nightmare. The Palestinian Jews, whether Zionist
pioneers or orphans of the Holocaust, saw the long wait for
the security of statehood finally rewarded. The Palestinian
Arabs, who for fifty years had watched the growth of this
alien presence on land they believed their own, saw the proposed Jewish state as a realisation of their deepest fears. A
half-century of sporadic violence was about to erupt into open
war.

The two communities may have been equally willing to
wage war; they were not equally prepared. The Arab hostility
of the previous decades had impelled the Jewish community to
organise itself for defence. The Haganah, born in the shadow
of the 1920 riots, came of age in the later, more serious outbreaks of 1929 and 1936. And as the years passed, its primarily
defensive orientation was subtly transformed by the nature
of the tasks it was called upon to perform. Defence against
guerrilla attacks is best served by counter-attack, and this the
Haganah learnt in the mobile units organised by the Russian
immigrant Yitzhak Sadeh and the fervently pro-Zionist British

officer Orde Wingate. The British government decision in 1939 to adopt a pro-Arab stance, though forcing the Haganah back underground, naturally accelerated the development of a Jewish military force. New part-time mobile units – the Hish – were formed, and the Haganah, acquiring a central command and formal structure, began to resemble an army in embryo.

During World War II British–Jewish differences were temporarily shelved, and some 27,000 Jews served in the Allied armies. In the process they learnt rudimentary tactics and the handling of modern weapons. A new full-time mobile force – the Palmach – was set up in 1941; it fought, as a unit, in the Syrian and Lebanese campaigns of that year, and received British training and weaponry in exchange for an undertaking to resist any future German occupation of Palestine. But Rommel never arrived and, the war over, Haganah activity was once more directed against Briton and Arab. The occupying power, prodded by a terror campaign conducted by the Irgun and Lehi Jewish splinter-groups, would eventually depart. But the Arabs had nowhere else to go. They would have to be defeated on the field of battle.

The Jewish forces were now strong enough to achieve as much. As civil war loomed the Haganah numbered some 43,000, of which 32,000 were in static local-defence units, 8,000 in the mobile part-time Hish, and just over 3,000 in the mobile full-time élite force of the Palmach. Weapons were still scarce: the Haganah had only 18,000 rifles by the end of 1947, less than a thousand machine-guns, and no artillery, tanks, anti-tank weapons or aircraft. But its fighters were better-trained, it had a centralised command and, most important, it represented a united community intent on survival.

The Palestinian Arabs were in poorer military shape. For decades they had been attacked by land-purchase orders, not by Jewish fighters; there had been no incentive to organise militarily. While the Haganah slowly gathered strength the Palestinian Arabs fretted at the constraints imposed by the British presence. Once independence was eventually granted, they believed, there would be no more Jewish immigration, no more exploitation of Arabs by the alien Jews. Accordingly, few Arabs thought it worthwhile to gain military experience in World War II; many of the leaders, Palestinian or otherwise,

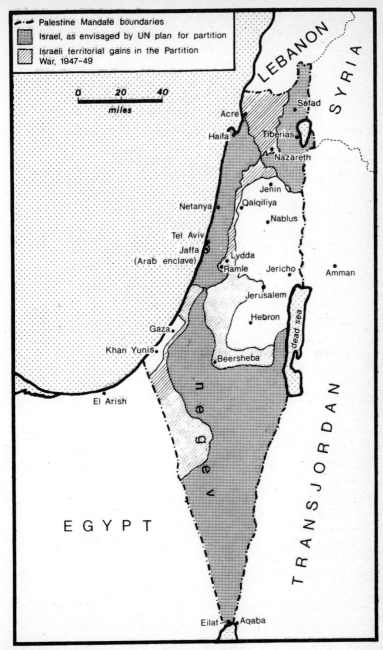

Palestine Mandate boundaries
Israel, as envisaged by UN plan for partition
Israeli territorial gains in the Partition
War, 1947–49

0   20   40
miles

LEBANON

SYRIA

Acre
Safad
Haifa
Tiberias
Nazareth

Jenin
Netanya
Qalqiliya
Nablus

Tel Aviv
Jaffa
(Arab enclave)
Lydda
Ramle
Jericho
Amman

Jerusalem
Hebron
dead sea

Gaza
Khan Yunis
Beersheba

El Arish

N e g e v

EGYPT

T R A N S J O R D A N

Eilat   Aqaba

1. The partitioning of Palestine

preferred to play politics with the Third Reich. After the war they watched the Jews fight the British with seeming indifference. It mattered little who won. A British victory would presumably be followed by implementation of the pro-Arab 1939 White Paper; a British exodus would leave the local Arabs, with help if need be from neighbouring Arab states, to solve the Jewish problem in their own sweet time. Rather than preparing to fight for their land, the Arabs patiently awaited a formal presentation ceremony. By the time it became apparent that they were to be presented with less than half of Palestine, it was too late in the day to organise a battle for the rest.

For some months this tardiness would not be apparent to the confident Arabs. Indeed, as the pre-partition plethora of local incidents coalesced into civil war, the advantages seemed to lie all with them. They had easy access to arms in the neighbouring Arab states, their geographical position was by far the stronger. The main areas of Jewish settlement, as shown in exaggerated form by the proposed new borders, were the coastal strip, eastern Galilee, the northern Negev, and Jerusalem.* These four areas formed large enclaves in Arab territory and were linked, naturally, by roads running through Arab territory. The optimal Arab strategy seemed self-evident. They would hold their own ground on the heights dominating these major roads and, by blocking the flow of Jewish supplies along them, force the enclaves' collapse through lack of water, food and weaponry. So, less than a week after the announcement of partition, the first Jewish supply train was attacked on the Tel Aviv–Jerusalem road. A week later similar attacks took place on the Jerusalem–Hebron road.

The Jewish response – the organisation of supply convoys – was less than successful. The roads wound through terrain ideal for ambushes; the convoys could only be defended as well as the severely limited number of weapons available allowed. Soon supplies were becoming scarce in Jerusalem and some of the outlying settlements.

Further cause for Arab satisfaction lay in the newly-formed

* The first three of these areas were allotted to the Jewish state; Jerusalem, with seventeen per cent of the Jewish population of Palestine, was to be under international control. But the Arab rejection of partition, so the Jews reasoned, implied that the fate of Jerusalem would also be decided on the field of battle.

Arab Liberation Army (A.L.A.), led by Fawzi el Qawuqji and financed by the Arab League, which in January 1948 began infiltrating into Palestine via Transjordan. It consisted of between four and five thousand irregulars – both Palestinians and volunteers from Syria, Iraq, Egypt (mostly members of the Muslim Brotherhood) and Lebanon – and was to operate in four main areas. Two forces, each around 800 strong, would be based in and south of Jaffa on the coastal plain. The two main groups, under Qawuqji himself and Abdul Kader Husseini, would operate in southern Galilee and the environs of Jerusalem respectively. And by early February these two latter groups were beginning to make their presence felt. Husseini's forces were strengthening the existing Arab grip on the Tel Aviv–Jerusalem road, and Qawuqji was preparing to take the offensive in the Beisan valley.

On 16 February Qawuqji attacked the Tirat Zevi settlement. He lost forty men for the death of a solitary Jew, before a belated British intervention enabled him to withdraw without too great a loss of face. But this first intimation of disaster did not reverberate through the Palestinian Arab community. While the morale of the better-informed Jews crept upwards, the Arab population celebrated Qawuqji's outrageous claim that three hundred Jews had been killed.

As the A.L.A. entered upon its short and erratic career, the British were slowly evacuating Palestine, town by town and region by region. Both Jews and Arabs sought to seize the military strongpoints they left behind, and here the Arabs often gained the advantage. Young British officers, imbued with the romantic legacy of Lawrence and embittered by Jewish terrorist activities, often let slip the 'secret' evacuation dates to local Arab leaders.

But this in the end proved a superficial blessing, for the manner of the evacuation as a whole favoured the Jews. It was not a departure marked by elegance. Power was not transferred, merely abandoned. The British simply jerked out the administrative plug, leaving no manuals behind them for those unversed in the ways of administrative electricity. For the Jews, who were already in most ways a competently self-governing community, this posed few problems. They merely extended their organisational apparatus into new areas. For the Arabs, who had no apparatus to speak of, it meant chaos. The lights, and the telephones, were going out all over Arab Palestine.

In the purely military sphere the story was similar. The Arabs were failing to keep pace with the growing Jewish military power. In February 1948 the Jewish community was fully mobilised; six Hish and three Palmach brigades, totalling some 30,000 men, were put into the field. At the same time the Jews were conducting a global search for second-hand weaponry, and Golda Meir was touring the United States and raising $25 million with which to pay for them. Such organisational thoroughness was not to be found on the Arab side. Both the local irregulars and the ill-coordinated A.L.A. functioned more on the lines of politicised banditry.

Still, during February 1948 the illusion of a well-matched contest lingered fatefully on. The Jewish convoys were failing to maintain an adequate level of supplies in the beleaguered enclaves. Only in early March, bolstered by new deliveries of smuggled weapons, did the Jewish High Command resolve to overcome these problems through an all-out offensive. Those areas allotted to the Jewish state by partition – and those containing substantial Jewish settlement – were to be seized and held in a series of brigade-strength operations. Israel had not yet been born, and already it was expanding.

There was no real choice. Arab rejection of partition had forced the Jews to fight for it. In the process the prospective borders, drawn on communal rather than military grounds, had lost all credibility. For the Jews to secure their allotted state, against Arab opposition, it became necessary to seize areas allotted to the Arabs. Hence the April offensive – Plan D – had as its objectives the securing of the heights overlooking the Tel Aviv–Jerusalem road, the seizure of a wide corridor between Galilee and the coastal plain, and the subjugation of the 'mixed' cities of Haifa, Tel Aviv, Jaffa, Tiberias and Safad.

All of this was to be accomplished by 15 May: day of the British exit and, most probably, of the Arab states' entrance. Most of it was. In the north Qawuqji, perhaps with the intention of severing the narrow Jewish-held corridor linking Galilee to the coastal strip, launched a week-long attack on the Mishmar Haemek settlement. His final, humiliating defeat on 13 April left the Jews free, for the rest of April and early May, to concentrate on clearing eastern Galilee of all hostile forces. In the process the mixed cities of Tiberias and Safad passed safely into their hands.

In the crucial Tel Aviv–Jerusalem corridor success was harder to come by. Operation *Nachshon* – the attempt to seize the dominating heights – commenced on 3 April with an attack on Kastel. The Jewish forces scrambled their way up the slopes to take the hill, but were swiftly dislodged by a counter-attack led by Husseini. On the 8th the story was the same, but on the 9th the Jews took the position and held it. Of more lasting importance to the Arab cause, Husseini was killed in the abortive counter-attack.

On the same day detachments of the Irgun and Lehi terrorist groups attacked the hitherto friendly Arab village of Deir Yassin some three miles away. Incompetence bred panic, panic bred bloodlust, and 250 of the inhabitants were slaughtered. Arab guerrilla leaders, wanting a free hand in the contested zones, had already advised the local populations to abandon their villages temporarily. Few had done so up until now. The massacre at Deir Yassin may not have set the Arab exodus from Palestine in motion, but it did turn it from a matter of tens to a matter of thousands almost overnight.

Meanwhile the Haganah, still absorbed in military pursuits, had succeeded in capturing most of the heights overlooking the road, and two supply convoys were able to reach Jerusalem before the Arabs re-closed the route on 17 April. In Jerusalem itself the Jewish position remained precarious. The food and water situation was rarely less than critical, the Old City was surrounded by Arab forces. The Haganah commander in the city, David Shaltiel, wished to evacuate the Jewish settlements on the Ramallah and Hebron roads, but was forbidden to do so by the High Command. Rather he was to keep both supplied, to keep Jerusalem itself supplied, to relieve the Old City, and to relieve the Jewish enclave on Mount Scopus a mile or so to the north-west. His difficulties were increased by both the paucity of Haganah troops at his command and the relative magnitude of the Irgun and Lehi detachments operating 'alongside'. Only in Jerusalem did the Jews match the Arabs' skill in dividing their own ranks. Predictably enough, neither side enjoyed much success. Incident followed incident – the worst of which was the slaughter of a Jewish convoy in Sheikh

Jarrah in retaliation for Deir Yassin – but the lines on the ground barely shifted.

In the other major cities it was a different story. In the last three weeks of the British mandate, as Tiberias and Safad fell in the north, Haifa and Jaffa fell on the coast. The Jews now had a firm grip on both eastern Galilee and the Mediterranean littoral. Only in the interior did Arab prospects look less than tarnished. The Tel Aviv–Jerusalem road was closed once again, and the Jewish hold on their future capital seemed far from secure. South of the city the Etzioni settlements, which had heroically but unwisely provoked the Transjordanian Arab Legion by attacking its arms convoys, were finally overrun on 13 May. The following morning the last British High Commissioner drove sedately out of Jerusalem. The mandate was at an end. That evening the strident, passionate voice of David Ben-Gurion announced the birth of the Jewish state of Israel. 'We offer only peace and friendship to all neighbouring states and people,' he said. The war entered a new phase.

II

On 15 May 1948 five Arab armies entered Palestine intent on the new state's swift demise. The official, and popular, motive was the protection of the rights of the Palestinian Arabs, but it was far from the only one. Most Arabs were certainly indignant at what they saw as the U.N.'s legitimising of a new colonialism; some noted that the nebulous cause of pan-Arabism would not be strengthened by an Israeli occupation of the Negev that effectively cut the Arab world in half. But in 1948 such sentiments only counted for anything if they happened to coincide with the interests of the ruling dynasties.

King Farouk of Egypt liked to keep his army at home, where it could serve the valuable purpose of propping up his shaky throne, but as the moment of decision approached he realised that too many enemies could make too much capital out of Palestine for him to sit regally aside. His main political opponents within Egypt – the Muslim Brotherhood – were already involved, 'heroically', in the fighting; his main adversaries in the Arab world – the Hashemite kings of Jordan and Iraq – were likely to intervene. Farouk decided to risk sending his army across Sinai. After all, in Palestine it could amuse itself using up those defective arms bought on the international black market at such a satisfying profit to the régime.

Farouk was not the only Arab ruler talking about Palestinians and thinking about fellow-rulers. Transjordan's King Abdullah and the ruling régime in Syria were as much concerned to deny each other Palestine as they were to squash Israel. Iraq tended to support Jordan, as both were allied to Britain and ruled by Hashemites; Syria tended to side with Egypt. Abdullah was relatively willing to accept partition as long as he got the Arab share, a point of view confided to Golda Meir in a secret meeting the previous November. It was not shared by the titular leader of the Palestinian Arabs – the Mufti of Jerusalem – who wanted to rule all of Palestine on his own. He looked to the Syrians for support, but they were more interested in Qawuqji, who they mistakenly believed would prove an effective military leader. The Mufti and Qawuqji had been intriguing against each other for over a decade.

This farrago of inter-Arab suspicion and hostility would, not for the last time, fatally prejudice any slim hope the Arabs had of achieving an apparently shared objective. The appointment of King Abdullah as nominal commander-in-chief of the Arab invasion forces was both ironic and superfluous. Ironic because Abdullah was the Arab leader least interested in a war with Israel, superfluous because none of the Arab leaders had the slightest intention of accepting any orders he foolishly chose to issue. With no common plan of campaign each army charged, rather slowly, into Palestine.

In the far north they might as well not have bothered. The Lebanese Army demonstrated its Arab solidarity with a token foray, and promptly stopped. The Syrians launched a two-pronged attack, one force crossing the Jordan to seize Mishmar Hayarden, the other attacking south of the Sea of Galilee. The first contentedly sat on its gain, the second was swiftly halted. The Iraqis marched into Samaria and occupied the 'Triangle' – the stretch of land between Tulkarm, Jenin and Nablus. Having done so they adopted a defensive stance, merely repulsing an ill-conceived Israeli attack on Jenin.

The Arab Legion, the most respected of the Arab forces, still trained and led by British officers, concentrated on staking out

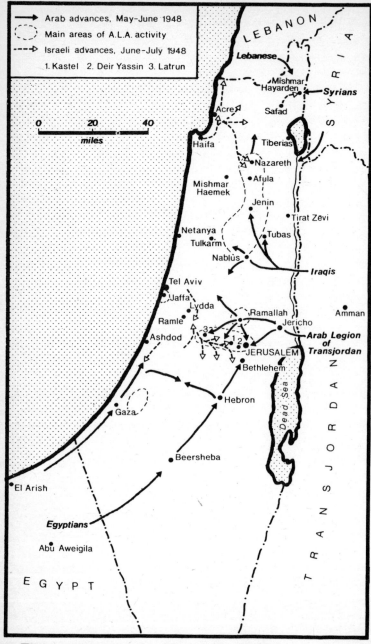

2. The partition war, May–July 1948

Abdullah's claim to the region bounded by Hebron, Latrun and Ramallah, including Jerusalem. In the Holy City itself the Legion quickly reversed an Israeli success in linking up Mount Scopus with the New City, and the position stabilised. The Tel Aviv–Jerusalem road remained closed, with both sides controlling significant stretches. Three Israeli attempts to take the Legion's Latrun stronghold astride the road were repulsed. In each attack the Haganah employed the unimaginative tactic of the frontal assault; an uncharacteristic lapse which cost Israel a high percentage of its casualties for the entire war.

In the south the Egyptian Army appeared to be making headway, as two major forces fought their way north-west, from Rafah up the coastal strip to Ashdod, and from El Auja through Beersheba and Hebron to Bethlehem. But unexpectedly stiff resistance from the Jewish settlements in their path slowed the Egyptian regulars, and at the beginning of June counter-attacks by the regular Israeli forces halted the two advances, the first twenty miles south of Tel Aviv, the second in the southern outskirts of Jerusalem.

In far-off New York the U.N. had spent most of May arguing the relative merits of an internationally imposed cease-fire. The Americans, afraid of an Arab victory, wanted one before Israel disappeared beneath the waves of communal hostility. The British, who wanted air-bases in the Negev, and thus at least a limited Israeli defeat – the Negev had been given to the Jewish state in the Partition plan – were reluctant to support a ceasefire until such time as the Arabs controlled the area in question. Only when the Egyptians seemed reasonably ensconced in the northern Negev did Britain support a cease-fire backed by sanctions.

This mistaken confidence in the durability of Egyptian control was both publicly shared by Britain's Arab allies and privately reinforced by the need for time to reorganise the badly dislocated invading armies. Abdullah's Arab Legion had taken most of the territory coveted by Transjordan, and now, critically short of ammunition – a situation partly caused by Egyptian seizure of a Transjordanian arms shipment – was confident of holding on to it only if no further offensive action was required. The Syrians, having hardly started, were admittedly reluctant to stop, but the Iraqis, complaining that they were operating on a 'vast front in different directions',[1] obviously needed time to consult a map. The Egyptians too were badly disorganised, their advances having compounded the logistical chaos that stretched back to Cairo. The Arabs agreed, magnanimously, to a month-long truce.

This suited the Israelis. Restrictions on the import of men and weapons had naturally been lifted in the wake of the British exit, and with every week the Israeli forces were growing stronger. On 15 May the number of Israelis in the field had approximately equalled that of the combined Arab forces, and now, as more Jews poured into Palestine, there was a growing disparity. The Arab régimes had already mobilised all those who could be spared from the more intimate tasks of preserving domestic stability. Of course the Israelis knew that sooner or later their enemy would have to be ejected from the Negev, from Galilee, from those positions that threatened the coastal plain. But time was on Israel's side, and a breathing space would be welcome. More weapons could be brought in, problems of coordination between the various brigades ironed out. The exhausted troops could be given a much needed rest.

The ceasefire came into operation on 11 June, and lasted for almost a month. It was terminated by the Arabs. Though their military leaders were hardly anxious to resume the war, their political superiors, having already announced enormous non-existent victories, felt obliged to justify their own propaganda. As a sop to the military it was conceded that the Arab armies should remain on the defensive. This ludicrous compromise was well summed up by Kurzman: 'The Arabs, of course, could not gain anything by such tactics, but with luck they would not lose anything either.' [2]

While the Arabs immersed themselves in such strategic debate the Israelis were preparing to resume the struggle with a series of offensives that would effectively win them the war. The moment the first Egyptian shots rang out in the south, these plans were put into operation. The Egyptians would be held; the Syrians and the A.L.A. in the north, and the Arab Legion in the centre, would be thrown back.

The most successful of these offensives was Operation *Dekel*. The objectives were the securing of the Vale of Zebulon and the capture of Nazareth; the opposition came from the irregulars of the A.L.A. After only a few days' fighting the objectives were attained, and western Galilee was firmly in

Israeli hands. In the far north the Syrians proved harder to shift, and Israeli attacks on Mishmar Hayarden were repulsed. But even this proved a blessing in disguise. It encouraged the British to oppose a ceasefire, thus granting the Israelis time to inflict a costly defeat on Britain's primary ally, Abdullah and his Arab Legion, in the crucial central region. Lydda and Ramle were seized by converging forces, and the Israelis exploited their success by pushing south and east, so widening the corridor connecting Jerusalem and the coast. Although another attack on Latrun failed and the main road remained closed, the alternative road constructed during the truce was now defended by a wide belt of territory. The Israeli forces in Jerusalem bungled an attack on the Old City and it remained in Arab Legion hands, but the New City was now securely held. The Israelis had claimed most of their allotted territory, and quite a bit more besides. Moreover, there seemed little chance of their being forced back by military means.

So, reasoned the ever-optimistic British, it was time for politics once more, and heavy pressure at the U.N. produced a second ceasefire on 17–18 July. This time it was clearly to the Arabs' advantage, but they did little to realise the potential benefits. The vague sense of solidarity apparent in May had now all but vanished, as each régime heaped blame on the others for the humiliating lack of success each had suffered. None really wished the war to continue, but none dared to be the first to accept peace. The Lebanese government actually went on record as agreeing to be the *second* government to make peace. The intrigues continued. Meeting in Amman in late August the Arab foreign ministers boosted each other's morale and enthusiastically decided to resume the war. Prudently they neglected to specify a date for the resumption. As September passed no moves were taken to set one.

Unfortunately for the Arabs, the Israelis were feeling decidedly less sanguine. One man, the Swedish diplomat Count Bernadotte, was threatening to pull the rug out from under their feet. He had been appointed by the U.N. to negotiate a Palestinian peace on the spot, but his supposed neutrality appeared to the Israelis to mask an indecent attention to British and Transjordanian interests. His revision of the original Partition plan had done nothing to allay such suspicions. Palestine and Transjordan together were to be carved into two states, loosely linked in a confederation. Jerusalem and the Negev were to go to the Arabs. As compensation the Jews were to receive western Galilee, most of which they had already taken.

The other Arab states did not think very much of Bernadotte's suggestions either, in that they countenanced a considerably enlarged Transjordan. But to the Israelis the new plan was more than an inconvenience; its implementation would deprive the new Jewish state of areas allotted it by the original partition, areas considered essential for survival and development. The Arab armies of course could never make the plan stick, but as long as they controlled the areas in question Israel remained vulnerable to international pressure. The U.N. might choose to legitimise the Arab presence – for example, by recognition of the Mufti's Palestinian Government, set up during the summer in the Gaza region with Egyptian encouragement – and then enforce such legitimacy with international sanctions. This dreadful possibility could only be effectively averted by an Israeli occupation of the Negev. Even the U.N., it was thought, would be hard pressed to legitimise Arab claims to territory they no longer controlled.

By mid-September the Israelis were ready to attack. The army was now better integrated, for, at Ben-Gurion's insistence, the semi-independent tendencies of the leftist Palmach brigades and the rightist terrorist organisations were being more or less forcibly suppressed. The troops in the field now numbered 90,000 – as against 60,000 Arabs – and were organised into four regional forces covering the North, Centre, South and Jerusalem. They no longer fought in the self-sufficient companies of a hundred or so men, but in task forces of thousands, sustained by all those service arms – intelligence, logistics, maintenance – typical of a modern army. If the artillery, armour and air arms were still somewhat skeletal, it was to be expected. Only fear of international counter-moves held back this army from concentrating against the smaller and woefully divided Arab armies one by one.

This fear was soon to be assuaged. On 17 September members of Lehi not yet reconciled to Ben-Gurion's autocracy assassinated Count Bernadotte in Jerusalem. Like Deir Yassin the action was roundly condemned by the Israeli government; like Deir Yassin it proved extremely advantageous. The Israelis were able to gauge the resolve of their opponents. International reaction was negligible; the Arabs shook their fists but did not move their armies. With the dead mediator's plan receiving sympathetic attention at the U.N., it was clearly both necessary and possible to move against the Egyptians in the Negev.

Operation *Yoav* was made easier by the Egyptian dispositions, which consisted of three long, thin and vulnerable lines. Two followed the roads already mentioned, from El Arish to Ashdod and from El Auja to Bethlehem. The third straddled a lateral road connecting the other two through Faluja and Bet Guvrin. The Israeli plan was to break through the lateral line, and drive south and east to cut the supply routes of the Egyptian forces on the Hebron road.

On 15 October the Israelis manufactured an incident in the Negev, and Operation *Yoav* began. The fledgling Israeli Air Force attacked, rather successfully, Egyptian air bases in Sinai, while on the ground the army launched diversionary attacks along the coast road and east of Faluja before delivering the main blow in the area of Iraq el-Manshiya. But to the Israelis' surprise the attack failed and, with pressure building at the U.N. for another ceasefire, a do-or-die assault was launched

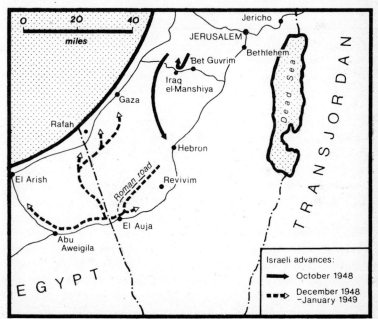

3. The northern Negev, October 1948–January 1949

in the stronger Faluja crossroads sector. This, despite heavy losses, was a success, and behind the punctured Egyptian line was open country. Israeli forces took the Arab town of Beersheba on 20 October. Only a deterring gesture by the Arab Legion saved Hebron from a similar fate.

A new ceasefire came into effect on 22 October, with both sides in possession of a substantial slice of the northern Negev. Around Faluja a sizeable Egyptian force had been encircled by the Israelis; the officer who negotiated on its behalf was one Major Nasser. He talked long and earnestly to his Israeli counterpart of the need to evict the British from Egypt.

The Israelis were still more concerned to evict the Egyptians from the Negev, and as their forces in the north 'liberated' all Galilee from the clutches of Qawuqji, the Syrians and the Lebanese, the High Command busily planned another venture in the south.

The Egyptian Army was now in a stronger position. It still held the coastal route, and the Hebron route as far as Revivim. Between these two roads was only impassable sand, or so it seemed. The Israelis would have to fight their way along the roads, strongpoint by strongpoint. It would be slow and costly.

At this point fortune favoured Israel. A reconnaissance patrol stumbled across an old Roman road traversing the 'impassable' sand. The Israelis energetically 'repaired' the road surface and on 22 December, after devising another suitable pretext for breaking a ceasefire, made use of it. Motorised units appeared out of the desert to attack the startled Egyptians in El Auja. The positions further north on the road, cut off from the rest of the army, mostly collapsed within a few days. The Israelis drove west into Sinai. Sweeping through Umm Katef the advanced Israeli units were threatening to seize El Arish from the south, and so cut off the large Egyptian forces still holding the coastal regions around Rafah and Gaza. This threat was staved off by the Israeli government, under intense pressure from the British and American governments. Opting for a second-best solution the Israeli military leadership sent forces up the El Auja–Rafah road. The capture of Rafah would achieve the same ends, but not so obviously. This transparent subterfuge failed. A British ultimatum stopped the Israeli forces in their tracks. The Arabs, it was decided, had already lost enough.

In early January the Egyptians sued for an armistice, and one by one, in the succeeding months, the other Arab régimes followed their example. One more operation was undertaken by the triumphant Israelis. In early March they seized the southern Negev, Eilat, and a few miles of coastline at the northern end of the Gulf of Aqaba.

The war was over, but its legacies made peace hard to entertain. A temporary military judgement had been passed on rival claims to the stretch of land between the Jordan and the sea. But it was not a judgement that could be politically sustained.

Chapter 2

THE UNPROMISED LAND
Palestine to 1920

I

Many people see the Palestine War as the origin of all the subsequent conflicts involving Israel and the Arabs. Certainly, it
did create irreversible change in the political complexion of
the Middle East. The refugee problem may only have been the
most tragic of these. But other factors made equal contributions to the maintenance of a hostile atmosphere and the outbreak of wars. The defeat of the Arab armies left a bitter
taste. The seizure of territory by both Israel and Jordan against
the aims of the United Nations partition plan did not help
either. At root, the problem was that the Palestine War forged
and gave shape to a new state in the Middle East – a state
whose very nature presented a challenge to the region's Arab
majority.

This state didn't just leap into being. It was certainly not
the product of any declaration of statehood or independence
on the part of the Jewish community in Palestine, but neither
was it created in the furnace of war. War allowed the State of
Israel to construct itself through the welding together of an
effective national army and the establishment of a system of
centralised command capable of addressing itself to the tasks
of political leadership and civil administration. It also created
the conditions for building an economic infrastructure. But
there was already a blueprint for this state, and well before
1948 the military, economic and political institutions that are
the absolute essentials of any state were already almost completely formed, waiting for the moment of birth. Before Israel
was born there had been conception and gestation, and we must
trace the Arab–Israeli conflict back to the moments of passionate desire that preceded (as such moments usually do) even
the conception of this unruly child.

II

> If I cannot bend the gods, I will let hell loose.
>
> (Virgil, *The Aeneid*)

During the last century the 'Eastern Question' was, in E. J. Hobsbowm's words, 'the most explosive issue in international affairs after the Napoleonic Wars, and the only one likely to lead to a general war'.[1] The 'Eastern Question' was how politicians of the nineteenth century spoke of the complicated set of international disputes created by the imminent demise of the once mighty Ottoman Empire. The Ottoman Turks emerged in the fourteenth century to pick up the bloody mantle that had been ripped from the shoulders of the Byzantine emperors centuries before. They spread their rule over Greece, the Balkans, North Africa, Palestine, Syria and Iraq by 1680 and, having been turned from the gates of Vienna in 1683, almost immediately went into decline.

Like all such empires, once the Ottomans found it impossible to expand any more they were confronted with the huge task of maintaining stable rule over a vast and culturally heterogeneous area. Internal rebellion and incursions from surrounding areas taxed a central administration (known, incidentally, by the quaint title of the Sublime Porte) which found it impossible to modernise and increasingly difficult to act effectively at all. The empire began to break up under the strain.

This process of disintegration would normally have been encouraged as empires still being born tried to seize great chunks of the empire about to die. However, the conflicting aims of the various emergent European powers impelled several of them actually to sustain Ottoman rule as an effective buffer against the others. The British, for example, sought stability and neutrality in the Eastern Mediterranean, For most of the nineteenth century this served the purposes of imperial communication with India. Britain carefully avoided direct military confrontation in the area, only resorting to arms when no other course was open to it. The British were even more concerned not to keep a military presence in the Turkish empire, for fear this would hasten the Ottoman decline. For most of the century the British attitude to Egypt could be summed up in Lord Palmerston's words: 'We do not want . . . it for ourselves, any more than any rational man with an estate in the north of England and a residence in the south would have wished to possess the inns on the north road. All he could want would have been that the inns should be well-kept, always accessible, and furnishing him, when he came, with mutton-chops and post-horses.'[2]

However, during the last quarter of the nineteenth century it became clear that the Ottoman Empire was falling apart most ungracefully, despite British efforts to hold it together. Neither threats of force nor force itself would prevent Britain's competitor powers from picking up the pieces. Then, and only then – when British interests could no longer be secured from outside – did Britain decide to hasten the demise of the Empire by seizing territory for itself.

There were two important areas: Egypt – where Britain had been faced with a rising tide of nationalism combined with the reckless modernisation programmes of a pro-French dynasty – and the Persian Gulf and Mesopotamia – where the natural threat of German or Russian intervention increased to crisis point in the years following 1870. In 1882, the British occupied Egypt, partly to secure control of the recently opened Suez Canal, partly to protect British investments in the Egyptian economy (especially in the important area of cotton production), and partly to oppose the threat of a radical, anti-European nationalist takeover. Ensuing years saw a struggle for control of the Persian Gulf area.

Eventually, Russia and Britain came to terms over Persia, but by this time the Turkish orientation towards Germany had become crucial. German involvement in the building of the Berlin–Baghdad Railway threatened not only British strategic interests in the Gulf by a rearguard assault, as it were, but also her access to the oil which had been discovered in the area in the late nineteenth century. Things reached a head in 1911, when Winston Churchill (then First Lord of the Admiralty in charge of the navy) decided that the British fleet would switch from coal-fired to oil-fired boilers. The navy had long been Britain's guarantee of its dominance as a world power. From 1911 on, British control in the Middle East was no longer just a matter of safeguarding 'imperial communications'. It was to become, quite simply, the foundation of Britain's power, if not the only guarantee of the British Empire's survival in any form whatsoever.

The inevitable war between Europe's great imperial powers was not long in coming. Like avaricious relatives around grandfather's deathbed, the European powers fought viciously for possession of the most valuable parts of Turkey's estate. The Turkish decision to side with Germany and Austria against Britain, France and Russia was probably an act of desperation. Only German victory could oppose the joint will of the three other powers to dismember the Ottoman Empire. But that decision set the seal on the fate of Turkey.

Turkey's alignment gave the British the excuse for the full-scale invasion of the Ottoman Empire which they had delayed for so long. Britain had four main aims in the area: (i) to protect the Suez Canal (ii) to secure territorial continuity between Egypt and India (iii) to hold back the French who supported the demands of some Arabs for a 'Greater Syria' occupying most of the Fertile Crescent and (iv) to secure oil supplies and an oil route from the Persian Gulf and Iraq to the Mediterranean.

Britain had been contacted in 1914 by Sharif Hussein, the Emir of Mecca. Hussein was a descendant of the Prophet Mohammed and, as nominal ruler of the Hejaz (the Eastern coastal strip of the Arabian peninsular including the holy cities of Mecca and Medina), he was able to offer considerable forces in the struggle against Turkey. The British became interested just as their armies began to meet with defeat in the battle for the Middle East. In a series of letters sent between Hussein and the British High Commissioner in Egypt, Sir Henry McMahon, a deal was arranged which seemed to promise a guarantee of Arab independence in exchange for an Arab revolt against the Turks under Hussein's leadership.

Through McMahon the British informally offered to support and recognise Arab independence in an area excluding only a vaguely defined region 'west of . . . Damascus, Homs, Hama and Aleppo' which, McMahon wrote, could not 'be said to be purely Arab'. The British had no intention of giving the Arabs independence, and never actually promised it. They preferred instead to split up the area into zones of French, British and Russian influence. Such a carve-up was arranged in

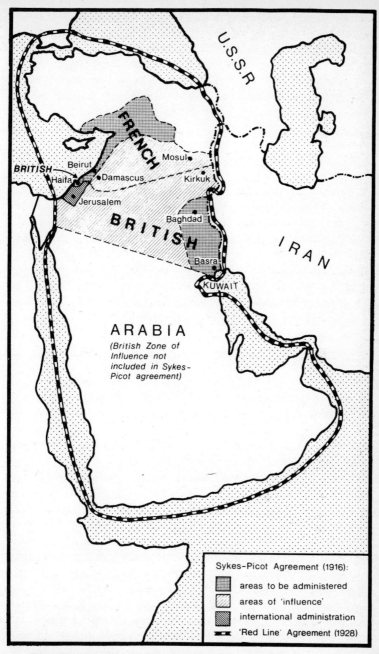

4. Middle East oil between the wars

the secret Sykes-Picot agreement of 1916 (see map 4). Sykes-Picot provides the most realistic picture of British aspirations in the Middle East. After the Bolshevik revolution of 1917, the Russians made the details of Sykes-Picot public and rejected any claims to territory in the area. The British then claimed that the agreement was no longer valid – but that did not prevent them from grabbing the territories allotted to them in this defunct agreement, even surreptitiously seizing the oil-rich Mosul area from the French in the final days of the war.

Meanwhile, the Arab revolt went ahead in 1916 as promised by Hussein. The British, with careful attention to their reputation for perfidy, promptly marched into Palestine with Hussein's Arabs as their right wing and almost simultaneously offered a part of this land to the Jews. Prompted by the diplomatic approaches of a leading Zionist, Chaim Weizmann (later to become first president of Israel), the British Foreign Secretary conveyed a note to the Zionist Organisation through Lord Rothschild. This was the famous Balfour Declaration of 2 November 1917, stating that 'His Majesty's Government view with favour the establishment in Palestine of a national home for the Jewish people'.

It was a triumph of studied vagueness. The Declaration committed Britain's 'best endeavours to facilitate the achievement of this object', providing that 'nothing shall be done which may prejudice the civil and religious rights of existing non-Jewish communities in Palestine, or the rights and political status enjoyed by Jews in any other country'. These were generalities and conditions that even the largest empire the world had ever known could hide behind.

It has often been argued that Palestine was included in the area that McMahon had claimed was not 'purely Arab'. True or false, the argument is irrelevant. The Balfour Declaration was a cunning piece of political sleight-of-hand, like the McMahon promise motivated by nothing so noble as consideration for Jew or Arab. As propaganda it was the product of a lengthy diplomatic exercise that had bought valuable Jewish allies in America and revolutionary Russia at a time when America needed to be edged into joining the Allied efforts and Russia needed to be dissuaded from dropping out. As a portentous proclamation of a British commitment in the Middle East it gave Britain a public justification for occupying the area. Neither McMahon nor Balfour offered any genuine promise of independence, and for Jew and Arab alike the documents were just as worthless. In January 1917, the British Prime Minister, Lloyd George, is reported to have said of Palestine: 'Oh, we must grab that. We have made a beginning.'[3]

The Middle East became a subject for discussion at several conferences following the 1918 Armistice. Hussein's son, the Emir Feisal, was accepted as a delegate to the Versailles Peace Conference. Feisal had already approached Chaim Weizmann on the advice of Edmund Allenby, commander of the British Middle East forces. Feisal and Weizmann struck up a friendship and agreed to present a united front to the British and French. Both men were careful not to use the expression 'Jewish State' in any negotiations, but Feisal undoubtedly realised that a state was precisely what the Jews wanted. He calculated that the Zionists could be a powerful lever on the British and he saw no reason to make unnecessary enemies in the face of an already complicated bargaining situation.

Clearly, Feisal was aware of Britain's duplicity, but he was a realist. The French insisted on the validity of the Sykes-Picot agreement but were prepared to forego their claims on Mosul and Palestine for immediate financial compensation. Feisal probably mistrusted the weak French more than the strong British and the withdrawal of their claim on Palestine gave him the opening he needed. He accepted that Palestine should become the site of the Jewish national home and he agreed that Palestine and a projected Arab state (taking in present-day Saudi Arabia, Lebanon, Jordan, Syria and Iraq) should both become British protectorates for a limited period. In return he demanded the establishment of Arab rule in the Arab state and eventual full independence. Palestine was a small price for Feisal to pay for a kingdom that would have stretched almost from the Indian Ocean to the Russian border. Especially when Palestine didn't belong to him and wasn't promised to him.

Feisal and Weizmann presented a joint document to the Peace Conference setting out their agreement on Palestine. Naturally, the document included a promise that the religious, political and economic rights of non-Jewish Palestinians would be protected. It is hard to imagine that either man took this promise too seriously. Feisal could clearly ignore a great deal to obtain his Arab state – including the obvious fact that a Jewish state would have to discriminate against non-Jews. Weizmann simply wanted to secure international acknowledgement of the Zionist Organisation's right to speak for Palestine. In the game of power politics nobody wins except the powerful and those whom the powerful choose to elevate to power.

As it happened, even this semblance of accord between Zionist and Arab nationalist aspirations was threatening to the British. One big Arab state was bad enough. In any case, there were the French demands to take into account, and then there was the fact that the Arab East was not as united as it might have seemed. It was split by dynastic and sectarian rivalries. It was divided into areas with completely different traditions, cultures and economies. Ibn Saud, ruler of the Najd or central area of the Arabian peninsula, was fighting Hussein and his Hashemite dynasty in the Hejaz. Like Hussein, Saud had the doubtful blessing of British support. In the north there was a strong movement to proclaim a 'Greater Syria' as the natural leader of the Arab world. The people of Mesopotamia had a civilisation whose history went back centuries, and they laid claim to their own independence. On top of all that, the oil reserves in Mesopotamia and around the Persian Gulf were becoming increasingly important to European industry and were being fiercely fought over by the British, French, Dutch and Americans.

The San Remo conference in 1920 reached a satisfactory compromise. The area was split up into different territories. The British were granted the mandates to Palestine, Transjordan and Iraq (formerly Mesopotamia). The French gave up their claims on Palestine and Mosul and received Syria, the Lebanon and a share of Iraqi oil. The Hejaz was granted independence and was eventually seized from the Hashemites by Ibn Saud in 1924. Feisal, who had been proclaimed King of Syria by the British before San Remo, was quickly kicked out by the French. Iraq was given nominal independence following a popular revolt which nearly succeeded in removing the British army and Feisal was made king. Hussein's other son, Abdullah – *en route* to Syria to avenge his brother – was happy to accept a diplomatic British offer of the Emirate of Transjordan instead. The French were less subtle and ran Syria and

Lebanon as virtual colonies – but what's in a name? Call them mandates, protectorates or colonies – the result was still the same. These were occupied countries.

And yet the mandate system had one important advantage. It made it look as though you were not actually occupying the country concerned, but simply looking after it. This illusion was fostered in Transjordan and Iraq by the establishment of puppet Hashemite régimes. British interests seemed to be safe, once more.

Chapter 3

STRANGERS IN A STRANGE LAND

Mandatory Palestine, 1920–1948

Probably the Battle of Waterloo *was* won on the playing fields of Eton, but the opening battles of all subsequent wars have been lost there.

(George Orwell, *The Lion and the Unicorn*)

I

There is a limit to the application of democratic methods. You can inquire of all the passengers as to what type of car they like to ride in, but it is impossible to question them as to whether to apply the brakes when the train is at full speed and an accident threatens.

(Leon Trotsky, *The History of the Russian Revolution*)

The Palestine Mandate seemed like a godsend to the British. There was very little of value in Palestine itself, but it commanded a strategic position overlooking the Suez Canal on the one hand and the land route to oil and India on the other. The Mandate ratified the Balfour Declaration and repeated its vague generalisations along with more of the same sort of thing. In 1920, Winston Churchill had written of a time when there might 'be created . . . by the banks of the Jordan a Jewish State under the protection of the British Crown'. Such an event, he continued, 'would be especially in harmony with the truest interests of the British Empire'.[1]

The fact was that the aims of the Balfour Declaration were *so* ill-defined and ambiguous that, in theory, the British could maintain a presence in Palestine indefinitely. They had, so it seemed, not just a mandate but a freehold on the property. True, the Mandate recognised the Zionist Organisation as the representative of the Jewish people in Palestine. It set up the Jewish Agency as a sort of administration within the administration. But it also insisted on fair-play for *all* Palestinians and nowhere did it acknowledge any more specific Zionist goal than 'the establishment in Palestine of a national home for the Jewish people'. This could mean anything from a fully-fledged Jewish state to a shack in Tel Aviv sign-posted 'National home – Jews only'.

The Zionist establishment knew what it wanted very well. Some Zionists argued that Jewish nationalism was racist and put forward the goal of some sort of bilateral, Jewish–Arab, state. They were asking for the moon – the most any Zionist congress called for was 'cooperation with the Arabs', and that only until 1929. Others demanded immediate Jewish rule, arguing that gradualism risked defeat. A group of these Zionists formed the 'Zionist Revisionist' tendency in 1925. They argued for a Jewish state on both sides of the Jordan, and proposed militant struggle against the British. Their spiritual heirs were the Irgun terrorists and the ideas of their leader, Vladimir Jabotinsky, gained political respectability in the shape of Mena-chim Begin's Herut (and later Likud) party. In the 1920s they would probably have been massacred in any serious engagement with the British.

Nevertheless, the drive towards setting up a Jewish state received a tremendous boost from the formal recognition of Zionism in the Mandate. The same Winston Churchill who had celebrated a Jewish state in 1920 drafted the infamous 1922 White Paper in his capacity as Colonial Secretary. 'Phrases have been used,' went the White Paper, referring to an earlier statement by Weizmann, 'such as that Palestine is to become "as Jewish as England is English". His Majesty's Government regard any such expectation as impracticable and have no such aim in view. Nor have they at any time contemplated . . . the disappearance or the subordination of the Arabic population, language or culture in Palestine. They would draw attention to the fact that the terms of the [Balfour] Declaration . . . do not contemplate that Palestine as a whole should be converted into a Jewish National Home, but that such a home should be founded *in Palestine*.'

In theory, British mandatory rule had seemed unassailable. But the theory failed to take account of the facts. The Zionist Organisation wanted the protection of the Mandate while they gained sufficient organisation, strength of numbers and military capability, but they rejected British efforts to put stumbling blocks in the way of ultimate statehood. Thus, until the 1930s Zionist leaders called for the strengthening of the British police forces and opposed the creation of representative bodies which would have lessened the power of the High Commissioner for Palestine. At the same time they created autonomous bodies under the Jewish Agency for the purposes of local government administration (the Va'ad Leumi), the organisation and welfare of the Jewish labour force (the Histadrut), and the defence of agricultural settlements (the Haganah). The Va'ad Leumi which was elected from among the members of a larger 'Assembly of Deputies' was empowered to collect taxes from the Jewish community. Even without the Zionist Organisation and its offshoots, these three bodies alone formed an embryonic state – and they had all been formed by the end of 1920. One fact that the British ignored, therefore, was that whatever the Zionist Organisation said to the contrary (and they unanimously accepted the 1922 White Paper) a Jewish state was already being built.

The Palestinian Arabs did not ignore this fact. They had been betrayed by Feisal who, sitting on his throne in Baghdad, mouthed anti-Zionist slogans while the British pulled the strings. They witnessed the deceptions of the Zionists who promised to cooperate with the Arabs and not to discriminate against them, but who then continued on their own separate road. They saw the building of a state apparatus which excluded the Arabs. Land that Arabs had once worked (or been unable to work for lack of funds) was bought up by Jews. Jobs were created, but Arabs were not allowed to compete for them. It is perhaps a fine point. After all, the Jews were not doing anything illegal or even, by most standards, immoral. They were simply looking after their own interests.

Legal and moral it may have been – but it was not fair. The Arabs lacked education; they lacked technical skills; they lacked organisation. Most of all, they lacked money. They had the will, but they didn't have the wherewithal. It wasn't that they were anti-Semitic – that, after all, is a Western concept. It was simply that they saw the Jewish immigrants using money, influence and education to get the things they felt should be theirs, too. Between 1920 and 1925, for example, the Zionists spent almost £1 million buying barren marshy land in the

Valley of Jezreel near Galilee. The British High Commissioner wrote that when he saw the valley 'in 1920 . . . four or five small and squalid Arab villages, long distances apart from one another, could be seen on the summits of the low hills here and there. For the rest, the country was uninhabited.'[2] Not surprising, in such a desolate area. However, within five years 2,600 Jews had settled in the valley. Three thousand acres of forest had been planted. Twenty schools had been opened, over 50 square miles of land had been cultivated. One can marvel at the amount of dedication and sweat that went into that effort, but think also about the money it must have cost – saplings, seed, building materials, tools, agricultural machinery, transport costs. There is no record of the amount but it must have been enormous – more money than the Arabs in those 'four or five small and squalid villages' could have dreamt of if they all dreamed together. And this settlement was only the first of many similar ones to come. What part were the Arab peasants and *fellahin* (tenant farmers) allowed to play in the unfolding of this magnificent Jewish dream? None. What benefits did they see the future bring them? Those of second-class citizens in a privately financed nation. Then to be told, as Feisal and Weizmann had told them, as the Zionist Organisation was constantly telling them, that their interests were the same as those of the Jews in Palestine was simply to add gross insult to traumatic injury. Little wonder that many Palestinian Arabs who had aspired to and been promised independence saw Zionism as their main enemy. It trampled on their dreams and threatened to burn their receipts – and Feisal sat in Baghdad. They did the only thing they could. They fought.

The separation of Transjordan from Palestine put a brake on the movement for a Greater Syria, which many Palestinian Arabs supported. Abdullah was firmly committed to Britain, and to informal union with Iraq, rather than with Syria. But an autonomous Transjordan was by no means universally applauded. For the Zionists it meant the loss of territory they had claimed on the east bank of the Jordan – territory that many argued was an integral part of Biblical Israel. Palestinian Arabs saw British patronage of the Hashemites as threatening their own aspirations. With the demise of Greater Syrian nationalism a specific Palestinian nationalism emerged as the area's most powerful ideological current.

Arab attacks on Jewish settlements had, until 1920, been isolated and desultory affairs – as often carried out by indiscriminate nomadic tribes scavenging for a living as by dispossessed Palestinians seeking some sort of revenge. The mandate of 1920 seemed specifically to exclude the Palestinian Arabs from any plans for the creation of national Arab entities. The establishment of Transjordan made matters worse. The disturbances accordingly increased and the British, having achieved their objective of getting formal recognition of their right to protect Palestine's burgeoning Jewish community, felt that the time was ripe for a change of emphasis. The newly appointed High Commissioner for Palestine, Sir Herbert Samuel (who was both Jewish and pro-Zionist), took action.

In September 1920, he set a limit to Jewish immigration – by May of the following year he found it necessary to suspend Jewish immigration altogether. He also introduced the first of several attempts to restrict the acquisition of Arab lands by Jews – the 1920 Transfer of Land Ordinance. These moves were not only designed as a sop to Arab opinion. In fact, a minority of that was actually in favour of Jewish immigration – especially among the urban Arab middle class (predominantly Christian) whose Western outlook and business interests were already being aided by Jewish money and expertise as well as by the influx of cheap *fellah* labour into the towns along Palestine's coastal strip. Probably just as important was the British calculation that the longer they prevented the Jews from attaining a majority in Palestine the longer they would be entitled to administrate the now mandatory obligations of the Balfour Declaration.

These were traditional British divide-and-rule tactics, but so far lacking in a vital ingredient. An Arab organisation would be needed to channel potentially violent anti-Zionism into peaceful institutions which the British could control. From 1920 on, the British made numerous attempts to set up Advisory and Legislative Councils including Arab and Jewish representatives. The first obstacle to be overcome was the lack of representatives from the Arab population sympathetic to the British aim. Herbert Samuel sought to create an Arab organisation to challenge the distinctly uncooperative Arab Executive. When the Mufti of Jerusalem died in 1921, Samuel seized his opportunity.

The High Commissioner needed the position of Mufti (the religious leader of Arab Palestine) to carry political weight. He created the title of 'Grand Mufti' and rigged the election so that his candidate, Haj Amin al-Husseini, won. It was, perhaps, one of the most foolish moves the British administration ever made in Palestine.

Haj Amin belonged to one of Palestine's leading Arab families. He had played a leading rôle in the 1920 demonstrations and, having fled the country, had been sentenced by the British to fifteen years' imprisonment. He had soldiered with the Turks *and* with Feisal. He was at one time an official in the British Military Government of Palestine and also presided over Jerusalem's Arab Club, which led the Palestinian campaign for a Greater Syria. Clearly, he was both adaptable and influential. His fifteen-year sentence was revoked. The British hoped to buy off his militant nationalism by giving him power and they hoped to create around him a British-approved Palestine–Arab organisation.

As 1922 dawned, the British authorities issued a decree establishing the Supreme Muslim Council. The Council was to administrate the affairs of Palestine's Muslim community in the same way that the Jewish Agency took care of the Jews. Haj Amin was, of course, elected president of this Council. But he was no Weizmann and the Palestinian Arabs were a far remove from the Zionists.

The Zionists were for a long time a small minority in Palestine. In 1922, they were no more than eleven per cent of the population. Naturally, they acceded to Britain's wishes and hoped that in doing so they would not undermine British authority and would win protection. If Britain wanted them to talk to the Arabs, they would talk. They would even sit on Legislative Councils, but they argued that Arab and Jewish interests were separate – if not yet incompatible. They demanded equal Arab–Jewish representation as a condition of their cooperation.

Most Arabs, seeing the relative weakness of the Zionists and opposing their aims, soon came to reject any council which involved inflated representation for the Jewish community. Not really understanding the devious routes taken by Western-style 'democracy', they refused to follow them. By 1923, all Arab representatives had become resolute in their rejection of 'power-sharing', preferring, if necessary, to throw themselves on the rough mercy of the British sense of fair play. It was a preview, in microcosm, of later, more violent disputes over partition.

Haj Amin al-Husseini made good use of his British-endowed position to further his own vast ambitions in the Arab world. When other Arab leaders agreed to drop their increasingly fruitless opposition to the establishment of a joint Legislative Council in 1929, the Grand Mufti conjured up a Jewish plot to take over Jerusalem and desecrate the Muslim Holy Places. The ensuing riots were the worst ever. In the most horrendous incident, fifty-nine Jewish men, women and children were killed and their bodies mutilated in the town of Hebron. With this incident a new era in Palestine began.

The Zionist leadership had, up to then, been concerned to secure the support of the 'left wing' of their organisation – especially the substantial minority of Jews who argued for an accommodation with the Arabs. To this end, they accepted the 1922 White Paper and agreed to a number of paper resolutions calling for 'Arab–Jewish cooperation'. This empty formula also increased their credibility with the British and other international communities.

After 1929, pressure mounted from the Zionist 'right wing'. The leadership had to keep a delicate balance. 'Cooperation' went by the board and while Zionists tried to maintain a publicly moderate face, signs of Jewish intransigence to Arab or British demands began to show themselves. The Passfield White Paper which the British issued after the 1929 riots proposed new restrictions on Jewish immigration and on land sales to Jews. These proposals could not be put into practice without Zionist agreement. But by this time the Zionists neither wanted nor needed to agree. Immigration could continue by means of a well-organised underground network. Land sales could not be effectively restricted because a large proportion of the available land was owned by absentee landlords happy to arrange for transfers to be made through third parties acting outside Palestine. The Passfield White Paper was the first British proposal to be rejected absolutely by the Zionist Organisation.

Arab pressure continued to increase. The first pan-Arab Congress was held in Jerusalem in 1931. It was explicitly committed to oppose 'Zionist colonisation of Palestine', but it too rejected Passfield (for not being tough enough). Meanwhile, the British, in a desperate attempt not to push the Jews into a militant position, performed yet another miracle of diplomacy. Prime Minister Ramsay MacDonald wrote to the Zionist Organisation in 1931 once again promising that the Balfour Declaration would be upheld despite the Passfield White Paper, which MacDonald astutely avoided repudiating. The British authorities could not go on for long with this spectacular tight-rope walk, however, since the wire was now being shaken from both ends. On top of everything, the gravest economic crisis in history had hit Britain particularly hard. The government began to think in terms of constructing safety nets against the inevitable fall.

Despite the MacDonald letter, the Zionists began to prepare for the day that the British would have to be attacked. It had been Zionist policy not to retaliate against Arab attacks. Instead, they had called upon the British authorities for protection. The British were less and less able to protect anybody in Palestine and, although reliance on the Mandatory power remained public Zionist policy, things had changed behind the scenes. In 1930, the Haganah began stockpiling smuggled weapons and the command structure of this loosely organised defence corps was centralised and tightened up. For some this was not enough. In 1931, the Irgun Z'vei Leumi split from the Haganah and began terrorist activities against the British. In 1935, the Zionist Revisionists under Jabotinsky split from the Zionist Organisation.

The Arabs, too, prepared to fight the British. When its president died in 1934, the Arab leadership split up. It had been rendered ineffectual by growing rivalry between the two main dynastic blocs who formed its leadership. These two blocs coalesced into two of the Palestinian Arabs' first political parties. For a few months they (and several smaller parties) jockeyed for power while the British continued their futile efforts to create some sort of representative body including both Jews and Arabs.

But Jewish immigrants soon began to arrive in Palestine in comparatively large numbers as they fled a new tide of anti-Semitism in Eastern Europe and Nazi Germany. It began to look as though the Arabs might soon be outnumbered. Between 1933 and 1936, the Jewish population of Palestine virtually doubled and reached to within a few per cent of one third of the total population. In the peak year of 1935 over 60,000 Jewish immigrants entered Palestine. Suddenly, the need for Arab unity became urgent. The six main parties and a number of influential individuals formed the Arab Higher Committee – successor to the Arab Executive. Haj Amin al-Husseini was the inevitable choice for chairman, as he commanded the respect of the most militant sections of the Arab population.

Under the threat of a Jewish majority the Arabs found an effective voice at last. The A.H.C. organised a general strike which paralysed the Palestinian economy and threatened to spark off revolt in Transjordan, Lebanon and Syria. The British moved in thousands of extra troops and used their influence on the rulers of Transjordan, Iraq, Saudi Arabia and the Yemen to pressure the A.H.C. to call off the strike. Without the support of these key Arab states (Egypt was not then thought of as a true Arab state and it certainly was not considered a part of the Arab East), the A.H.C. could no longer command the Palestinian workers who saw no immediate benefit from the continuation of their strike action. The A.H.C. was also split by the old dynastic rivalries. Support for the Hashemites became the main plank of opposition to Haj Amin. After the strike was over, the pro-Hashemites seceded from the organisation, leaving Haj Amin and his followers to resort to large-scale terrorism against British and Jews alike.

But the strike succeeded in worrying the British a great deal. With a European war looming they needed to keep a tight hold on the Middle East. First they tried a partition plan envisaging separate Arab and Jewish states, a British-controlled zone around Jerusalem with a corridor leading to the Mediterranean, and a British zone round Aqaba. The Arab state was to be linked to Transjordan and a limit was to be set on Jewish immigration for five years. The Zionist leadership agreed to consider this plan, since it was most favourable to them, but objected to the immigration restrictions. The Arabs found the whole idea of partition objectionable, especially when it acknowledged the Jewish right to lands, most of which were not yet Jewish-owned and the rest of which they considered to have been taken unfairly. The Transjordanian connection was an equally troublesome thing. In a few months the British dropped the plan as unworkable.

As each day went by it became more and more important to reach agreement with the Arabs. Haj Amin had fled the country in 1937 – he was later to turn up as an adviser to the Third Reich on Muslim matters – but his followers posed a threat to British interests in the whole of the Middle East. By 1939 the situation was desperate. No one could doubt that Britain would soon be locked in combat with Germany and possibly with Russia. Egypt had become nominally independent in 1936 and moved closer to Fascist Italy with each day. Ethiopia had fallen to Italy a year before. Nobody could tell what France might do, especially since its mandates were due to end in Syria and the Lebanon. It was essential for Britain to secure Arab support throughout the Middle East for all the same old reasons of oil, trade routes and empire.

The British government calculated, not unreasonably, that it could count on Jewish support in any struggle against Nazi or pro-Nazi forces, no matter what. In fact, a handful of right-wing Zionists among the ranks of the Irgun and its even more extreme breakaway group, Lehi (better known as the Stern Group), argued that Britain was the main enemy. Some even seem to have been attracted to the idea of entering some sort of alliance with Italy. But the vast majority of Zionists were prepared to enter a temporary alliance with Britain for the sake of defeating the greater evil of Nazism. The British, therefore, issued a White Paper in May 1939, proposing that an independent Palestinian State would be set up within ten years based on the existing population ratio of two Arabs to each Jew. To this end, Jewish immigration and land purchase would be restricted.

The Zionists naturally regarded the White Paper as a complete betrayal, but there was little they could do about it, except bring in immigrants illegally, stockpile arms and ammunition, and wait until the coming war was over. The future first Prime Minister of Israel, David Ben-Gurion, spoke for most Zionists when he said: 'We will fight with the British against Hitler as if there were no White Paper; we will fight the White Paper as if there were no war.'[3]

II

> No more distressing moment can ever face a British govern-
> ment than that which requires it to come to a hard and fast
> and specific decision.
>
> (Barbara Tuchman, *The Guns of August*)

The White Paper gave formal British support to a policy which
would have led, everything else staying equal, to an Arab
Palestine with a substantial Jewish minority. But everything else
did not stay equal. The wilder policies of the Grand Mufti and
other Palestinian Arab leaders had severely discredited them.
The British, far from creating a malleable Arab leadership, had
been forced effectively to destroy the chances of any possible
Arab organisation inside Palestine. The *fellahin* and the
nationalists within the country had begun to lose faith in
British promises well before the 1939 White Paper. When Haj
Amin al-Husseini and the Lebanese-born Palestinian leader,
Fawzi Qawuqji, joined a pro-German rebellion in Iraq in 1941,
the British lost all faith in *them*. By 1945, any countervailing
power to the Zionists could only come from outside the
country.

Shortly after the British had forcibly put down the Iraqi
rebellion they took steps to ensure that such a countervailing
force would indeed appear. Somehow they could not resist
playing the old high-class game of deal and double-deal, despite
(or, perhaps, because of) the gradual dawning of an awful
realisation – the realisation that the Depression of the thirties
and the great war that followed it had ushered in the economic
and political bankruptcy of the British Empire.

Having occupied the best part of the Middle East during the
early years of the war (including Syria and the Lebanon which
had to be protected from the pro-German rule of Vichy
France), Britain set about creating a political union of Arab
states. It was a curious reversal of British policy towards Sharif
Hussein's dream of one big Arab state. Egypt, under the young
and popular King Farouk, was growing increasingly antagon-
istic to the British presence – which, despite a new treaty signed
in 1936, by which Britain would evacuate Egypt in twenty

years – increased dramatically as Rommel's armies advanced across North Africa. (Before the reversal of German fortunes in late 1942, it was even rumoured that Rommel had a room booked in his name at Cairo's Shepheard's Hotel.) Farouk had a distinct preference for the company of Italian suitors over the stifling security of his British guardians. Other Egyptians, including the then junior army officer Anwar Sadat, were tempted by offers of a German alliance against the British. Under these circumstances the British were prepared to back Egyptian demands for an alliance with the states of the Arab East – which would connect Egypt with pro-British Transjordan across the planned Palestinian state.

Between 1942 and 1944 a series of talks was held by Egypt and various Arab states with a view to setting up an 'Arab League'. The League duly came into being in March 1945, and included Egypt, Iraq, Saudi Arabia, Yemen, Transjordan, Syria and Lebanon – all the Arab states that were formally independent. (Other Arab states joined the League as they became independent.) By no stretch of the imagination has it ever been possible to describe the Arab League as a full union. For example, its Charter specifically states that no League decision is binding on dissenting members – Arab rivalries being so deep-rooted, member states could never be guaranteed to abide by anything less than a unanimous decision. So the League was designed to carry out a minimal programme of Arab demands. The Arabs professed a hunger for unity, but the League was hardly a snack – still less an *hors d'œuvre.*

Britain considered it would serve her purpose well enough if she could be sure that the League would throw whatever weight it had behind the demands of other Arab communities for independence. These demands, which were the one thing Arab League members could agree on, were in most cases directed against France, America and Russia. France held on to its North African possessions and still laid claim to Syria and the Lebanon. U.S. oil interests and the astute use of hard cash were buying America power in the Middle East. Russia's proximity to Iran (part of which it had occupied during the war, and for a short time after) threatened Britain's interests in the Persian Gulf. The British could hardly afford a full-scale occupation of the Arab world. The League, with its headquarters in British-occupied Egypt and with an Egyptian as its Secretary General, could ensure that no other nation would easily take Britain's place.

But the Arab League's support for independence didn't stop at the borders of countries not dominated by Britain. For one thing, Egypt continued to press for the removal of some 80,000 British troops stationed around the Canal Zone. For another, the demand for an independent Arab Palestine, while initially directed against the U.S., inevitably involved Britain in yet more tortuous diplomacy.

The 1939 White Paper had shocked a good many people and Britain's consistent refusal to admit Jewish refugees from Hitlerism galvanised many more. The tragic victims of an unimaginable cruelty were shuttled back and forth across the oceans in overcrowded, stinking ships right the way through the war and for some three years after its end. Those, like the passengers on the now legendary ship *Exodus*, who sought refuge in Palestine became especially poignant symbols in the light of Zionist demands. The British refusal to admit such refugees and the arrests and deportations of others who had entered Palestine illegally were seen as particularly cruel. In fact, the Mandatory authorities in Palestine were neither more nor less cruel than a score or more of national authorities who operated immigrant quota systems in countries across the world. The United States, Great Britain, South Africa, Mexico, India, Australia, Chile, Turkey and Cuba were just a few of the countries restricting Jewish immigration to a greater or lesser extent from 1937 on. All of them condemned many Jews to death after they had escaped the hangman's noose once. But the Zionist dream itself, the promise of a Jewish homeland, seemingly shattered when it was most needed, gave the Palestine quota an extra bitterness.

And yet, in the world of politics no disaster is catastrophic enough to prevent some people gaining from it. 'Hitler was the true father of the Jewish State,' it has often been remarked – and with a deal more reason than might at first appear. In May 1942, at an Extraordinary Zionist Conference held at the Biltmore Hotel in New York, the Zionist Organisation adopted a programmatic resolution urging 'that Palestine be established as a Jewish Commonwealth integrated in the structure of the new democratic world'.

The 'Biltmore Programme', signalling Zionist orientation towards the U.S., was the first official, public and explicit demand for Palestine to become a Jewish state. Most of the cards were face-up on the table now. Only one remained in the hole, but it was the most important card of all, the card that revealed whether the Zionists were bluffing or not, the one that made all the difference between a royal flush and nothing. On this card you could read whether or not the Zionists had the military strength to back up their demand.

Very few people thought they had. Despite terrorist attacks (which the Irgun started up again in 1944) and persistent Zionist non-cooperation with the Mandatory authorities, the British thought their Arab League could win the trick. The imminent independence of its Indian colony made little practical difference to British interests in the Middle East. Trade routes and oil supplies were still its economic life-blood. Britain was fighting against the rising influence of America and the Soviet Union. Both of the new superpowers saw a use for Zionism. The Soviets under Stalin (renowned neither for his humanitarianism nor for his pro-Jewish sympathies) saw support for a Jewish state not so much as a possible toehold in the Middle East but more as a means of getting the British out of the area. The Americans had equally devious motives for supporting such a state. Firstly, America had a large and influential Jewish constituency whose political power could not be ignored. The Nazi persecution had made Zionism a major political issue in the U.S. Secondly, America's 'special relationship' with Britain was predicated on the continued decline of British power. While Britain dominated the oil-rich Middle East, it remained a threat to American hegemony. American support for a Jewish state would provide a well-placed client to supervise Arab allegiances. Who knows, if the State of Israel was born against Arab wishes, the Arabs might in any case reject Britain and be forced into the American camp?

Britain was the past-master at diplomacy and must have been aware of these considerations. The British were also aware that neither the United States nor the Soviet Union would make an indelicate move for fear of upsetting the Arabs. But most of all they knew that to lose Palestine was to risk losing power in the post-war world. Prime Minister Attlee was not, in fact, convinced of Britain's need to remain in the Eastern Mediter-

ranean, but his Foreign Secretary, Ernest Bevin, thought otherwise – especially in view of the Soviet threat. Bevin sent Field-
Marshal Montgomery to Egypt in June 1946, to assess the
military and political situation. 'Monty' met with little
sympathy from the Egyptians and he concluded that the Suez
Canal Base should be evacuated, leaving it under the peacetime
control of Egypt. He judged that it would take five years to do
so and also argued that it would only be possible if Britain
maintained troops or bases in Libya, Transjordan, Malta,
Cyprus and Palestine. Moreover, he supported the argument
that a British presence in the Sudan would be vital to the
security of British interests, 'so as to be able to control the Nile,
the life-blood of Egypt'.[4]

Montgomery's opinions represented one extreme. The other
– that such a scale of military involvement was economically
crippling, impractical and relevant only to the inveterate imperialists who stalked the dusty corridors of the Colonial Office
– increasingly attracted Attlee. In the end, a typically British
compromise was reached involving a half-hearted withdrawal
from Egypt. It collapsed because of Egypt's insistence on union
with Sudan. But an essential part of that compromise was the
continued effective British occupation of Palestine.

As things stood Britain had promised to end the Mandate by
1949. There were two ways to do this and still retain influence
in the area. The first required a situation in which a specific
level of conflict was maintained between Jew and Arab. This
conflict had to be serious enough to call for policing but not
severe enough to lead to uncontainable violence of the sort the
British were experiencing in the last days of the Mandate.
Various suggestions were put forward for such a solution – all
of them involving either a binational state or some sort of
partition. The British proposals were all variations on the sug-
gestion that they maintain the binational state as a protectorate
or that they occupy a special zone in the partitioned territory.
In those proposals Jerusalem was usually included in British-
occupied territory.

All of these plans were violently rejected by one or both of
the warring communities. Jewish and Arab impatience steadily
increased. A state of open warfare seemed unavoidable. The
Jews smuggled in arms and immigrants and waged a guerrilla
offensive against the Arabs and the British. The Arabs, sup-

plied with arms and money by the Arab League, fought the Jews. Even the 100,000 British troops then stationed in Palestine could not easily subdue rebellion on such a grand scale and their task was made even harder by Britain's tacit support for the Arabs. Pressure mounted from the U.S., the U.S.S.R. and world opinion sympathetic to the plight of the European Jews. The British Labour Government threatened to split over the Palestine question. Slowly the British fell back to their second and far more serious plan.

Since there seemed to be no solution acceptable to both Jew and Arab, one or the other would eventually have to dominate, or both perish in the attempt. Britain would abdicate all responsibility for carrying out the terms of the Mandate and would toss the problem to the newly-created United Nations Organisation (successor to the Mandating authority, the League of Nations) for it to solve. The U.N. would have no better luck than the British and would formulate a solution unacceptable to Arab or Jew or both. War would break out but the British would leave on a previously specified date. Their exit would be followed by an invasion by the forces of the Arab League who would win a resounding military victory over the Jews and create a *de facto* Palestinian Arab state under the protective wing of the pro-British Arab League.

The key to this plan was Abdullah's Transjordan, granted independence but formally allied to Britain in March 1946. If it worked, the Transjordanian Arab Legion would drive a wedge through Palestine from the River Jordan to Gaza and Sinai. Should the Arab Legion not conquer the whole of Palestine, the British might have to be called back to police an actual, not a paper, partition. So much the better. In either case British troops would be able to evacuate Egypt for the relative security of a Transjordanian-protected Palestine. Egyptian demands would be satisfied. The British would remain within striking distance of Suez. A land-bridge would be opened connecting Egypt to Transjordan and Transjordan to the Mediterranean. The perfect solution.

We have no way of gauging the accuracy of this precise picture of British decision-making, but there can be little doubt that something of the sort passed through the minds of the decision-makers. The point is not that such a scheme demands schemers of unbelievably Machiavellian proportions, nor that it is too fantastic to be true. In fact, it was the last in the long series of compromise solutions that make up the unhappy history of British involvement in Palestine.

It was completely consistent with all Britain's efforts to remain in the area, and explains the essential motive behind the uncharacteristically hasty British withdrawal from Palestine. They left precisely because they did not think they were leaving at all. In the post-war world, colonial power was forced to transform itself into more subtly influential forms. But the British, in creating their Commonwealth and their spheres of influence, were left with a not-too-distant memory of the times when they not only rode the waves but ruled them, too. To such fading emperors a sphere of influence is not a sphere of influence without at least the possibility of a military presence.

The events of the Palestine War related in a previous chapter show how close the plan came to reality and exactly why it failed. The British did not count on the dedication and unity of the Zionists, devoted to the idea of 'their' state. They failed to understand that self-interest might weld the U.S. and Soviet governments into a temporary union as easily as it created disunity and hostility amongst the Arab League members. They had taught the world how to govern by deceit, but the world had deceived them.

In April 1947, Britain turned the whole sorry Palestinian mess over to the U.N. The General Assembly formed a special Commission with representatives from Australia, Canada, Czechoslovakia, Guatemala, India, Iran, the Netherlands, Peru, Sweden, Uruguay and Yugoslavia. The Commission was not unanimous – the majority report recommended yet another partition plan while a minority favoured the closer links of a bilateral, federal state. The Zionists agreed to partition, despite their evident refusal to accept a proposed economic union with the Arab state and knowing full well that partition along the lines recommended without economic union would be unworkable. The Palestinian Arabs, thinking that the British withdrawal would even out the odds, rejected both proposals out of hand.

At the last moment the Palestinian Arabs realised that the U.N. was about to impose a partition plan on them and tried to forestall the outcome by agreeing to federation. It was too late. The Arabs had lost support in the General Assembly by taking what appeared to be a cavalier and stubborn attitude towards the U.N. and international agreements in general. On 29 November 1947, the U.N. General Assembly, mindful that partition was easier to implement than federation, received the required two-thirds majority in favour of partition. The U.S., U.S.S.R. and France voted with the majority. Britain abstained.

Chapter 4

JEWISH STATE, ARAB WORLD
Zionism and Arab Nationalism to 1956

Conferences, adjournments, ultimatums,
Flights in the air, castles in the air,
The autopsy of treaties, dynamite under the bridges,
The end of laissez-faire.
(Louis MacNeice, *Autumn Journal*)

I

Be very careful, Messieurs Zionists, governments disappear
but peoples remain.
(Nassif Bey al-Khalidi, 1914)

The Jewish State was the title of one of the seminal works of
Zionism. Written by a Viennese journalist, Theodore Herzl, in
1896, its very title indicates that the goal of a Jewish state had
been important to the Zionist movement well before 1948.
Despite that, Zionism has never been a monolithic movement,
and Herzl's great achievement was not to prescribe a unanimously approved goal for the persecuted Jews of the nineteenth
century, but to develop the tactics and organisation essential to
the pursuit of their freedom.

Zionism was the bastard child of nineteenth-century
nationalism and the Judaic tradition – illegitimate because the
two are totally incompatible. For centuries many Jews had
looked to Palestine as the Holy Land, the ancient home of the
Jewish nation in the days when religious and political estab-
lishments were indistinguishable. Through a unique chain of
circumstances the Jewish religion and holy books had survived
while all traces of other pre-Christian faiths from the Middle
East had disappeared. But the Jewish empire had sunk into
decline long before the Roman conquest of Britain. The Jews

had been scattered throughout the territories of the empires that had subjugated them. This dispersed nation is known as the Diaspora.

The Diaspora Jews looked forward to the time when divine intervention would restore their lost empire. They injected into their faith a belief in the Messianic promise of the Kingdom of Heaven on Earth. Even the most assimilationist and irreligious Jews nurtured a deep commitment to the Holy Land. It reinforced the cultural message of Judaism – that a Jew was, first and foremost, Jewish and only German, Russian or Spanish by accident of birth. Even the assimilationists (like Herzl himself) with their three-piece suits and European manners were assimilationist *Jews*.

During the early and mid nineteenth century a small number of Jews went to Palestine as agricultural settlers for practical or spiritual reasons. In the 1870s, however, several European governments developed anti-Semitism as a weapon in their armoury against social revolution. Particularly notable were the Russian, German and Polish régimes whose countries included a large (several millions strong) and easily recognised minority of Jews. Long considered by Christian orthodoxy to bear the guilt for Christ's death, the Jews in these countries were now officially burdened with additional responsibility for liberalism, secularism and anti-monarchism. Many of them did actually become revolutionaries in the wake of vicious pogroms and state-sanctioned persecution. Some Jews – usually in the more democratic countries of Western Europe – urged more vigorous efforts to assimilate. Others found a less radical interpretation of the lessons of the French Revolution.

Most Russian and Eastern European Jews (the vast majority of the world's Jewish population at the time) had been totally excluded from the political, economic and cultural life of their societies. They occupied their own villages, often spoke their own language (Yiddish) and maintained their own religious and folkloric traditions. How could these people hope to be assimilated? They stuck out like a fifth limb on the social body – the best they could hope for was amputation and eventual decay. More likely, they would be chopped off bit by bit, and each time the wound would be cauterised by arson, pillage and rape.

Those who understood the plight of these truly oppressed

people saw an alternative. The limb could be transplanted. After all, the Jews had their religion and their language (in this case, Hebrew – the liturgical tongue). They had a strong cultural identity – which was one essential condition of nationalism. They lacked a territory, a geographical identity – the other essential of nationalist movements. But then the Bible testified, so they thought, to a legitimate claim on Palestine. All the Jews needed was to occupy the land to have all the qualifications necessary for a declaration of their very own republic.

And so the anomaly of Zionism was born. It was a nationalist movement without a material base. There was no Jewish land, no Jewish economy, no Jewish political organisation. Zionism was a marvellous piece of sleight-of-hand. A Jewish *national* identity was conjured up out of the past when such things did exist, and used to justify the occupation of Palestine. This archaic national identity would then be magically transmuted into a modern national identity by the fact of occupation. It all seemed quite convincing – as long as nobody saw the way in which conflicting ideas of nationhood were swopped around in the middle of the trick.

To be fair, Palestine was not always the goal of Zionist aspirations. As one of the formative influences on Zionism, Yehuda Leib Pinsker, wrote: 'The goal of our efforts must not be the *Holy* Land, but a Land of *Our Own*.'[1] Nonetheless, Palestine had undoubted benefits over other, proposed territories. 'Its name alone,' wrote Herzl, 'would be a powerful rallying cry for our people.'[2] In fact, the programme adopted by the first Zionist Congress in Basle in 1897 (organised by Herzl) specified Palestine as the site of the future Jewish State.

Clearly, persecuted Jews in Russia or Poland could not organise themselves into a state somewhere thousands of miles from where they lived. As Pinsker wrote: 'The creation of a Jewish home could never happen without the support of governments.'[3] Herzl's Zionist Organisation accepted the need to orient itself towards whichever power controlled (or was likely to control) Palestine, and so formulated the basic tactic of 'Political Zionism'.

Unfortunately, until 1917 no government was much interested in Herzl's offers to help colonise Palestine for them. The temptations of Jewish labour, money or political support, although attractive, were firmly refused by the Ottoman Sultan as early as 1896. One major problem was that Palestine was already occupied by a population, largely consisting of Muslim Arabs, who had their own nationalist aspirations. 'The Turkish Empire does not belong to me,' Sultan Abdul Hamid wrote to Herzl, 'but rather to the Turkish people. I cannot distribute one piece of it. Let the Jews save their billions! When my Empire is divided up, they will be able to have Palestine for nothing. But what is divided up will be only our cadaver. I will not allow a vivisection.'[4]

Political Zionism, accepting its enforced limitations, became 'Practical Zionism' in anticipation of this time. Herzl had written in his diaries: 'When we occupy the land, we shall bring immediate benefits to the state that receives us. We must expropriate gently the private property of the estates that receive us. We shall try to spirit the penniless population across the border, by procuring employment for it in the transit countries, while denying it any employment in our own country . . . The property-owners will come over to our side. Both the process of expropriation and the removal of the poor must be carried out discreetly and circumspectly. Let the owners of immovable property believe they are cheating us, selling us more than they are worth. But we are not going to sell them anything back.'[5]

This is exactly what happened. The Zionist Organisation collected funds from sympathetic Jews, paid highly inflated prices to willing absentee landlords living in Beirut or Damascus, and made every effort to attract Jewish immigrants as settlers. The object was to present whichever government controlled Palestine with a *fait accompli* – a Jewish occupation of substantial areas of the country.

They were not overly successful in their efforts. For example, during the revolutionary upheavals between 1904 and 1906 an estimated five million Jews fled Russia and Eastern and Central Europe. A few thousand headed for Palestine (including a young man named David Green from Plonsk in Poland) but most arrived in Britain or America. So great was the flood that, in 1906, the Conservative government under Arthur Balfour imposed a restriction on Jewish immigration into Britain. America willingly accepted all the valuable labour it could get. In 1882 the Jewish population of Palestine was around 24,000.

It climbed unsteadily to some 84,000 by 1922. The Muslim Arab population of Palestine in 1922 was, by contrast, nearly 590,000. There were also over 71,000 Christians, 5,000 Druzes and an estimated 30,000 nomadic Bedouin.

Immigration would not improve dramatically until the 1930s, but the Zionists continued their informal occupation of Palestine and their diplomatic manoeuvring, awaiting the inevitable arrival of the British. The 1897 Congress adopted a programmatic resolution specifying a series of gradual steps to be taken towards 'the settlement of Palestine', 'the organisation and unifying of all Jewry', 'the strengthening of Jewish national feeling and consciousness' and 'preparatory moves towards obtaining' the support and consent of governments. In addition, the Congress voted to set up a private company to purchase and finance the development of land in Palestine. This was the Keren Kayemet or Jewish National Fund (J.N.F.). The J.N.F. was formally constituted in 1901 and made its first land purchases in 1904/5. It was the first concrete piece of the future Jewish state.

Despite differences over the exact political nature of the Jewish national home – differences that were to plague the Zionist Organisation until 1948 – Zionism without the ultimate goal of a Jewish state would have been meaningless. The Jewishness of Zionism was basic – whatever the political ambitions for Palestine's Jewish community, all were agreed on that. Zionism was born out of anti-Semitism and it was sustained by a notion of the intrinsic nationhood of Jews everywhere. But by the nineteenth century, nationhood *meant* statehood and while the Jews believed themselves to be an innately separate grouping of humanity, statehood meant statehood for them *as Jews.* While much of the rest of the world struggled for the political rights of economically dispossessed classes, for their independence from imperial powers or for new forms of political union to suit the new times, Zionists struggled for political union itself, based on the primacy of their Jewishness. Only a sovereign Jewish state could solve the problem of anti-Semitism, as they saw it. Any other kind of political union would merely shift its location.

This arguable proposition seemed to become increasingly self-evident as Palestinian Arabs began the struggle for their own self-emancipation. Those Jews who may not have accepted it in the first place – the ones who argued for true socialism, or for a truly secular state including Jews and Arabs on an equal footing – soon found themselves in the minority. The occupation of Palestine by Zionists stoked the fires of Arab hostility and violence. Anti-Zionism became identified with anti-Semitism in the minds of many Jews and Arabs, simply because Zionism was so determinedly Jewish. And as anti-Zionism grew so the need for Zionism became more apparent to many Jews. It was a vicious circle. The Zionists bequeathed to the future children of Israel an inheritance which would forever have to be defended by force of arms, at the cost of many lives.

As the true child of Zionism, the State of Israel's only security was its strength. Despite protestations to the contrary, Israel could only have been born at the expense of Palestine's Arab population, whose very existence is a threat to the Jewishness of the Jewish state. As long as Israel continues to be both a state and Jewish, it can only survive by the unremitting pursuit of military superiority. It is a tragic irony that this Jewish State, conceived in the bloodshed of nineteenth-century anti-Semitism, was born in bloodshed and has only been sustained through further bloodshed.

II

There is but one safe thing for the vanquished: not to hope for safety.

(Virgil, *The Aeneid*)

The seizure of Eilat in March 1949, the final Jewish conquest in a long and bloody war, marked the end of Israel's birth pangs. Nobody could argue that it was a clean or easy birth. Neither did Israel seem to be a healthy child – but it was alive, and for Zionists that was the main thing.

If Herzl had fathered the state and the British carried it, then the midwife and wet-nurse was undoubtedly David Ben-Gurion. Born in Poland in 1886 and formerly known as plain David Green, he arrived in Palestine in 1906. Like many Jews of his generation and background he combined acute political vision with an almost mystic, if essentially non-religious, attachment to Judaism. In 1920 he became the first Secretary-General of the Histadrut; in 1930 he was one of the creators of Mapai (the Israeli Labour Party which was the dominant force in Israeli politics for the first thirty years of statehood). He played a leading rôle in the formulation of the Biltmore Programme and established Zionist orientation towards America and, later, Israel's orientation towards France. In 1948, he became Prime Minister and Minister of Defence in Israel's Provisional Government and took upon himself the task of forging a workable state in the heat of the struggle for survival.

Throughout 1948, Ben-Gurion argued that two things were crucial to the Israeli enterprise. The first, the unification of Israel's military forces under a single command, he helped achieve by creating the Israeli Defence Forces (I.D.F.) around a nucleus of the old Haganah. In September 1948 the independent, right wing force known as the Irgun was abolished by Ben-Gurion. That same month members of the even more extreme Lehi assassinated the U.N. mediator Count Bernadotte in Jerusalem. Nobody was ever convicted of this murder, but it gave Ben-Gurion the opportunity to suppress Lehi, too. In October the Kibbutz-based commando corps, Palmach, was disbanded – thus removing the last vestige of independent command within the Israeli armed forces. These were essentially political, not military, decisions – as can be seen from the late stage at which they were implemented and the fact that the Haganah command had been effectively centralised some eighteen years earlier.

The second was the strengthening of the civil administration – perhaps the least honourable of Ben-Gurion's achievements during 1948. It was effected largely at the cost of creating a refugee problem of tragic proportions. Until April-May 1948, the Jews were probably more interested in seeing Palestinian Arabs remain in Jewish-occupied territory than in throwing them out. In fact, the more Arabs they could persuade to stay in predominantly Jewish areas the better it was for their public image as benevolent rulers. Nonetheless, during that period an estimated 200,000–250,000 Palestinian Arabs fled from their homes. Many of these were doubtless responding to Arab League calls to leave so that they might later return as conquerors. Some must have fled out of fear and others merely because they were in the way of bullets. However, the Declaration of the State of Israel and the large-scale seizure of land and property that went with it changed the picture. In May 1948 less than seven per cent of Palestine's total land area was controlled by Jews. Even excluding an estimated 400,000 Arabs living on the West Bank and in Transjordan, 150,000 living in the Gaza Strip and 250,000 already seeking refuge, there were still some 500,000 Arabs left on territory the Israelis sought to occupy. It would have been difficult, to say the least, to ensure that those 500,000 Arabs accepted the authority of a civil administration representing not many more than 600,000 Jews. On the other hand, if the Israeli version is true and those 500,000 were told that they would be welcome to remain in their homes under Jewish rule, it is not credible that only a handful did actually remain. History, if not common sense, testifies to the fact that people do not readily leave their houses and jobs to become refugees – even on the assumption that they will soon return to them. And yet U.N. figures estimate that the total number of Palestinian Arabs 'displaced' between the announcement of the U.N. partition plan in 1947 and the cessation of hostilities in 1949 was between 700,000 and 750,000. That is to say that very nearly all the Palestinian Arabs who had not fled their homes by 14 May 1948 subsequently became refugees. Either they were intensely hostile towards Israeli rule – in which case the Israelis would surely have helped them on their way – or the Israelis, seeking to control areas with large and *potentially* hostile Arab communities, persuaded them to go.

In any case, they did go – fleeing in their thousands to Gaza, the West Bank and the surrounding Arab states. The creation of a strong civil administration throughout the territory controlled by Israel in 1949 demanded the smallest possible hostile population. The refugee problem was (and is) entirely compatible with the aim of establishing and securing a specifically *Jewish* state – whether or not that aim was the actual cause of the problem.

Within the months following the defeat of the Arab League states, Ben-Gurion's government enacted a series of fundamental laws that, in the absence of a formal constitution, clearly defined Israel's foundations in the Jewishness of its people.* The Law of Return (1950) grants all Jewish immigrants the right of immediate citizenship. Excluded from this is anyone 'who acts against the Jewish nation'; anyone who may 'threaten the public health or State security'; anyone who has a criminal record and 'is liable to endanger the public welfare'; and, of course, anyone who is not Jewish. 'The Law of Return,' Ben-Gurion wrote, 'identified the historical destiny of the State of Israel as the ingathering of the exiles.'[6] The Israel Nationality Law (1952) includes the provisions of the Law of Return, while imposing a number of stringent conditions on the granting of citizenship to non-Jews. The Zionist Organisation Status Law (1952) formally acknowledges the interdependence of the state and the Zionist movement and declares that 'Israel regards itself as the work of the whole Jewish people and its gates are open to every Jew who wishes to come'. Israel's Marriage Laws forbid marriages between people of different religions.

The aim of these laws was simply to preserve the Jewish character of the State and to ensure a constant flow of Jewish immigrants to provide an essential labour force. At other times Ben-Gurion would also encourage a higher birth-rate to counter the Arabs' tendency to reproduce themselves more rapidly than the Jews. In 1971, he wrote that 'any Jewish woman who, as far as it depends on her, does not bring into the world at least four healthy children is shirking her duty to the nation, like a soldier who evades military service'.[7] The association between motherhood and military service is a revealing one, displaying a belief in the essential militarism of Israeli society. Israel is a country where, as Yigal Yadin once put it, 'every civilian is a soldier on 11 months' annual leave'.[8] But it is not just the existence of an army reserve that is important.

* For Israeli legal purposes it is not necessary to practise or even believe in Judaism (the Jewish religion) to be classified as a Jew. However, since the only workable definitions of 'Jew' and 'Jewish' are religious, this has often led to conflict within Israeli governments, who are invariably dominated by political parties of a distinctly secular persuasion. In fact, Israeli law and most Zionist writings are explicit in their rejection of the idea of a religious State. There is a striking contrast between Israel's insistence on its Jewish character rooted in Biblical and religious tradition and its parallel refusal to accord Jewish religious authority any civil or administrative rights. Political crises, often taking the form of conflicts within coalition governments including minority religious parties, frequently arise because of this traditional Israeli ambivalence towards Judaism.

The besieged State of Israel was forced to think and plan in military terms – it had to become, in many respects, like a gigantic fortress ringed by armed encampments and ordered by a discipline which verged on military command. This certainly was Ben-Gurion's vision. He was the first of many Israeli prime ministers who combined that office with the post of Minister of Defence. During the years following 1948, he sought to impose greater centralisation and state control on the Israeli community and promoted the establishment of armed agricultural settlements to 'defend' Israel's borders.

But the first problem to be met was the depletion of Israel's resources and manpower. Reinforcements were necessary, and no amount of exhortation would help Jewish mothers to reproduce faster than nature permitted. The single most important decision of Israel's first Parliament (Knesset) was to double the population in four years. Agricultural production had been severely hit by the flight of the *fellahin*. Old agricultural areas needed to be redeveloped and new settlements (especially in Galilee and the Negev) had to be established.

A number of measures were taken to secure Arab lands for Jewish settlers. Certain ordinances surviving from the Mandatory period (notably, Colonial Defence (Emergency) Regulations of 1945) were used for this purpose and in later years the Knesset approved more specific measures for the expropriation or military control of Arab land, such as the Law of Absentee Property (1950) and the Emergency (Security Zones) Regulations of 1949.

The influx of immigrants in the early years of the State actually exceeded expectations. Between 15 May 1948 and the end of 1951 nearly 700,000 Jews arrived in Israel, virtually doubling the population within three years. After 1951, this early flood subsided and immigration has since been effectively boosted only by Israel's military victories.*

The majority of Jewish immigrants until 1954 came from Africa and Asian countries (including a number of Arab countries – most notably the Yemen). They provided an in-

* The immigration problem underlies the bad relations between the USSR and Israel. The USSR's refusal to allow the free emigration of Jews (dating from 1967) is actually threatening to Israel. Soviet Jews represent the largest available source of likely immigrants into Israel – most Western Jews being too well-established in their own countries to wish to move, and the supply of Asian and African Jews being limited.

valuable source of cheap labour, in the absence of an adequate number of Arabs. The westernised Jews who made up the majority of Israeli society in those early days would not readily accept a low wage economy. But Israel started life as a Third World country, dependent on aid, loans and charity from the West. The country's economy was largely agriculture-based, and even agricultural production was in a mess. To develop at all, Israel needed to take drastic action. Accepting its position as an 'export platform' for the West in the first years of the State, the Israeli government introduced severe austerity measures combined with the immigration policy which supplied the necessary cheap labour.

Over 250 agricultural settlements were established in the four years to 1952, compared to just over 300 in the years between 1870 and 1948. Most of these were in the Negev and Upper Galilee – in pursuit of government policy to settle the border areas and secure routes into the Negev and on to Eilat. The Negev and Eilat were especially important for Israel's long-term planning. The desert areas represented sixty per cent of the territory controlled by Israel before 1967. And while its shipping was prevented from using the Suez Canal, the Gulf of Aqaba provided Israel's only viable route to its 'natural' sphere of economic influence – East and Southern Africa and Asia. The development of a port at Eilat (which today handles ten to fifteen per cent of Israel's foreign trade and the majority of its oil imports) was essential to the full realisation of the Zionist dream – that Israel should become the dominant nation in its area, free of any dependence on greater powers, a developed country transported to a so-called 'developing' region. The whole Negev area was, therefore, the way to Israel's future as well as a potential agricultural and mineral storehouse.

Egypt, of course, had other plans for the Negev. Particularly, it still cherished the dream of a land-bridge connecting it to the Arab East. Apart from that, the development of Eilat made the Suez blockade into an empty gesture. Egypt claimed that Israel had seized Eilat illegally – after they had signed the 1949 Armistice Agreement. Israel claimed that Eilat had been seized from Jordan, *before* that particular Armistice Agreement had been signed. The U.N. upheld Israel's position. Undeterred, the Egyptians fortified the entrance to the Gulf of

Aqaba and imposed a blockade on Israeli shipping (but not cargo) in 1951. Equally undeterred, Israel continued to build up Eilat and develop the Negev.

Development usually entailed the occupation of border areas by armed settlers, sometimes including regular members of the I.D.F. In Galilee, an Israeli scheme to drain the Huleh swamp provoked a Syrian assault in 1951 after Israel had intruded into areas declared to be demilitarised zones in the 1949 Syria–Israel Armistice Agreement. Israel, in turn, took retaliatory measures on Syrian villages. In 1953 an Israeli plan to divert the Jordan River headwaters to irrigate the Negev caused a further escalation of conflict. The project was halted in a matter of weeks, after the U.S. suspended economic and military aid to Israel, but was restarted a few years later.

Settlements established in the Negev – particularly along the border with the Gaza Strip and in the El Auja (Nitzana) demilitarised zone – caused further friction between Israel and Egypt. For some years, however, the conflicts stayed on a small scale – confined in the main to attacks by Palestinian Arab raiding parties and Jewish settler-soldiers.

The combined effects of the 1950 Tripartite Declaration by the U.S., France and Britain to restrict arms sales in the Middle East, the general economic situation of Israel and the Arab States alike and the influence of the Western powers (notably the U.S. and Britain) in containing Arab nationalism and controlling the Israeli economy, ensured the low level of conflict in the area.

War is not just conflict on a larger scale, however, it is conflict on a higher level of social organisation. In the wake of the Palestine War the societies of Israel, Egypt, Jordan and Syria were in disarray. But by 1953 qualitative changes had taken place in the Middle East which made full-scale war increasingly likely.

Curiously, the success of Israel's immigration programme had disastrous effects. The expense of absorbing the immigrants combined with Israel's massive defence allocation were crippling an already stilted economy. Housing and education were the two areas of most concern and immigrants were crowded into camps where the first stages of their absorption (through education) became the object of competing attentions from various political groupings within the country.

The 1949 Compulsory Education Law, adopted on 21 September 1949, provided a state-organised system of universal education. There were a number of different 'trends' – each one aligned to a political party. The trends competed vigorously for the right to educate immigrant children held temporarily in relocation camps. Particularly vociferous in this struggle were the religious parties who condemned 'evil instructors and clerks' and 'the unclean life of Israel'.[9] The government coalition under Ben-Gurion insisted on its right to control the education of immigrants, but the political conflicts on the issue eventually forced the government's resignation. The next coalition was headed by Ben-Gurion again, but included increased representation of the religious parties. This coalition proved to be equally unstable and Ben-Gurion seemed to despair of ever uniting Israel behind what he saw as its essential tasks – the attraction and absorption of immigrants. In 1953 he resigned, leaving the premiership and defence posts in the more moderate hands of Moshe Sharrett and Pinchas Lavon, respectively.

This swing towards moderation was possible partly because of the Arab States' internal weaknesses and mutual conflicts. During 1953–4 Arab–Israeli relations seemed to be improving, but the lack of a strong leader like Ben-Gurion also served to harden the resolve of Israel's military leadership who became increasingly distant from the diplomatic manoeuvring of the coalition government. While this rift between Israeli civil and military policies deepened, the Arab world began to undergo profound and far-reaching changes.

III

> I'm wondering if there's anything more I could have done to prevent this.
>
> (Anthony Eden, 1939)

The decrepit and corrupt Egyptian régime of King Farouk had fallen in 1952 to a coup instigated by a number of junior officers in the Egyptian army. These men had formed a loose organisation called the Free Officers' Movement some years before – men like Nasser, Sadat and Hakim Amer – whose goal had been hardly more radical than to democratise the process by which army officers were promoted to positions of real authority. But the Palestine War had shifted a certain amount of attention on to Farouk's rôle in Egyptian society. During the late forties his behaviour had become increasingly scandalous. His authority had been constantly undermined by the British, who despite the 1936 treaty occupied the country in force and still effectively ruled Egypt. He had been shamed and belittled and he seemed to make a virtue of his lack of power and responsibility.

During the Palestine War, Farouk divorced his popular wife, had Egyptian troops arrange a summer residence for himself in the middle of the embattled Gaza Strip and reputedly bought inferior weapons and pocketed the profits. These scandals were only overshadowed by the whole manner of the king's evidently degenerate life-style. Glandular disorders and a monstrous appetite had turned him into a figure of Rabelaisian proportions. He was as unable to govern his carnal lust as he was to govern Egypt. He had lost all the respect and popularity with which he had ascended the throne and sought only to cling to power and wealth for the sustenance of his gross desires.

His attempts to negotiate an evacuation of British troops were continually hampered by Britain's insistence on remaining in the Sudan and by the increasing corruption of Egypt's political parties. But Egypt's economy was in ruins. Defence expenditure was only one side of the problem. The Korean War had raised Egyptian cotton prices to an artificially high level. Despite the short-term benefits of this it was only a matter of time before it drove Egypt further into debt as more and more wheat had to be imported to offset the effects of speculative investment in cotton production and the ever-growing Egyptian population (noticeably swollen by the influx of Palestinian refugees). The Egyptian leadership responded to its internal problems by taking up an increasingly anti-British stance.

Progress towards the evacuation of the Suez Canal Zone was further impeded when the Conservatives under Winston Churchill regained power in the 1951 British elections. Churchill and his Foreign Secretary, Anthony Eden, were even less prepared to reach a negotiated settlement with Egypt than the Labour administration had been before. The American Government, meanwhile, tried to draw Egypt into some sort of pro-American alliance. They offered aid and their support in Egypt's struggle against Britain if Egypt would join the newly-formed Middle East Defence Organisation (M.E.D.O.) along with Turkey, France, Britain and the U.S. Since the first three named members of M.E.D.O. were precisely those countries who had been most responsible for Egypt's current plight, the Egyptians were not too happy with the proposal. They rejected it and stepped up the fight against the British presence.

Egypt's ruling political party, the nationalist Wafd, called for the formation of 'Liberation Squads' to attack British positions in the Canal Zone. The British retaliated and, after one particu-larly bloody assault on an Egyptian police station, the people of Cairo set fire to some four hundred buildings in the centre of the city. Their targets included property and buildings asso-ciated with foreign rule – including the famous Turf Club, Shepheard's Hotel and many shops and restaurants owned by Italians, Greeks and Jews. The damage was extensive – some £23 million worth. The Wafd had let loose forces beyond its control. Farouk entertained at his palace throughout the riots, showing no apparent concern. He fiddled while Cairo burned.

After the riots had subsided, Farouk stepped in and suspended the Wafd-controlled parliament. But it was too late. He had merely adjusted the set and settled back in his seat to watch the same old programme.

Of course, the greatest threat to Farouk came from his people – not from the British who were more or less convinced that the Suez Base could only be maintained with a full-scale invasion of Egypt. This was something they could not afford. But for the thorny problem of Sudan, the British would doubt-less have packed up and left the day after the Cairo riots. But British and Egyptian claims to Sudan were totally incompatible. The Egyptians demanded 'Nile Unity' while the British re-quired a link between its Middle Eastern and East African spheres of influence. Farouk, no doubt, would have accepted a British presence to protect his throne, but he was also facing the possibility of insurrection if the British refused to leave. He managed to suppress most of the threatening political organisa-tions in Egypt, but by the time he discovered the existence of the Free Officers they were ready to move.

When they did move, in July 1952, Farouk's régime collapsed like a house of cards. It had taken but the faintest breath to shatter the unstable edifice of Egyptian rule.

The Free Officers were nominally led by the respected General Neguib. In fact, the most influential member of this small band of soldiers was Gamal Abdul Nasser. Nasser argued from the start for a rapid return to parliamentary democracy in Egypt. But nobody had been prepared for the way in which the old guard had so quickly and completely collapsed. As Nasser noted in 1953, the Free Officers wanted no more than 'to purge the army, rid the country of foreign occupation and establish a clean, fair government which would work sincerely for the good of the people. Once in power,' he continued, 'we found ourselves faced with the difficult problem of establishing a political, social and economic programme.'[10] Within months the Free Officers became the sole instrument of government. The monarchy was abolished, political parties were suppressed and Nasser himself became Prime Minister and, in 1954, President.

They were hardly leaders of a revolutionary hue. They introduced some moderate land reforms, took drastic action against striking workers, came to an agreement with the British over Sudan and seemed set to reach a viable agreement on the evacuation of the Suez Base. Western governments found the Neguib–Nasser régime a welcome change. The British, despite a certain amount of paternalism, responded favourably to the new Egyptian leadership. The Free Officers were naïve in the ways of politics, but at least they were inspired to get things done. For the briefest historical moment it seemed as though a new, vigorous and independent Egypt might trip happily into the Western camp. Even Moshe Sharrett found the new masters of Egypt amenable to Israeli reason, and peace talks were held during 1953 and 1954.

Jordan, under Abdullah's grandson Hussein, and Egypt, under Nasser, introduced measures designed to minimise border crossings by Palestinians from the West Bank and the Gaza Strip. Both countries sought to normalise their relations with Israel. Early in 1954 Sharrett and Nasser sent representatives to Paris for secret talks aimed at bringing peace to their border and opening the Suez Canal to the passage of Israeli cargo (though not Israeli ships). During the course of the year it became clear that Britain would soon agree to an evacuation of the Suez Base. The Eisenhower administration in America looked even more favourably on the aims of Arab nationalists than Truman's Democratic government had. Dominated by Foreign Secretary John Foster Dulles's rabid anti-communism, American policy became increasingly obsessed with creating an 'iron curtain' around the U.S.S.R.'s southern borders. Without forsaking their commitments to Israel the Americans remained studiously aloof from British negotiations with Egypt, promising only to institute an Egyptian aid programme if and when agreement was reached with the British.

Dulles's first move towards creating an American sphere of influence in the Middle East was a tour of the region in May 1953 – four months after Eisenhower's inauguration and just over two months after the death of Stalin. Prime Minister Churchill was so upset by American moves that he took it for active encouragement of Egypt's anti-British stance. He wrote to Eisenhower saying so and threatening that 'Britain would disclaim all responsibility' from any 'bloodshed' that might result from American support of Egypt's demands.[11]

Despite Churchill's hysterical hatred of 'the Egyptian dictatorship', negotiations on the Suez evacuation continued in secret. The Israeli defence establishment (notably its intelligence wing) shared Churchill's misgivings, however. In July 1954 a number of incendiary bombs were placed in public buildings and the offices of the U.S. Information Service in Alexandria and Cairo. The campaign was carried out by Egyptian Jews and Israeli espionage-agents in order to create ill-feeling between America and Egypt and to defer the evacuation of the Suez Base. The responsible Israeli authorities thought that the presence of foreign troops in the Canal Zone was a barrier to Egyptian military action against Israel. They also calculated that with Egypt in control of the Canal even the limited access which Israel still had to the waterway would be threatened. In any event, the Egyptians immediately withdrew from their secret talks with Israel and arrested eleven Jews for the acts of sabotage. Two were hanged and six others sentenced to long prison terms. A few weeks before the hangings, six Egyptian members of the Muslim Brotherhood had been executed for an assassination attempt on Nasser following the signing of the long-awaited Suez Base evacuation agreement. Nasser was walking a narrow line indeed.

Sharrett had not known of the sabotage operation, and he immediately set up a committee to investigate the affair. It appears that after the failure of the operation the head of Israeli intelligence, Colonel Givli, and the Israeli Chief-of-Staff, Moshe Dayan, conspired to remove the relatively moderate Lavon from his post as Defence Minister. This may well have been the original purpose of the operation, we don't know – it was certainly the result. Lavon was forced to submit his resignation and Ben-Gurion returned from retirement to fill the vacant Ministry. Within days of his return in February 1955 the first large-scale military operation against the Egyptian army since 1948 was mounted. Israeli forces entered the Gaza Strip under cover of night and levelled an Egyptian army camp on the outskirts of the city of Gaza itself.

Whatever chances for peace there had been as 1954 dawned – and there are many who say they were considerable – Israel's confused and ham-fisted dealings with Egypt had put paid to them by the beginning of 1955.

The militarist argument in Israel was clearly winning the day. In August 1954 the Israelis made the first of many arms deals with France. The deal was actually financed by the U.S. and probably went through as a result of an earlier deal the U.S. had made with Iraq. However, orientation towards France was supported by Ben-Gurion who was disturbed by America's conciliatory attitude to the Arabs. For some years later, Israel received the majority of its weapons from France. A few weeks after the French deal was signed and just before Egypt and Britain reached agreement over Suez, the Israelis sent a ship (the *Bat Galim*) through the Canal. The ship was arrested and the crew held for three months. British intentions to leave the Suez Base did not waver, and the Israelis discovered that the Suez blockade would not end and would probably intensify with Egyptian control of the Canal. The complete closure of the Suez Canal and the Gulf of Aqaba was reason enough for Israel to go to war. With the gradual crumbling of the Tripartite Declaration, the means to wage such a war were becoming available.

The Suez Base evacuation agreement was signed on 19 October 1954. Two weeks later, the U.S. announced a 40-million-dollar aid programme to Egypt, and Britain resumed supplying arms. But Egypt's military inferiority to Israel was still obvious. The Gaza Raid only hammered that message home when Egyptian reinforcements were wiped out .by Israeli troops on their way to relieve the Gaza garrison. America, however, refused to supply Egypt with the modern arms and aeroplanes that it required unless Egypt entered some form of pro-American alliance.

This was the nub of the matter. 'How can a great power ally itself with a small state like us?' Nasser asked. 'This would not be an alliance – merely subordination.'[12] He was right.

The U.S., in a logical and geographic extension of the Truman doctrine which had guaranteed Greece and Turkey against Soviet intervention, saw the creation of a pro-American union among the so-called 'Northern Tier' states as its prime concern. A number of alliances were set up involving these states – Turkey, Iran and Pakistan – through 1953 and 1954. In 1955 Iraq and Turkey signed the 'Baghdad Pact' and this mutual defence agreement under U.S. supervision later attracted the other Northern Tier states (which, like Turkey, are not Arab) and Britain. Iraq, with its oil and its staunchly pro-British Prime Minister, Nuri es-Said, now became the Arab state of key importance to Britain.

'Our general policy in the Middle East', Anthony Eden wrote some years later, 'was founded on the need to protect British interests in Iraq and the Persian Gulf.'[13] The Suez evacuation – due for completion in June 1956 – and the Iraq–U.S. arms deal pushed Britain further into the American orbit. But the Americans were mindful of their commitments in Saudi Arabia. For them, Middle East oil meant an economic investment and the industrial welfare of their European allies. But oil routes were not a lifeline because, at that time, America was a net exporter of oil (as was the U.S.S.R.). Unlike the British, the Americans were able to take a dispassionate look at the Middle East. If Egypt refused to join a pro-American alliance, that was all right. The Northern Tier provided an adequate buffer against Soviet expansion in the area; Arab nationalism was, at that stage, directed against Britain and France – and American oil interests had, in the past, only benefited by anti-British feeling. Britain, on the other hand, was still reeling from Mossadeq's nationalisation of the Iranian oil industry. Mossadeq had been toppled by the C.I.A. in 1953 and America was moving into Iran. If Arab nationalism was victorious, Nuri could all too easily fall in Iraq. The Persian Gulf States might follow. Britain could kiss goodbye to its influence, its oil supplies and its economic revival.

However, Nasser had objected most vociferously to any attempt to persuade Egypt to join the Baghdad Pact. He had vehemently condemned Iraq for its membership of the Pact and for the preceding arms deal with the U.S. The British could do little to change his mind without American support, but they could at least quieten him down. In April 1955, Eden promised Nasser to forgo further pressure on Arab States to join the Pact in return for a cessation of anti-British propaganda. The two men agreed and Eden promptly turned his attention to persuading Jordan to join the Pact.

The complex web of intrigue was being woven exceedingly fine. Nasser declared himself for a policy of 'non-alignment' and attended the Bandung Conference along with other Asian and African leaders who sought independence from both the U.S.S.R. and the U.S. Sometime during 1955 he also approached the U.S.S.R. for arms, and informed American representatives that their Government's policy might force him to buy Soviet weapons. In October he announced a weapons deal with Czechoslovakia. Meanwhile, border incidents in the West Bank, Sinai and Gaza multiplied alarmingly. A full-scale Israeli occupation of the El Auja demilitarised zone on the Egypt–Israel border seemed to presage an imminent war. The Egyptian response to Britain's persistent attempts to induct Jordan into the Baghdad Pact was to sign a mutual defence pact with Syria. The Syrians, too, started buying arms from the U.S.S.R.

The British were more concerned about Jordan than anything else. 'My main purpose was to draw Iraq and Jordan closer together,' Eden recalled later.[14] The problem was that the mass of the Jordanian population, and especially the half-million or so Palestinians, had no desire whatsoever to be drawn closer to Iraq. Hussein was quite prepared to accede to British requests and join the Baghdad Pact – after all, his army and air force were trained, equipped and officered by the British; his throne itself was propped up by British money, men and weapons; and he had family ties with the Iraqi monarchy. But the closer he drew to signing the necessary alliance, the more violent became the ensuing riots. Nationalism had become an irresistible force in Jordan and Hussein was obliged to bow to it – despite himself but in order to save himself.

Eden, who had become Prime Minister in April 1955, saw the hand of Nasser at work. His worst suspicions were confirmed when Hussein sacked Glubb Pasha, the British commander-in-chief of the Jordanian army, in March 1956. Glubb had been charged with putting down the anti-Baghdad-Pact riots that had swept Jordan, and his dismissal coincided with a visit to Cairo by Foreign Secretary Selwyn Lloyd. Flying to London, Glubb told Eden that Saudi money and Egyptian manipulation were behind the increasing force of Jordanian nationalism. Two equally unsatisfactory outcomes seemed possible. Either the British would be forced to leave Jordan by popular pressure, or the Jordan–Israel border troubles would escalate to a war which could well involve Britain on both sides. Eden seized gleefully on the chance to blame Nasser for this disastrous state of affairs. He had once seen Nasser as a sort of Egyptian Cromwell – now he talked of the Arab leader as an Egyptian Hitler. 'What's all this nonsense about isolating Nasser or "neutralising" him,' Eden shouted at one of his civil servants at the time, 'I want him destroyed, can't you understand?'[15]

Similar cries could be heard ringing through the French and Israeli corridors of power. Nasser was openly supporting the nationalist rebellion in French Algeria. The discovery of considerable oil and gas reserves in Algeria in 1955 made France even more determined not to lose this valuable colony. The Israelis – once again under Ben-Gurion's premiership – saw the 'Czech' arms deal and the growing possibility of some Nasser-dominated political union between Egypt, Syria and Jordan. Ben-Gurion's response to this was typical – he simply increased the frequency and intensity of retaliatory raids into Arab territory. In September 1955 Nasser closed the Gulf of Aqaba to Israeli cargo as well as ships and, soon after, Ben-Gurion and Dayan started planning a so-called 'pre-emptive strike' into Sinai.

The last act in this shabby drama opened with John Foster Dulles finally and firmly withdrawing the U.S. and World Bank promise of aid to help build a vast irrigation and hydro-electric dam at Aswan on the Upper Nile. Unlike Ben-Gurion or Eden, Dulles and Eisenhower were happy to 'isolate' Nasser. Active antagonism would have hindered their credibility among the Arabs (specifically, within the Saudi leadership) and they calculated that the withdrawal of aid would bring Nasser to his senses or, failing that, to his knees. Despite Eden's characterisation of Nasser as pro-Soviet, the Americans realised this was far from the truth. Nasser had, in fact, acted against the Egyptian Communist Party and continued to express his opposition to any form of great power alignment. But the Americans did not realise that Nasser was even more determined to survive than he was to avoid alignment. And they also failed to appreciate that Stalin's death had loosed forces in the U.S.S.R. whose ambitions lay in the direction of increased trade with the non-Communist world. To the extent that men like Khruschev and Bulganin sought to increase Soviet ties with the rest of the world, they were willing to overlook the internal affairs of régimes like Nasser's.

Within seven days of Dulles snubbing the Egyptians, Nasser nationalised the lucrative and, by then, Egyptian-managed Suez Canal. Britain and France – joint shareholders in the Canal – decided on war. Israel was determined that Suez or Aqaba must be opened to Israeli shipping. The 'madman' Nasser had to be taught a short and sharp military lesson. In early August 1956 the Israeli Government assured France of its support in the coming war. But America was making every effort to avoid a large-scale conflict with Egypt; and the Russians, when not preoccupied with suppressing rebellion in Poland and Hungary, threatened to intervene if France and Britain attacked Egypt.

The French devised a cunning plan calling for an Israeli invasion of Sinai. A joint Anglo-French assault on the Canal Zone would follow some days later under the guise of a policing action. The British and the French would swear blind that they were only in Egypt to separate the Egyptian and Israeli forces. But they would stay in Egypt nonetheless.

On 24 October 1956 Britain, France and Israel signed the Sèvres accord setting out the details of their planned operation against Egypt. The British and French would have been happy to agree on a handshake. But Ben-Gurion could trust no one. Israel was surrounded by enemies. He had demanded the perfidious promises in writing. At Sèvres, he got them.

Chapter 5

BEN-GURION'S WAR

The Sinai Campaign, October-November 1956.

Persuade her; cut her throat, but persuade her.
(Joe Orton, *Entertaining Mr Sloane*)

I

In the early fifties the Arab states were primarily concerned
with freeing themselves from the lingering grip of colonialism.
But Israel had not been forgotten. For one thing the two issues
were seen as being interrelated, for another the trauma of
1948–9 could only be exorcised from the collective Arab psyche
by military success. Sooner or later the armies would have to
meet once more.

This underlying tension received permanent reinforcement
along the uneasy frontiers between the various Arab states and
Israel. Cynics had noted that 'the boundary lines had been
drawn with a thick chinagraph pencil on a small-scale map',[1]
and certainly the haphazard manner in which they drove
through farms and villages provided support for such an
assertion. Chinagraph pencil or not, they were hard borders to
defend and easy ones to cross.

Soon after the 1948–9 war ended, Arabs started crossing
them. At first they were mostly Palestinian Arabs paying return
visits to their former lands. These, they thought with some
justification, were more likely sources of nourishment than the
dry hills and valleys of Samaria, to which they had been so
summarily banished. In their footsteps came a host of less
justified day-trippers: bands of thieves eager to benefit from
the blind eyes turned by officialdom on the Arab side of the
border. Ineffective Israeli retaliatory measures encouraged the
process, and soon a major trade in loot and murder was
flourishing. Israeli casualties, almost all civilian, mounted

steadily. In the three years 1951–3 they totalled 464, or over half as many as Israel would incur in the entire June War.

These Arab raids received no official endorsement, nor possessed a directly political purpose, but it was inevitable that the Israelis would see them as an expression of the general Arab hostility. They retaliated, with mounting effectiveness and ferocity, against Jordan, the source of the vast majority of raids.

The Egyptian frontier was generally quiet at this time, but Ben-Gurion, eager to demonstrate Israeli power to the new Nasser régime, wanted action there as well. The result was the Gaza Raid of February 1955. This ill-conceived operation, far from achieving either its stated or unstated aims – the termination of Arab incursions and the cowering of Nasser respectively – merely provoked an Egyptian reply in kind. Within a short space of time the *fedayeen* (freedom-fighters) were raiding into Israel with both official encouragement and a directly political purpose.

They did not achieve much in military terms, but they did keep the Palestinian grievance in the newspapers and, more significantly, their much-exaggerated exploits provided a welcome glimmer of Arab pride, and a much-needed morale boost for the Egyptian Army. Wishful thinkers could point to the *fedayeen* as clear proof that the Arab armies of 1948–9 had been reflections less of the Arab military character than of the corrupt régimes then in power. And if the *fedayeen* represented the advance guard of the new post-1952-revolution Arabs, then a new Egyptian Army of similarly dynamic energy was surely in the process of completion.

This was wishful thinking with a vengeance. The Army was certainly better equipped than it had been in 1948–9; the 'Czech' Arms Deal having provided a useful force of armour (some 150 T-34s and around a hundred Su-100 self-propelled guns) and the basis of a modern air force. Also the upper stratum of the military hierarchy was more knowledgeable, and more likely to be selected on merit than in Farouk's day. But beneath this stratum the junior officers and N.C.O.s were generally lacking the necessary technical training, and the mass of *fellahin* infantry regarded military service as a particularly onerous portion of life's burden. The deep divisions within Egyptian society were faithfully recreated in the Egyptian

Army. Cooperation and communication had little reality in the social context, hence they had little reality in the military. The concept of a national policy was still the prerogative of the few. The Egyptian soldier fought because he was ordered to. The 'new' Egyptian Army was, not for the last time, a myth.

II

Israel was bent not on recovering lost land or national self-respect, but on the more basic business of survival. Social divisions, as prevalent in Israel as elsewhere, had been suspended in the face of the external threat, and both State and Army were created amidst an all-encompassing sense of social and national unity. The political consequences of a unity reinforced by external enmity – the provisioning of Israel's ruling group with a vested interest in national paranoia – would of course contribute to Middle Eastern instability, and so prove both self-justifying and self-regenerating. But at the same time the military consequences of that unity – the creation of an army whose *esprit de corps* was virtually unique – would save Israel time and again from the consequences of that instability. The Israeli Defence Forces (I.D.F.) would never suffer like its enemies from a shortage of social cohesion or motivation.

There were problems, however. The most obvious was manpower. The 'War of Independence' had been won by the nation-in-arms, but no nation can forever remain in arms. The victorious army of 1948–9 was mostly disbanded, its members returning to those civilian pursuits that add up to a society. Yet the threat remained. Israel was still surrounded by enemies intent on removing it from the map, who would not recognise or make peace with a Palestinian cuckoo state. Somehow a way had to be found of producing a nation-in-arms at the drop of a hat.

The method adopted was a three-tiered system of regulars, conscripts, and a large civilian reserve. The regular force was small, comprised exclusively of officers and specialist N.C.O.s. Each year it received a new intake of conscripts to train, and after serving their term these retired into the civilian reserve without relinquishing their membership of specific units. Each year they would return for refresher courses and further train-

ing. In such a manner the regular army, with its current conscripts, always formed a skeleton ready to receive, at a
moment's notice, the flesh and bones of the civilian reserve. The
I.D.F. could match Arab manpower in a matter of hours.

This rational, as opposed to conventional, approach
epitomised Israeli military thought in these early years. It was
a new army, unfettered by the dead hand of tradition, able to
tackle problems with the simple genius of common sense. The
British had taught the Egyptians how to stop Rommel, and
now the Soviets were teaching them how to fight on the North
European plain; the Israelis were teaching themselves how to
fight in the local areas that mattered. With weaponry the same
principles operated. The Israelis bought what they wanted,
modifying if need be to suit their particular needs, whereas the
Arab states tended to take what they were given, even down to
amphibious tanks for use in Sinai.

Pragmatism was installed at the heart of the Israeli military
machine, and despite Ben-Gurion's determined efforts to build
a traditional army untainted by the egalitarian ethos of the
Palmach, it proved unshakeable. Certainly discipline was tighter
than it had been during the 1948–9 war – the use and maintenance of modern weaponry requires as much – but the formal
discipline of European armies was never very noticeable in the
I.D.F. The unique social cohesion of Israeli society made it
unnecessary, and the alternative – 'internal' or 'self-imposed'
discipline – was much more conducive to the spreading of
initiative down through the ranks.

The pragmatic approach was well illustrated by the birth and
career of 'Unit 101'. In the immediate post-war years, as we
have seen, the main problem facing the I.D.F. was border
infiltration. Attempts to deter these raids by retaliatory attacks
on Arab villages, police stations and army installations proved
largely unsuccessful. For one thing the Arab states were not
very susceptible to local deterrence measures, and for another
the Israeli regulars proved singularly adept at bungling the
measures themselves. If the army of 1948–9 had not forgotten
its military skills, then it was giving a very passable imitation.

Only the I.D.F. would have come up with a solution like
'Unit 101'. The leadership, despairing of the regular force under
its command, invited a reserve battalion leader, one Ariel
Sharon, to recruit a small private army, and for several months

in late 1953 Sharon's 'Unit 101' conducted a series of successful night-raids into Arab territory. At the end of the year the unit was merged with a paratroop battalion, still under Sharon, as the 202nd Paratroop Battalion. Through 1954 it conducted more successful operations. The major reason for these initial successes was a remarkable capacity for improvisation:

> Instead of using the dynamic leadership and *esprit de corps* of the paratroopers to enhance the value of conventional tactics, these assets were used to the full by adopting bold high-risk tactics which Israeli superiority in morale made possible. In other words, Sharon's tactics were 'relational', rooted in the specific strengths and weaknesses of the adversaries. Egyptian and Jordanian soldiers were trained regulars who fought stubbornly and well so long as they were holding fortified positions according to plans prepared in advance. By relying on shock and surprise instead of conventional tactics, Sharon exploited the enemy's inability to improvise amidst confusion.[2]

These 'relational tactics', along with the other characteristics of '202' – high morale, unconventionality, democratic informality – became a paradigm for the entire I.D.F. during Moshe Dayan's tenure as Chief of Staff.

But the I.D.F., and Dayan, still had certain blind spots. By 1955 the problems of conscription/mobilisation, morale, organisation, and infantry-fighting qualities had all been largely solved. To Dayan, an infantryman at heart, albeit a motorised one, this meant that all the problems had been solved. But to any student of the recent world war there were two rather startling omissions from this list: tanks and planes.

In 1955 the Israeli Air Force and Armour Corps were still suffering for their relative failure in the 1948–9 war. The Israeli armoured force in that war had consisted of thirteen tanks which frequently broke down, and whose crews spoke a bewildering variety of languages. Faith in tanks had not been enhanced by this unit's performance. Despite the acquisition of a sizeable number in the post-war years the I.D.F. leadership continued to think tanks both too unreliable and too slow for Israel's mechanised and motorised infantry units. The armour would only be used in an infantry support rôle.

The crews, of course, knew better. Their tanks were faster *on the battlefield* because they could advance into enemy fire. And this fact, they knew, would eventually penetrate their superiors' skulls. In the meantime the enthusiastic members of the Armour Corps took their tanks to pieces, put them back together again, drove them over every conceivable type of terrain, and discussed, practised, modified tactics to the last armoured nuance. Here again the Israelis were benefiting from their ignorance, building a tactical doctrine from the basics upwards, a 'relational' doctrine geared to themselves, their machines, their terrain. In the war games of 1952 and 1953 the Armour Corps put it all into practice, effectively winning both for their respective sides. The military hierarchy, echoing the conservatism of Guderian's superiors in the 1930s, merely censured the tankmen for spoiling the manoeuvres. The Armour Corps was not deterred. If the Sinai Campaign plan should give them little scope for self-justification, then they would have to ignore the plan.

The I.A.F. had not been particularly successful in 1948–9 either, but it was realised that its future rôle would be a crucial one. Wars in the Middle East were likely to be short, and planes were fast. They were also sophisticated weapons, giving the edge in air combat to the more sophisticated culture. And as the military geography of Israel would force the I.D.F. to accept the exposed rôle of the attacker, the I.A.F. would have to provide that cover which the desert would not.

What sort of planes were required? The I.A.F.'s one great success in 1948–9 had been the immobilisation of the Egyptian Air Force (E.A.F.) on the ground at the beginning of Operation *Yoav*. To repeat this feat the I.A.F. would require planes with a substantial bomb 'pay-load' – fighters would not suffice. But as the I.A.F.'s primary rôle after such a strike would be that of ground-support, then highly mobile planes were essential – bombers would not suffice. Since Israel could not afford both fighters and bombers the I.A.F. would be built around fighter-bombers, the most modern available, from the Mystère through the Mirage to the Phantom.

The I.A.F. has always been, unlike the Army, a regular force, and in the years prior to the Sinai Campaign the emphasis on technical perfectionism and producing pilots of the highest quality were first laid down. By 1956, like the Armour Corps, the I.A.F. thought itself equal to any Arab challenge. It also found such faith unreciprocated at the highest level. But vindication for both was soon to come.

III

The reorganisation of the Israeli and Egyptian armed forces was interrupted by the campaign in Sinai. The political background to this strange alliance between Israeli virility, French desperation and British senility has already been discussed. Here it must be noted that strong military reasoning guided the Israeli decision to seek a clash of arms with Egypt in the wastes of Sinai.

A state of war still existed between the two nations, posing, so the Israelis felt, a grave threat to the security of their state. In the summer of 1956 it took three forms: the *fedayeen* raids, the Egyptian stranglehold on the Straits of Tiran, and the growth of Egypt's military resources in the aftermath of the 'Czech' Arms Deal. Sharon's reprisal raids, though usually successful at a local level, were proving no deterrent to the overall level of *fedayeen* activity. Moreover, 202's tactics were becoming increasingly familiar to the enemy, and the unit's losses were mounting. The near-disaster of the Qalqiliya operation in early October 1956 was a warning not to be ignored. 'It is clear to all of us', Dayan noted in his diary, 'that we have reached the end of the chapter of night reprisal actions.'[3] The alternative course – already agreed at Sèvres – was all-out war.

The problems of the Straits also admitted of only one solution. Given the configuration of the Sinai communication system – the only good road to Sharm el-Sheikh led down the Gulf of Suez coast – the forced opening of the Gulf of Aqaba implied the prior conquest of Sinai *in toto*. This of course would involve a sharp check to Egyptian visions of military potency.

The Israeli war-aim was thus to 'confound the organisation of the Egyptian forces in Sinai and bring about their collapse'.[4] The method would consist of attacks along the three major trans-Sinai routes. On the first day, 29 October, 395 paratroopers from '202' would be dropped at the entrance to the Mitla Pass, with the dual purpose of threatening the Suez Canal (the Israeli contribution to the Anglo-French hypocrisy) and causing the maximum psychological turmoil in the Egyptian High Command. Before the latter could react, Sharon would lead the rest of his brigade via El Kuntilla, El Thamad and Nakhl to link up with the Mitla force. By the evening of

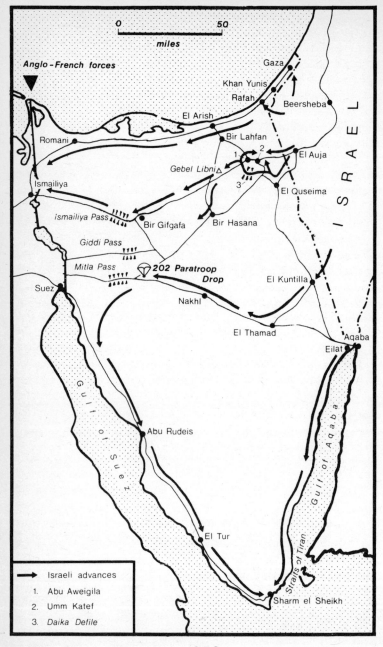

0   50

miles

Anglo-French forces

Gaza

Khan Yunis

Rafah

Beersheba

El Arish

Romani

Bir Lahfan

1   2

El Auja

Gebel Libni

3

Ismailiya

El Quseima

Ismailiya Pass

Bir Gifgafa

Bir Hasana

Giddi Pass

Mitla Pass

202 Paratroop
Drop

El Kuntilla

Suez

Nakhl

El Thamad

Aqaba

Eilat

ISRAEL

Gulf of Suez

Abu Rudeis

Gulf of Aqaba

El Tur

Straits of Tiran

Sharm el Sheikh

→ Israeli advances
1. Abu Aweigila
2. Umm Katef
3. *Daika Defile*

5. The Sinai campaign, 1956

30 October the British and French would be distracting the Egyptians with their phoney ultimatum, and the Israeli motorised infantry could begin to force its passage through the two main defence positions (Rafah and Umm Katef) on the northern and central routes. The only all-armour force, Ben Ari's 7th Armoured Brigade, was initially given no rôle at all in Sinai. It would act as a decoy on the Jordanian border. But Dayan was eventually persuaded to allow it a breakthrough-exploitation rôle, once the infantry had cleared Umm Katef. The I.A.F. was allocated purely ground-support duties. Ben-Gurion did not trust it to defend Israeli air space, preferring an arrangement with the French.

The Egyptian strategic reaction to this onslaught would be limited by the time factor; only about twelve hours passing between realisation that this was more than a large reprisal raid and the overshadowing effect of the Anglo-French ultimatum. Reaction would be mostly tactical – the Egyptian forces in Sinai would defend themselves when attacked. At the moment of invasion they consisted of strong infantry forces manning the fortified positions in eastern Sinai, backed by fifty Shermans on the El Arish–Rafah axis and seventy T-34s at Bir Gifgafa.

On the afternoon of 29 October Sharon's paratroopers duly dropped out of the sky near the Mitla Pass, and the rest of the brigade rolled over the frontier near El Kuntilla. The pass was more strongly defended than had been expected, and Sharon's vehicles broke down with alarming regularity – logistics and technical expertise were not priority concerns during Dayan's tenure as Chief of Staff – but late the following day the two groups managed their planned rendezvous at the entrance to the pass, and proceeded to dig in against a possible counter-attack.

The same day, 30 October, El Quseima was taken with difficulty by the infantry, and the remarkable odyssey of 7th Armoured Brigade began. Forbidden to motor on into Sinai until Umm Katef had fallen, Ben Ari decided to speed the process by a night drive through the Daika defile and into the rear of the Egyptian positions. Despite this assistance, the Israeli infantry proved incapable of capturing the Egyptian defences on 31 October – according to a contemptuous Dayan, 'their heart was not in it' – and Ben Ari decided to use up the time available with an armoured incursion into Sinai. While one unit took the Rouaffa Dam position behind Umm Katef the rest of 7th Armoured Brigade raced west to Bir Hasana and the Gebel Libni crossroads.

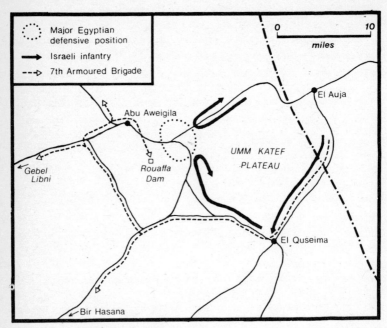

6. Umm Katef, 1956

Ben Ari was not the only Israeli commander disobeying orders that day. Sharon had been forbidden to assault the Egyptian-held Mitla Pass, but valour proved more than a match for discretion or obedience, and under cover of permission to 'reconnoitre' he sent a large force in against the Egyptian defenders. The paratroopers managed to wrest the pass from the enemy after a bitter fight, but thirty-eight Israeli deaths were rather a high price to pay for an objective not included in, or necessary to, the Israeli plan.

That evening, 31 October, the Israelis also launched their attack on the Rafah positions, and the Anglo-French air attacks on Egypt began. Early the next morning Nasser ordered all uncommitted units in Sinai to withdraw westwards over the Canal for action against the expected Anglo-French landing.

The contest in Sinai was over, although committed Egyptian units in the Rafah–El Arish and Umm Katef areas continued to fight through the day. On the central route Ben Ari's tanks engaged Egyptian T-34s in the main armoured battle of the war, and forced their retreat.

The Israelis mopped up. Gaza and El Arish fell on 2 November, Khan Yunis the following day. The I.A.F. took a fearful toll of the retreating Egyptians, whose own air force was fully engaged on the far side of the Canal. Israeli forces moved down the Gulf of Suez and Gulf of Aqaba coastlines towards Sharm el Sheikh. On 5 November, some hours before the British and French paratroopers landed around Port Said for their short-lived occupation, Sharm el-Sheikh fell to a dawn assault. All Sinai, but for the ten-mile-wide stretch east of the Suez Canal, was in Israeli hands.

IV

The Sinai Campaign had unusual military consequences. Normally it is victory that brings complacency and defeat a new willingness to learn, but in this case it was almost the reverse.

The Egyptians could not ignore their enforced withdrawal from Sinai, but they could, and did, confuse its causes. Too much emphasis was placed on the distraction of the Anglo-French threat and too little on the actual course of events in Sinai. The Egyptian leadership, military and political, found it easier to concentrate on the fact the E.A.F. had been facing three other air forces, than to dwell on the poor performance of individual squadrons in air combat against the I.A.F. They preferred to revel in the repeated Israeli failures to take Umm Katef, than to consider the consequences of the ease with which it had been bypassed by Ben Ari's armour. Perhaps the staggering of the Israeli assaults encouraged Egyptian faith in the strong fortifications along the frontier, but the speed with which all but Umm Katef were overcome should have suggested adoption of the defence plan submitted by the régime's German military advisers in 1953–4. The major defences, they had argued, should be sited on the more defensible line of the Central Ridge, not on the frontier. Even to reach such a line the Israelis would have to traverse eighty miles of desert; *their* supply lines would be long, *their* vehicles worn out by the appalling 'roads', not the Egyptian. But this sensible advice was disregarded. It offended Egyptian pride, it ruled out the possibilities of attack. The Egyptians continued to agree with their new Soviet advisers that more and better fortifications on the frontier would prove adequate in the future.

The Israelis, in contrast, had learnt a great deal, from both their successes and failures. The mechanical, logistical and command problems encountered during the campaign would be rigorously studied and overcome. And the new-found potency of the I.A.F. and Armour Corps would provide the nucleus of Israel's striking force in the years to come. It would be a faster and more devastating force than either of those that had already, twice, broken through the Egyptian defences guarding the approaches to Sinai.

Chapter 6

NASSER'S PEACE

The Aftermath of Treachery, 1956–1958

I say, you can't be sure the war will ever end. Of course it may have to pause occasionally – for breath as it were – it can even meet with an accident – nothing on this earth is perfect. A war of which we could say it left nothing to be desired will probably never exist.

(Bertolt Brecht, *Mother Courage*)

1

We are not at war with Egypt. We are in armed conflict.

(Anthony Eden, 1956)

Despite the military defeat suffered by the Egyptians in the Suez and Sinai campaigns, the propaganda victory belonged exclusively to them. Nasser's personal and political stock leapt in value as a result of the Anglo-French-Israeli alliance (thenceforth remembered by Arab propagandists as the tripartite aggression), and Arab nationalism found itself an unsullied hero. His determination, the unconditional support he received from the U.S.S.R., his very ability to survive military blows and diplomatic threats fuelled the struggle for self-determination throughout the Arab world. One by one, the ruling parties in Jordan, Syria, the Lebanon and Iraq saw social unrest break into outright rebellion. Only Hussein managed to survive intact, thanks to assistance from Saudi Arabia and from the U.S. Sixth Fleet which sailed into the Eastern Mediterranean at the first sign of trouble in 1957. But even Hussein was forced to recognise the minimal demand of his people for more democratic government.

In Syria, the pro-Western régime of Adib Shishakli had fallen in 1954. Concern over both the possibility of Western intervention and the growing power of the Syrian Communist Party created the conditions under which the Syrian Ba'ath Party could push its demands for increased Arab unity. Nasser was also worried by the possibility of either a pro-Soviet or a pro-Western takeover in Syria. In 1958, the two countries, both already receiving aid from the U.S.S.R., entered a curious union under the name of the United Arab Republic. With Cairo as its capital, and a cabinet consisting of seven Egyptians and one Syrian, the U.A.R. was effectively an instrument for the Egyptian protection of Syria. (The Yemen joined later in 1958 for similar reasons.) Nevertheless, under the auspices of the U.A.R., the pan-Arab Ba'ath Party increased its influence considerably.

A Nasserite faction in the Lebanon, probably with Syrian support, demanded that their Government approach the U.A.R. The demands were backed by outbreaks of violence. The Lebanese rebellion, which reached its peak in mid 1958, was put down with the assistance of British and American troops. (The U.S.S.R. vetoed the use of U.N. forces.) But from then on, the Lebanese government was reorganised as an uneasy coalition of the pan-Arab left and the pro-Western right.

The Hashemite Iraqi régime, dominated by Prime Minister Nuri es-Said, was thus increasingly threatened by its solidly pro-Western stance. Membership of the Baghdad Pact placed Iraq firmly in the enemy camp as far as Egypt, Syria and many Iraqis were concerned. To counter the establishment of the U.A.R. and the growing influence of pan-Arabism, Nuri's government hastily engineered a federation with Jordan. But a group of army officers under Brigadier Kassem and Colonel Aref took the opportunity of an order to march into Jordan during the Lebanese crisis to turn their troops on Baghdad. Despite Kassem's appearing to be a second Nasser, unlike his mentor his ambitions were largely personal. He was eventually overthrown in 1963 by a coup led by the Iraqi Ba'ath Party, but not before Iraq had followed Egypt and Syria some way into the Soviet camp.

Russian and American ambitions in the Middle East were given a helping hand by the Sinai War. Because Britain and France were permanent members of the U.N. Security Council they were able, in the early part of November 1956, to veto any Security Council resolutions aimed at the cessation of hostilities in Sinai and the Canal Zone. Even the General Assembly could only pass vague resolutions calling for immediate ceasefires or instant withdrawals. They had good intentions but little muscle. The U.S. and the U.S.S.R. felt obliged to take their own action in order to stop the fighting. Both superpowers were eager to impose a peace on the four combatants – the U.S. because it saw the likelihood of Egyptian influence in the Middle East spreading even faster if the fighting continued, and the U.S.S.R. because it needed to support Nasser without actually becoming involved in a war.

The U.S. used a variety of pressures available to it – including the withdrawal of aid from Israel and the withdrawal of oil supplies to Britain and France. The Soviets contented themselves with what was more or less a propaganda exercise – they declared their total support for Egypt and threatened to intervene after all the major battles had been fought and a ceasefire was about to be signed. In fact, America held all the trump cards. The Israelis could not hope to sustain their armies without American support and, in any case, by 5 November they had achieved all their objectives. Britain and France, who had taken the brunt of the fighting after 5 November, were almost totally dependent on American oil, once the Suez Canal had been blocked by sunken ships and the Syrians had blown up the oil-pipelines crossing their territory. Even the Baghdad Pact countries agreed to boycott Britain. For some time after the Suez affair, oil and petrol were severely rationed in Britain. Many people argue that the British economy has not yet recovered from the blow.

American persuasion was reinforced by a dramatic split in the ranks of Britain's ruling Conservative Party. Eden, in a misguided attempt to avoid repeating the mistakes made in supporting the appeasement of Hitler, plunged Britain into a crisis unparalleled in the quarter-century following World War II. He was condemned by the public and his colleagues, attacked from the left, right and centre. Key civil servants resigned in protest. His competence to lead was thrown into openly-expressed doubt. Even if the government survived the crisis, Eden could not.

Any hopes that the British might have had of retaining their influence in the Middle East were well and truly crushed by the

Suez adventure. With the Tripartite Declaration in a shambles and the Security Council stymied by British and French veto-ing, Russia and America struggled to seize the whip hand in the region. In early March 1957 the 'Eisenhower Doctrine' was approved by the U.S. Senate. Under its terms the U.S. guaranteed to protect the political independence of all Middle East States – by force, if necessary. It was 'Son of the Truman Doctrine'. Most Arabs were vigorously and often violently opposed to it. Without any doubt, the Eisenhower Doctrine encouraged the rebellion which swept the Middle East in the next few months as much as, if not more than, Nasser did.

America's persistent attempts to isolate Nasser led it to increase effectively its support for Israel. An equally important consequence of American policy was that newly-emergent Arab leaders (whether Nasserite, nationalist, socialist or merely populist) seeking to shed the harness of great power control rejected all American attempts to deal out aid in return for promises of allegiance or treaties of friendship.

The U.S.S.R., on the other hand, gained a great deal of credibility with the (loosely-speaking) 'anti-imperialist' movements of the Arab world. The Russians sought to extract no promises, nor to make any bargains. They realised that acceptance of aid itself was a sufficient guarantee of the Arabs' continued dependence on them. They even overlooked the rabid anti-communism of most emergent Arab leaders. By the end of the fifties the U.S.S.R. was heavily involved in Egypt, Syria and Iraq. Of the seven original Arab League states only Saudi Arabia, Jordan and the Lebanon maintained a pro-American stance – and it was a precarious one, at that.

II

There is one thing about being president – nobody can tell you when to sit down.

(Dwight D. Eisenhower)

The Sinai War was the beginning of a new and more critical stage in the history of the Middle East. Rather than put an end to Arab hostility against Israel, the Israeli victory heralded increasing polarisation in the area. The eventual settlement left no doubt in Arab minds that true independence could not be achieved while the State of Israel existed. Despite the extreme caution, not to say duplicity, with which Eisenhower and Dulles dealt with Israel, Ben-Gurion's Government managed to extract assurances from America and the U.N. which amounted to an occupation of Egyptian territory and a guarantee of American protection for Israel.

Little difficulty was encountered in the negotiations for the Anglo-French withdrawal from Egypt. But Israel was a different matter. While agreeing in principle to a total withdrawal from Sinai, Ben-Gurion and his Foreign Minister, Golda Meir, voiced concern over the matter of the Gaza Strip and the Gulf of Aqaba. The Israelis demanded U.N. guarantees to safeguard their right of passage through the Gulf and to ensure the cessation of Palestinian Arab raids from the Gaza Strip. The American attitude was conciliatory in the extreme. Having assured Israel of support at the U.N. General Assembly, Dulles and Eisenhower proceeded to demand Israel's full and unconditional withdrawal from Sinai and Gaza.

In fact, Israel could not afford the expense of a continued occupation. The withdrawal of the Anglo-French force towards the end of December 1956 left Israeli troops vulnerable to attack. Without American support (aid had been suspended in October) the chances of Israeli victory in case of such attack could only deteriorate as time passed. By the end of January 1957 Israel had pulled back from all of Sinai except for the Gaza Strip and Sharm el-Sheikh (which overlooked the only navigable entrance to the Gulf of Aqaba through the narrow Straits of Tiran).

The Israelis thought that in evacuating most of Sinai they were making a concession which would be rewarded by a softening of the American attitude. They were wrong. America had too much to lose in the Arab world by showing itself to favour Israel. American support for Israel might be expressed behind closed doors, but in the councils of the United Nations or in the public eye it was (and is) important for America to display no partiality. Dulles and Eisenhower insisted that Israel accept the U.N. General Assembly resolution that demanded the immediate withdrawal of all troops from the Sinai Peninsula. While the U.N. found itself unable to guarantee the security of Israeli borders or Israel's 'right of free and innocent passage' in the Gulf of Aqaba, America refused to make similar guarantees outside the framework of U.N. resolutions. To a large extent the U.N. had become an instrument of America's will, but the appearance of impartiality which sanctified the legalistic mumb-jumbo of U.N. decisions had to be maintained. It would not do for America actually to deploy its troops in this situation, for example. Such a solution was only acceptable in the face of a threatened Soviet takeover or the imminent collapse of a pro-American régime. The Arab-Israeli confrontation was on the one hand too sensitive and on the other insufficiently critical to call for direct American intervention.

Dulles had assured Golda Meir that the U.N. would deal with the problem of the Gaza Strip. He had told her that the Egyptians could be relied upon to raise their blockade of the Gulf of Aqaba. He had even expressed an official opinion that the Gulf of Aqaba 'comprehends international waters'. 'In the absence of some overriding decision to the contrary as by the International Court of Justice,' he had written, 'the United States, on behalf of vessels of U.S. registry, is prepared to exercise the right of free and innocent passage and to join with others to secure general recognition of this right.'[1]

But all this had to be conditional on Israel's prior withdrawal – a withdrawal involving 'no promises or concessions whatsoever to Israel by the United States'.[2] If the Israelis wanted firmer assurances (and they did) no progress would be made. As long as there were pressing reasons for Israel to evacuate the Gaza Strip and Sharm el-Sheikh, they would have to take American support on trust. In the end the Israelis did exactly that. They lived to regret their act of trust, however. They did not make the same misake in 1967.

Having already withdrawn from most of Sinai, Israel still needed to consolidate its victory. The withdrawal seemed to indicate Israel's acceptance of the U.N. position – at least, in principle. This amounted to a rejection of the idea that military occupation was the proper way to prevent *fedayeen* raids from the Gaza Strip or to ensure Israel's freedom of passage in the Gulf of Aqaba. Even disregarding American pressure, an Israeli occupation of Gaza, though possible, would have raised enormous problems. With well over 200,000 Palestinian Arabs living in the Strip, Israel would have faced insurmountable administrative difficulties if it remained in occupation. In 1957 the country was neither economically strong enough to take on the burden of running the Gaza Strip under a military administration, nor was it populous enough to accept 200,000 Palestinian Arabs eligible for full citizenship. Given the mood of the time, any more drastic solution to the presence of so many Arabs on Israeli territory was unthinkable. Moreover, the *fedayeen* problem could always be managed by small-scale military operations from Israeli territory – especially if Israel remained in El Auja, as it did, commanding the westerly route into the Gaza Strip.

Israel's bargaining position was weak. Matters were not improved by Ben-Gurion's flat refusal to accept U.N. troops on Israeli territory. If a ceasefire was to be policed, he insisted, it would have to be policed from the Egyptian side of the border. The U.N. Secretary General, Dag Hammarskjöld, had already agreed with Nasser the terms under which the United Nations Emergency Force (U.N.E.F.) would occupy border posts in the Sinai. They reached a 'gentleman's agreement' generally known as 'the good faith accord'. Hammarskjöld accepted, in principle, that Egyptian consent was a necessary condition for a U.N. presence. Nasser informally agreed to 'be guided, in good faith, by acceptance of' the U.N. General Assembly resolution of November 1956, setting up U.N.E.F., although he admitted no limitation on the right of Egypt to withdraw its consent. Accordingly, Israel handed over the Gaza Strip to U.N.E.F. on 6 March 1957.

The following day U.N.E.F. troops arrived at Sharm el-Sheikh. The situation there was both more urgent and more complicated than it had been in Gaza. From the start of negotiations, Ben-Gurion had made it clear that Israel would go to war to keep the Gulf of Aqaba open to its ships and cargo. The withdrawal of Israeli forces from the rest of Sinai had left Sharm el-Sheikh cut off and vulnerable to attack. But it was not a border area and that made it difficult for anybody to insist that Egypt agree to an occupation by foreign troops. The Israelis could not stay in Sharm el-Sheikh, but they did not want to go either, for fear that the Egyptians would simply march in and reimpose the blockade. Even Dulles's assurance that, in his opinion, the Gulf was an international waterway did not help matters. It was an opinion, no more, and never tested in any court of law. The Straits of Tiran were still Egyptian territorial waters and the Egyptians maintained that whatever the status of the Gulf they had the right to prevent the passage of strategic materials to a hostile country in time of war. There has never been a peace treaty between Israel and Egypt (or, for that matter, any Arab state) and from time to time Egypt has felt itself justified in asserting that right.

Be that as it may, Nasser and Hammarskjöld reached agreement towards the end of March. The Gaza Strip would be handed over to an Egyptian administration, in line with the demands of the Strip's Palestinian inhabitants.

In return, Nasser gave his consent for U.N.E.F. to remain in Sharm el-Sheikh. Once again, Nasser accepted no limitation on his right to withdraw such consent and, in consequence, there was no specific guarantee that the Straits of Tiran would remain open. The most that could be said was that as long as U.N.E.F. troops remained in Sharm el-Sheikh, Israeli shipping would be allowed to enter and leave the Gulf of Aqaba.

The result of four or five months of hectic negotiations was a peace of sorts. It was a complicated patchwork of agreements which, like the Armistice Agreements of 1949, would in future years be interpreted and re-interpreted, invoked and broken. Of course, the truth is that these agreements were not the real guarantors of peace in the area, any more than the Armistice Agreements had been. If the object of the U.N. had been to impose a negotiated peace consistent with all the resolutions passed in the Security Council and the General Assembly, its actual achievement was to create enough loopholes for several armies to march through. The fact that these armies paused from time to time in their irresistible progress was simply a matter of logistics. They needed rest, they needed fresh supplies, they needed reinforcements. Neither diplomacy nor great power pressure actually attacked the political rationale that guided those marching armies. At best, diplomacy and pressure blocked the roads, requiring the armies to take diversions. Usually they simply constructed an elaborate system of excuses for *not* fighting – excuses which were only useful as long as nobody wanted to fight. As many people discovered years later, even the U.N.E.F. troops were little more than a symbolic presence. With less than 4,000 men on Egyptian territory, it could hardly have been otherwise – especially when the U.N. itself has never had the power to mobilise troops on its own accord and depends on the good will of its member nations to provide the necessary forces.

Fortunately, in the months following the Sinai War, Israel and the Arab States felt disposed to maintain a mutual peace. There were more urgent problems to be faced at home. But it was a jerry-built peace. The shaky foundations of Israel's existence still remained. The main disputants – the Palestinians and their Arab patrons on the one hand and Israeli Jews on the other – refused to recognise each other's claims. The Arabs still denied the State of Israel's right to exist and Israel refused to accept the Palestinians' assertion of their nationhood. With this basic problem unresolved, renewed conflict was inevitable. As long as the Palestinians' cause was still espoused by the Arab states, sooner or later that conflict would again involve the confrontation of nations – in other words, the next war was only a matter of time.

When it did break out, in the summer of 1967, Israel revealed that it had learnt more than a military lesson from the Sinai War. It had also learnt the lesson of a shaky peace.

Chapter 7

HOUSES DIVIDED

Middle Eastern Developments, 1957–1967

> The art of leadership . . . consists in consolidating the attention of the people against a single adversary and taking care that nothing will split up that attention.
>
> (Adolf Hitler, *Mein Kampf*)

I

> The basic problems facing the world today are not susceptible to a military solution.
>
> (John Kennedy, 1963)

Nasser's position as a charismatic leader gave the Arabs an unprecedented opportunity to submerge their differences under the shadow of a common banner. Had Egypt been powerful enough, had it possessed vast reserves of oil as well as labour, for example, Arab unity might have worked. But by one of those ironies that always make the best tragedy, Nasser's claim to moral leadership, unsupported by independent economic or military power, was also one of the most divisive influences in the post-1956 Arab world.

Even Soviet sponsorship was unable to weld the Arab States into a united front and, as cracks began to show on the surface of unity, once more the Arab leaders turned to Israel for explanation and excuse. And Israel, too, the beleaguered little state, found no more helpful solution to its own internal crises than the invocation of a common enemy. The lesson of ten more or less peaceful years in the aftermath of the Sinai War was that peace was distinctly bad for business. It was a lesson that was well remembered.

The Egyptians had not really wanted war in 1956, and even

the Israelis had treated the whole matter with a certain lack of conviction. But once a war has happened it cannot be easily wiped from the slate. The militancy of both Arab and Israeli could be held in check by the two superpowers, but memories of defeat and victory lingered.

The domination of Middle East politics by the U.S. and the U.S.S.R. was marked by the almost surreal atmosphere of a boxing arena. Here were two giants tiptoeing about the ring, assessing each other's strengths and weaknesses, occasionally feinting with a right uppercut or a left to the body but never following through. It all had a dreamlike quality to it – like a shadow-play. And all the time they kitted out their seconds with gloves and gum-shields and the seconds made great show of their mutual hatred while clinging to the corner ropes. Once again, nobody really wanted to start a new round, but nobody could forget the last one.

The Soviet Union flooded its client states with military and economic aid. The face of the Arab world began to change dramatically – the Aswan Dam and the vast Helwan steel complex were being built in Egypt, the Euphrates Dam was planned for Syria. The U.S.S.R. supplied weapons, machinery, technicians and all manner of technical aid. Much of its assistance was given in the form of barter deals, swopping aid for oil, phosphates or cotton. This system did not strain the shaky Arab economies – but it did tend to increase Arab reliance on the Soviets, since they would often commit themselves to production for years to come in order to get immediate aid. Indeed, the Russians were eager to make these sorts of deals and when, in 1967, the Americans refused to supply Egypt with vital wheat for the second year running, the U.S.S.R. jumped in with an offer to barter Egyptian cotton for the necessary wheat.

Clearly, Soviet interests were strategic and economic rather than ideological. Their traditional concern to open up routes to the Eastern Mediterranean, the Red Sea and the Persian Gulf was made more urgent by the increasing Soviet demand for oil. As Russia's western oil-fields passed their peak output the country turned to the Middle East for supplies. From this point of view alone it became important for the U.S.S.R. to develop good relations with oil-producing countries like Iraq and Iran, and also to maintain stability throughout the Middle East, to develop naval stations and land and sea routes and

actively to assist other Middle East countries like Egypt and
Syria in their oil explorations. The U.S.S.R.'s relative indifference to the politics of the Middle East's ruling régimes was a
direct result of its pursuit of these goals.

Of course, the Russians always prefer a sympathetic leadership and they never actually withdrew recognition from any
pro-Soviet Arab Communist Party. But when it was convenient
to their wider aims they would readily turn a blind eye on the
suppression of these Parties. By the early sixties the Russians
had even found it possible to form close ties with Turkey and
Iran – both members of CENTO (the Central Treaty Organisation, as the Baghdad Pact became known after the Iraqi coup)
and two of the most staunchly pro-American countries in the
Middle East. By the late sixties Russia had entered into a
number of major trade deals with Iran, and was busily exchanging capital equipment for oil and gas. Turkey and
Pakistan had also begun to deal with the U.S.S.R.

There were three things that attracted Middle East countries
to the U.S.S.R. The first and least important was geographical
proximity which not only made trading easier and extensive
trade links more logical, but gave the U.S.S.R. a military
presence it was difficult to ignore. The second was the flexibility
of the U.S.S.R. as far as the internal affairs of its clients and
customers went. The third was the stability of the U.S.S.R.'s
own political system which made it a far more reliable partner
than America could ever be. In recent years America has tried
to undermine this stability from within, as it were, by giving
open support to the Soviet dissident movement. This emphasis
on 'human rights' serves the dual purpose, as far as the Middle
East is concerned, of checking those dictatorial régimes (like
Iran's) that have used American support (not to say paranoia)
to strengthen their own rule while developing progressively
greater economic ties with America's competitors in the area.

The peculiar nature of the U.S.S.R.'s relations with its Middle
East clients seemed, at first, to have much to commend it.
Egypt and Syria looked set for a period of remarkable growth.
The establishment of the U.A.R. in 1958 suggested new hope
for the pan-Arab movement. Since the Soviets did not seek to
impose any particular political system on the countries within
their sphere of influence there, it seemed likely that the Arabs
would be allowed to follow a policy of self-determination lead-

ing to a genuine and workable union of Arab states. However, Russia's conciliatory attitude really involved a tacit acceptance of Nasser as the 'strong man' of any Arab union. He was the best educated, the most forceful and the most politically able of all the new Arab leaders. Khruschev was particularly attracted to his strength of purpose and his commitment to anti-Western policies. Egypt was the most modern, the most developed and the most populous of the 'progressive' Arab states and it seemed their natural leader. The Russians lavished attention on Egypt, but by the time they were prepared to promote Nasser to the ranks of the Soviet Communist vanguard in the mid-sixties it was already too late.

Despite Nasser's many and obvious qualities, the competition for leadership of the Arab world continued unabated. Soviet sponsorship only emphasised the opposing claims. In particular, Nasser found himself ranged against the pan-Arab Ba'ath parties of Syria and Iraq and Kassem's régime in Iraq. The Ba'ath (or Renaissance Party), although not achieving leadership in either Syria or Iraq until 1963, played a major rôle in the political life of both countries. It was especially influential in the Syrian and Iraqi armies. The Ba'ath emerged in Syria during the forties and was the first non-Communist political organisation in the Arab world specifically to espouse the doctrines of socialism and pan-Arabism. In fact, the Ba'ath was firmly anti-Communist and declared itself in favour of 'Arab socialism' – a hybrid doctrine that bore similarities to left-wing Zionism and displayed many of the same inconsistencies. The fact that the Syrian Ba'ath Party's fear of an imminent Communist takeover in 1958 impelled it to urge union with Egypt neither diminished its claim to lead the pan-Arab movement nor reduced its suspicious appraisal of Soviet ambitions.

Nasser found himself inevitably drawn into the Soviet orbit. His attempts to derive an independent, neutralist and 'socialist' form of Arab nationalism were hardly more than a series of improvisations on an ill-absorbed series of themes. His ambitions for Egypt forced him to become increasingly reliant on Soviet aid and the more that Egypt benefited from the munificence of the U.S.S.R. the more clearly Nasser saw Egypt's leading rôle in the Arab world. The legitimate claims of the Ba'ath were overlooked as Nasserism grew to be inseparable from Nasser and increasingly identified with Egyptian aspirations to dominate the Arab world. By 1963, the U.A.R. had split asunder as coup followed coup in Syria and rival factions in the army and amongst the population at large seized power – first in 1961, then in 1962 and twice more by March 1963. Egypt continued to style itself the U.A.R. despite Syria's secession and Nasser still sought to impose an Egyptian-dominated unity in the Arab world. He began to harbour a profound mistrust of the Ba'ath for its part in the break-up of the Egyptian–Syrian union.

For his part, Kassem nurtured a similar distaste for the Iraqi branch of the Ba'ath Party. But he also had ambitions for Iraq as a leader of the Arab world and refused to play second fiddle to Nasser. His only alternative was an alliance with the Iraqi Communist Party. It was an alliance that he carefully stage-managed by first banning and harassing the Party and, when all its teeth had been pulled, legalising it under the chairmanship of his own appointee. The Communists naturally acquiesced to this treatment, since any opposition would have run counter to Soviet aims.

By early 1963, resistance to Kassem's increasingly tyrannical and incompetent rule had become so strong that Iraq was in a state of virtual anarchy. Kassem was in dispute with the rest of the Arab world over his claim on newly independent Kuwait. He was in dispute with the U.S.S.R. over his treatment of Iraq's Kurdish minority (there were Kurds in Turkey and Iran, too, and the U.S.S.R. offered them support in the hope that they would disrupt CENTO). He had alienated the West by his vacillation and by the way he had unilaterally broken long-standing agreements on Iraqi oil concessions. And, of course, he had suppressed political activity in the country and reneged on most of his early promises of internal reform. In February 1963 he was toppled by an army-Ba'ath alliance, organised in part by many of the same officers who had been involved in the 1958 coup. The new régime was vehemently anti-Communist and anti-Soviet. It lasted less than a year in power and was replaced by another military government which returned to the Soviet fold.

For a short time during the ascendancy of the Ba'ath in Syria and Iraq it seemed as though the promise of Arab unity, shattered by the 1961 split in the U.A.R., had been revived. A federation between Egypt and the two Ba'athist countries was proposed, discussions went ahead and high-sounding declarations were made in April 1963. They came to nothing and the Iraqi coup of late 1963 was staged from an apparently Nasserite platform. In all events, rival claims to leadership of the pan-Arab movement and faction-fighting within the Ba'ath soon put paid to any hopes of Iraqi–Syrian union around specifically pan-Arab questions. An Egyptian–Iraqi union, declared in 1964, met a similar fate. It seemed that conflict within the ranks of even the 'progressive' Arab States was insurmountable, despite an apparent dedication to common aims and the espousal of similar means for their achievement.

The trouble was, of course, that there was no real basis for unity. The internal problems of Arab States could not be solved by union. On the contrary, union had to proceed from stable political systems based on reconstructed and growing economies. But political organisation and economic development were precisely the areas over which Arab régimes had no control.

The political systems which Nasser and other Arab leaders had inherited were created in the torpid atmosphere of imperial rule. They were corrupt, self-seeking and inept. Arab societies were semi-feudal where they were not totally feudal and the task of creating any sort of democracy without the involvement of a politically active middle-class, working-class or peasantry was an impossible one. Colonial rule had kept Arab societies at an artificially backward stage of development. As the great empires retreated, the Arab states found themselves thrust naked into the modern world – without the means to survive in it.

Under those circumstances, it was not surprising to find soldiers making all the political running. They were the nearest thing to an organised middle-class in most Arab countries. Educated and ambitious, they could use armed force and military discipline to threaten the decaying order that had limply gathered up the reigns of power from the hands of the British and the French. But they could not impose even a facsimile of parliamentary rule on countries where modern political and economic institutions had been purposefully strangled at birth. It was inevitable that the new military régimes, having disposed of colonial rulers and their royal puppets, would find totalitarianism the only alternative to the collapse of their societies.

Men like Nasser could only avoid imposing their will on the people they ruled at the cost of the social reforms and the progress they so earnestly sought. The tragedy was that in order to carry out those reforms and to make that progress they created around themselves a clique, a ruling caste, that could only survive if reforms were half-hearted and progress minimal. The state apparatus that Nasser and the others built was itself an instrument of the further oppression of the Arab masses. And the bureaucrats and officials who peopled that apparatus in ever-growing numbers became the targets of coup and attempted coup carried out by those who followed the only road to power in totalitarian and backward societies.

It is quite clear why Nasser, the Ba'ath leadership and Kassem would only accept Arab unity on their terms. Simply: the idea of a democracy consisting of separate totalitarian factions is an absurdity. Any Arab union would have had to be either totalitarian or, in some form, democratic. A workable union of totalitarian régimes was inconceivable.

The economic backwardness of the Arab countries was at the root of this sorry state of affairs. Egypt, for example, had a plentiful supply of manpower, but its other resources were (and are) pitifully limited and its economy was disfigured by centuries of colonial rule. If Egypt was to industrialise in the fifties and sixties it could only do so through the receipt of aid. But the more aid it received, the more its economy was tied to the demands of its 'benefactor'. It was not even necessary that Egypt should build up a financial debt.

For example, by bartering cotton for machine tools the Egyptians became increasingly dependent on cotton production. Despite the fertility of the Nile Valley it was virtually impossible to increase cotton yield significantly. For centuries two or three crops a year have been cultivated in the Nile Valley. Even the lands fertilised by the Aswan Dam hardly made up for the growth in population, let alone Egypt's spiralling import bill. In the fifty years to 1968, annual cotton production increased by just over ten per cent. Between the Sinai War of 1956 and the June War of 1967, wheat imports alone increased by one thousand per cent! On top of an archaic social system, chaotic and severely limited agricultural production and runaway expenditure on food and industrial imports there was Egypt's weapons expenditure. In the years leading up to the

June War, Egypt's major weapon imports averaged around 100 million dollars annually – five times the equivalent figure for the years 1950 to 1955. Little wonder that the Egyptian economy was in a mess.

By the beginning of the sixties, things were so bad that rioting broke out in Egypt's major cities. Nasser was forced to take drastic measures in a fruitless attempt to reduce inflation and meet some of the reasonable demands of the Egyptian workers and peasants. But there was little he could do. The wheat shortage got so severe that it reached famine proportions. The Americans thought that they could block Egypt's wheat supplies in an attempt to force him back into the Western camp. (They became particularly concerned about Egypt's involvement in the Yemen War.) They only succeeded in pushing Egypt further into the Soviet sphere of influence. Nasser could see no alternative but to raise the banner of Arab unity once more, and he understood that Arab unity could only be effected in the face of an external threat.

In May 1962 Nasser wrote a draft charter for the U.A.R. extolling 'the Egyptian people, the creator of civilisation', and declaring Egypt's leading rôle in the Arab nationalist movement. To differentiate his philosophy from that of the Syrians or the Iraqis he characterised it, for the first time, as 'scientific socialism' – an expression redolent of East Germany. He placed a great deal of responsibility for Egypt's problems on the failure of pan-Arabism. He declared that Israel was a tool of 'the imperialists', who meant it to be 'a barrier dividing the Arab East from the Arab West, and a constant drain on the energy of the Arab nation, diverting it from positive construction'.[1] At last Nasser had found a cause worthy of his predicament.

It was around the same time that Egypt became involved in the struggle in the Yemen. This involvement was partly a result of the Yemen's membership of the U.A.R. It was partly an exercise for the benefit of the by now well-equipped but unpractised Egyptian army. But most of all it was a declaration of Egypt's hostility to Saudi Arabia – a country that many Arabs had correctly identified as America's chief client in the Arab world.

Saudi Arabia had a real claim to Arab leadership, and this was a definite threat to Nasser's new offensive. While the

Saudis had a comparatively small population (possibly a fifth of Egypt's – there has never been a census in the country) they had immense amounts of oil money. Potentially, they were extremely influential, but they shrank at the mere sound of the word 'progressive', and socialism was comlete anathema to them. They supported the monarchist establishment in the Yemen, while Egypt fought with the republican rebels. The war dragged on, costing Egypt enormous sums of money it could not afford, but it was a crucial trial of strength that Nasser could not shrink from. With luck, Nasser's open opposition to Saudi Arabia and Israel would bring him the fruits of union that peace had so far denied him.

II

> It is politics which beget war. Politics represents the intelligence, war merely its instrument, not the other way round. The only possible course in war is to subordinate the military viewpoint to the political.
>
> (Von Clausewitz, *On War*)

Israel, too, had its problems. For some time after the Sinai War all was peaceful on Israel's borders. The occasional foray into Gaza soon became unnecessary when the Israelis realised that U.N.E.F. was doing its job and that armed *fedayeen* raids had been voluntarily stopped. Nasser doubtless found the U.N. presence a convenient excuse for not attacking Israel with any more potent weapon than rhetoric. The Jordanian, Syrian and Lebanese borders were quiescent if not absolutely peaceful and Israel tried to apply itself to the tasks of economic development. But despite the many differences Israel had with the Arab States, they did share a tendency towards economic crisis and political breakdown.

The major task confronting Israel in the aftermath of its second major war was the development of the Negev. As with other Israeli projects this required an enormous capital expenditure which would not be recovered for years. Furthermore, the major item of Government expenditure continued to be the defence budget, followed in second place by the education budget, neither of which promised immediate returns to offset large-scale investment. In consequence, Israel suffered a continual and severe trade deficit which was only met by substantial foreign-aid programmes, German reparations payments to victims of the Nazi persecution and charity from Zionists and Zionist sympathisers abroad.

Nevertheless, by 1962 the situation was bad enough to call for a substantial devaluation. For a while things improved – foreign currency reserves increased, the trade deficit dropped noticeably and wages rose without affecting the level of employment. The vital construction industry went through a minor boom as a result of the growth in industrial projects and to some extent due to a short-lived rise in immigration from 1961 to 1963.

Among the major construction projects were the resurrected Jordan waters scheme, the port of Eilat, the Beersheba–Dimona railway line and the Dimona nuclear reactor – all part of the overall development of the Negev. The devaluation, however, raised the prices of imports necessary to the completion of these and other large-scale projects. An inflationary price spiral began. In 1965, the substantial German reparations payments came to an end and as the major construction projects reached completion more and more people were thrown out of work. The situation was not improved by a general decline of international interest in Israel and by a sudden drop in immigration in 1965. By 1966 over ten per cent of the labour force were unemployed. In development areas and among the substantial number of Asian and African Jews who had come to Israel, the figure was closer to twenty per cent. Prices went rocketing up and wages followed at increases of up to twenty-five per cent.

Naturally, the Government (now led by Levi Eshkol) came under severe criticism. Towards the end of 1966, the Government presented a three-year economic plan that proposed stringent measures in an attempt to set the economy to rights. 'The recession,' Eshkol said in explaining the plan, 'is having the effect of fresh air in sobering people up and making them see things with open eyes.'[2] Within six months from the announcement of the plan, unemployed workers rioted in Tel Aviv, surrounding the Town Hall and bombarding it with stones and other missiles. Within another three months, Israel was at war.

Of course, there is no simple and direct connection between economic crises and wars. In this case, however, there was a link. Israel's wars have always served a useful purpose in stimulating the interest and support of Diaspora Jews. Only when Israel appears to be on the verge of extinction can it rely on the whole-hearted support of Jews across the world. They are, if you like, Israel's foul-weather friends. But there is an even more important connection between the 1966–7 economic crisis and the outbreak of the June War. Hostility and small-scale conflict are easily transformed into war when a political leadership is threatened. In much the same way that Nasser revived his ailing fortunes by taking up the cudgels of anti-Israel rhetoric, Eshkol and the political leadership of Israel found that internal dissension could be spirited away if external hostility was faced in strength and unity.

Curiously enough, the political crisis that Eshkol confronted in the spring and summer of 1967 was rooted in the 'Lavon affair' that had preceded the Sinai War over a decade before. Lavon's enforced resignation back in 1955 had signalled the return of Ben-Gurion to government. Lavon had been the defence minister held to be responsible for an abortive sabotage operation carried out by Israeli espionage-agents in Egypt. There had been some doubt as to Lavon's real knowledge of the affair and it seemed possible that he had been taken for a patsy by the actual perpetrators – Ben-Gurion's men in the Israeli defence establishment.

In late 1960, Lavon claimed to have unearthed new evidence proving his innocence in the matter. He linked his earlier resignation with proposals he had then been making for the reformation of the I.D.F. and the Defence and Foreign Ministries. In particular, Lavon claimed that he had uncovered a hive of corruption within the high ranks of the Israeli defence establishment and argued that, when he had sought to destroy this hive, evidence had been manufactured to discredit him and remove him from his post.

Eventually, a committee of ministers was set up to investigate Lavon's claims. Ben-Gurion dismissed Lavon's story and firmly opposed the establishment of this so-called 'committee of seven'. When the committee found in favour of Lavon, Ben-Gurion resigned. He argued that the government – which had endorsed the committee's decision – was not competent to judge the matter. New elections to the Knesset were called in 1961.

At first, it seemed just like another government crisis. When the Mapai central committee dismissed Lavon from his post as Secretary-General of the Histadrut so that Ben-Gurion could return as Prime Minister, that suspicion seemed confirmed. It was just a question of internal bickering. Lavon was in the right, but he would be pushed aside in order to guarantee the minimum of disturbance to the virtually autocratic rule of Ben-Gurion and his supporters. Things would continue as if nothing had happened and Israeli citizens would read their newspapers, mutter something about all politicians being crooks and go back to the sports page.

For a few months, that is exactly what happened. But as Israel began to sink first into difficulties and then into crisis, confidence in the government began to ebb. In 1963 Ben-Gurion once again resigned – citing 'personal reasons' as he had in 1953. Ben-Gurion recommended Levi Eshkol to replace him. Eshkol was another early Zionist settler with the usual wide-ranging background in the Zionist Labour Movement and its political and defence organisations. But compared to Ben-Gurion he was a moderate. During the early years of the state he had been responsible for founding Israel's weapons industry, but for eleven years until 1963 he had been Minister of Finance, concerned with the positive aspects of Israel's development rather than with the negative aspects of the country's attitude to its Arab neighbours. Faced with the most troublesome period in Israel's development since its foundation, Eshkol increasingly resorted to compromise.

His reputation for taking the middle way became almost legendary. Stories lampooning Eshkol became common currency. For example, it was said that when Eshkol went to a café and was asked if he wanted tea or coffee, he would pause thoughtfully and, after a moment's consideration, reply: 'Half and half.'

Eshkol's leadership style was a far remove from Ben-Gurion's. Ben-Gurion was a militarist and a believer in strong government. Eshkol saw no virtue in subordinating the requirements of civil government to the demands of the military. He felt that if there was corruption among holders of high office it should be brought out into the open and not glossed over for the purposes of maintaining an appearance of solidarity and strength. Ben-Gurion's concern with the Lavon affair had little to do with the rights and wrongs of Lavon's case. On the contrary, he was concerned that any cracks in the I.D.F. or the Government be papered over or, preferably, filled with the cement of militaristic zeal. He saw no reason for the I.D.F. to be accountable to the civil government – in fact, he considered such a situation dangerous because he saw the military establishment as the real backbone of Israeli society.

Accordingly, in 1964 Ben-Gurion mounted an attack on Eshkol's handling of Government affairs. In particular, he demanded that Eshkol, as Prime Minister and Minister of Defence, set up a committee of inquiry into the recent handling of the Lavon affair. Eshkol refused – saying that the original committee of seven and the government had been perfectly competent to judge the behaviour of members of Israel's defence establishment. Ben-Gurion took the issue to the 1965 Mapai Party Congress where he failed to obtain a majority for his position. With Moshe Dayan, the former Chief of Staff and Agriculture Minister, at his side, Ben-Gurion took his supporters out of Mapai and set up the rival Rafi Party ('The Israel Workers' List'). Mapai then merged with the left-of-centre Ahduth Ha'avodah to form the so-called 'Alignment' government of 1965. The Alignment was immediately confronted with the burdensome tasks of checking the rapid decline of Israel's economy and the equally swift deterioration in border security. Eshkol's resourcefulness and the quality of his leadership would be tested to the limit in this confrontation.

The rot in Israeli–Arab relations had set in once more by the beginning of 1964. The Jordan waters scheme, carried out in defiance of the Arab states which shared access to the rivers' headwaters, attracted a considerable amount of active opposition from Syria, Jordan and the Lebanon. In January 1964 the first 'Summit Conference' of Arab heads of state was convened in Cairo. The main discussion item was the Jordan waters scheme. Israel had completed construction of its National Water Carrier in December 1963. By the spring of 1964, water began flowing from the north of the country for use in the irrigation of the Negev.

This scheme had a long and difficult history, dating back to

1953. Under a plan prepared by an American special envoy in 1955, Jordan, Israel, Syria and the Lebanon were each allocated a certain proportion of the water involved for irrigation purposes. The Arab states refused to accept this plan, because it would have involved an implicit recognition of Israel. Nonetheless, Israel went ahead with a construction programme designed to implement the plan unilaterally.

The Arab states meeting at Cairo agreed to take countermeasures aimed at diverting the sources of the Jordan and thus denying Israel access to the crucial water. Diversion work started in 1965 and Israel began to use the opportunity of an increase in border incidents to mount airborne assaults on the diversion works in Syria and the Lebanon.

In fact, serious border clashes had begun to increase steadily in frequency from as early as 1960. The Palestinian refugees had been disappointed by the failure of peace moves. In particular, unified Arab pressure had shown itself to be a non-starter and the 1960 American election campaign (between Kennedy and Nixon) had been carried out in an atmosphere thick with pro-Zionist vote-catching promises. After Kennedy's inauguration he became considerably more conciliatory towards the Arabs, to be sure, yet America's basic orientation towards Israel (and towards the conservative Arab régimes in Jordan and Saudi Arabia) became increasingly evident. By 1962 America had become involved, against its former assurances, in supplying Israel with modern weapons. The Cuban missile crisis in the second half of that year only served to define and consolidate American and Soviet spheres of influence. As far as the Arabs were concerned it was a further indication of America's unwillingness and Russia's inability to pressure Israel into making any concessions. The Palestinians became increasingly concerned to get Israel to accept their status as a 'national entity', entitled not merely to relocation or compensation but to a land of their own.

Clearly, Israel could never accept that – under the circumstances it could only have entailed the loss of Israeli territory. The Palestinians began to feel once more that their only available means of persuasion was attack. Even if they were not strong enough to secure Israel's submission, they could at least force the hand of the Arab states by provoking Israeli retaliation. It was vital, as the guerrilla organisation al-Fatah later announced, to 'materialise the enemy [Israel] before the masses'.[3]

Syria was the focus for much of this activity. Many of the border incidents happened in the spring and summer months when Israeli settlers undertook their seasonal cultivation of lands round Galilee. Such settlers usually carried rifles in plain view on their tractors. Often the tractors would stray, possibly accidentally, into Syrian territory. In any case, the Arabs still maintained that most of the area round the eastern shore of Lake Galilee and the area further north to the east of the new town of Kiryat Shimona (near the reclaimed Hula Swamp territory) were demilitarised zones. To carry weapons in these areas could easily be interpreted as a provocation.

By 1965, following a further Arab Summit in Alexandria, the situation had moved on a stage. A unified Arab military command had been set up under the Egyptian General, Hakim Amer. The Egyptians had also pressed for the formation of an umbrella organisation for the Palestinians. This organisation, the Palestine Liberation Organisation (P.L.O.) was established in 1964. Its headquarters were in Gaza and the chairman was the erstwhile Saudi Arabian ambassador to the U.N., a certain Ahmed Shukeiry.

At this stage Egypt's main concern was the reconstruction of the pan-Arab movement under Egyptian leadership. The P.L.O. was designed as the nucleus of a future Palestinian Arab state. Its military arm – the Palestinian Liberation Army – was divided into units under the independent command of the Egyptian, Syrian and Iraqi general staff. Accordingly, the P.L.O. was not actively engaged in guerrilla operations against Israel, and the Egypt–Israel border remained quiet until 1967.

The military aspect of the Palestinian struggle fell to al-Fatah – an underground organisation formed in 1958 under the leadership of Yasser Arafat. In late 1964, Arafat had separate talks with the Ba'ath Government in Syria and with their help began to organise fighting against Israel. The relative success of the Fatah operations gave the lie to Nasser's rhetoric which carefully side-stepped the issue of transforming his propaganda war into a shooting war.

'They say, "Drive out U.N.E.F.!"' Nasser pleaded in March 1965. 'Suppose that we do, is it not essential that we have a plan? If Israeli aggression takes place against Syria, shall I attack Israel? Then Israel is the one which determines the battle for me. It hits a tractor or two to force me to move. Is this a wise way? We have to determine the battle.'[4]

But the Syrians were not going to let Nasser's arguments dissuade them from their bid to lead the Arab world. In February 1966 the right-wing Ba'ath Government fell to a pro-Soviet Ba'ath coup. While some changes were made, the new Ba'ath régime inherited its predecessor's desire to espouse the Palestinian cause more vigorously than any other Arab state. The new President, Dr Nureddin al-Attassi, began to call almost immediately for a 'popular war of liberation' against Israel. This cry was a two-edged sword. While Attassi declared total support for the Palestinian struggle, the particular form of his wording did not commit him to provide regular Syrian troops to the cause of liberation.

In fact, The Syrians' improved relations with Nasser's sponsors, the Soviet Union, probably acted as a check on their militant ambitions. The U.S.S.R. is hardly likely to have sought a Middle East war, especially since the Syrian coup meant that its foothold in the area had improved. But Soviet attempts to bring about a reconciliation between Syria and Egypt would undoubtedly magnify the chances of war.

Meanwhile, Nasser still tried to avoid the issue of war. For one thing the fighting in the Yemen was going badly. It was becoming a severe drain on Egypt's economy and it was conspicuously failing to endorse Nasser's claim to Arab leadership. His inability to reach agreement with the Saudis could prove to be disastrous. He had neither the desire, nor the resources, to become involved in another war. On the other hand, the Saudis – playing Nasser at his own game – began to press their claim to leadership in the region by calling for the creation of a pan-Islam movement. This would have involved non-Arab Muslim states like Iran and Turkey and Arab states like Jordan and Saudi Arabia itself. Their pro-American presence would have far outweighed the influence of a handful of weak, pro-Soviet states. In response to increased Syrian pressure, Nasser argued that military action would be ineffective unless the armies of one Arab country could cross the territory of another. Hussein refused even to consider granting such permission – which could have been fatal to his régime. The Syrians began to make aggressive noises against

Jordan, and Nasser, who now found himself playing off Arab unity against Arab disunity, agreed to sign a mutual defence pact with Syria.

Nine days later, on 13 November 1966, Israel mounted its largest retaliatory operation to date. Surprisingly, the target was not in Syria but on the West Bank of the Jordan not far from the Negev. The village of as-Samu was virtually razed by a combined land and air operation involving tanks and planes. The object of the exercise was ostensibly to destroy an active guerilla base, and it has been argued that Israel did not mount a similar operation in Syria because, given the Syrian terrain, such an attack would probably have led Israeli forces to the outskirts of Damascus. It is more likely that Israel wanted to dissuade Jordan from entering the recently signed defence pact between Syria and Egypt. Despite Ben-Gurion's declared aim of several years earlier that Israel should be able to take on all its Arab neighbours at once, a three-pronged attack with the benefit of the Arabs' vastly improved weaponry was still a threat.

But the Samu raid, far from cowing Hussein, pushed him towards militant involvement. Predictably enough, Nasser had already invoked the memory of 1948 and Abdullah's 'stab in the back'. Now Hussein entered the fray and pointedly attacked Egypt for hiding behind U.N.E.F.'s skirts. Nasser retaliated with taunts of 'U.S. puppet' and declared that U.N.E.F. was only a symbolic force and could do nothing to stop Egyptian troop movements. The war of words went on. Syria demanded that Nasser prove his assertions about U.N.E.F. Nasser was being attacked from right and left. The last chance to achieve his cherished dream of Arab unity under Egyptian leadership was slipping away.

By the beginning of 1967 there was a virtual border war going on between Syria and Israel. In the spring Israeli settlers came out as usual to cultivate, doubtless bearing small-arms among their agricultural implements. On 7 April a Syrian artillery battery seems to have opened fire on some Israeli tractors from the Golan Heights. It was the signal for a major air battle. Israeli Mirages flew over Damascus. Even the Syrian account admits to the loss of four MiGs. It was, by any account, an important clash of forces. Not unreasonably, Syria invoked its mutual defence pact with Egypt.

The Russians seem to have found the situation extremely threatening. As conflict escalated, Russian loss of face became more and more likely. Their weapons were being destroyed with alarming ease. Their relations with Syria and Egypt were being strained by an evident inability to unite the two. Their reputation as a world power was in danger of being dealt a deadly blow by their inability to protect their clients. Syria worried them most of all. Despite the Syrian leadership's aggressive show of strength, their position was extremely insecure. Popular feeling was running high. There was a constant risk that disaffected groups would seize the opportunity of Israel's military incursions to foment open revolt. The Ba'ath Party's declared positions with respect to Nasser, Arab unity and Israel were all being shaken by the complex and extreme nature of the 'border war'. Riots broke out in Damascus in the first week of May, inspired by an unholy alliance of big merchants, land-owners and religious leaders. There were calls for a general strike; troops and armed workers patrolled the streets of the capital and other major Syrian towns.

The Russians seem to have decided that their only option, short of direct intervention, was to create a pretext for Egypt and Syria to bury their differences. This, at any rate, seems to be the only logical explanation for the part that the U.S.S.R. played in a curious incident during the second week of May 1967. At this time, Nasser was evidently informed of a build-up of Israeli troops near the Syrian border. The implication was that Israel was preparing for an invasion of Syria within a few days. The source of the information seems to have been Soviet intelligence, although there is no evidence that it was accurate. The U.S.S.R. had accused Israel of harbouring such troop concentrations on other occasions in the recent past. This time the accusations served not as propaganda but as direct pressure.

Whatever the rôle of this spurious intelligence, on 13 May Nasser made the first of a number of fateful decisions. To coincide with Israel's Independence Day celebrations he would send a large contingent of troops into the Sinai. There was to be no secrecy or subterfuge. The troops would travel in plain view through the open streets of Cairo. This in itself would serve as a strong reminder of Egyptian force. The Israelis would at least have second thoughts about repeating their recently expressed threats of reprisals against guerrilla raids. The raids (mostly by al-Fatah forces) were clearly worrying the Israelis. At the very least, Nasser would share some of the Palestinians' glory. At most, he might scare the Israelis into silence – if not actual submission.

Once in the Sinai, the Egyptian troops would have to occupy the border areas and Sharm el-Sheikh. There would have been no point in mounting such a public manoeuvre if it was to pull up short of the U.N.E.F. positions. Once Egyptian troops occupied the U.N.E.F. positions, U.N.E.F. itself would be forced to withdraw altogether. Nasser's agreement with Hammarskjöld permitted no other possibility. This much must have been obvious, and if it went no further the exercise might well have achieved Nasser's limited aims. What Nasser did not count on was the response of the Arab world to these tentative moves. No sooner had Egyptian troops begun to move than the praise and the plaudits started. Within days the clamour of Arab approval was deafening. It came from all sides. Nasser even had an excuse to remove his wretched troops from the Yemeni imbroglio and send them to Sinai as reinforcements. The sense of power was exhilarating and liberating. Obstacles seemed to melt away in the face of the Egyptian march. By 22 May Nasser had decided, to the surprise of all his friends and advisers, to re-impose the blockade of the Gulf of Aqaba. It was a decision that led, inevitably, to war.

Suddenly, Arab unity was a reality. Even Jordan and Saudi Arabia acknowledged Nasser's leadership. By simply lifting his finger Nasser had won a famous victory. It was as if the Sinai War had never happened. American and Soviet diplomats rushed about offering their respective clients encouragement mixed with caution. 'Don't be the first to strike,' was everybody's advice, because nobody wanted a war. Not even Nasser. But as the end of May drew on and the Israelis had made no move, the Egyptian President, intoxicated by the suddenness of his rise from the pits of desperation, discovered new life in the old rhetoric. 'We are now ready to deal with the whole Palestine question,' he said in a speech on 29 May 1967, as if to dictate terms to an already defeated Israel – offering a silent, hopeful prayer that Israel would not fight, would not be goaded into striking the first blow despite his constant goading.

The days dragged their feet and no blow came. 'This is Arab power,' Nasser had triumphantly declaimed. But it was also the agony of waiting. Israel would not give up without a fight, he knew that. Israel could not give up without a fight. Nasser began to have second thoughts. He sent emissaries to America. The Russians had a fit of nerves. Still the Israelis made no move.

Something had to break soon. In Israel, the Cabinet held exhausting, fitful meetings. The threat was real enough, the cause was good enough and the nation was united enough. But the political leadership was in disarray. They turned to the U.S. for help, possibly a solution. The moderate Foreign Secretary, Abba Eban, visited London, Paris and Washington to plead Israel's cause. But while his government at home began to worry about an Egyptian invasion, Eban, for a number of reasons, stressed only the Egyptian blockade.

The Americans considered they had two options: either to 'unleash Israel' or to re-open the Gulf of Aqaba themselves in Israel's name. They preferred the second alternative, but they demanded time to negotiate. Time was the one thing the Israelis did not have. They became increasingly aware of the Arabs on their borders, but a long mobilisation would be economically crippling – a second defeat to add to the re-imposition of the blockade. Some Arabs, like Ahmed Shukeiry ('a real son of a bitch' as one Russian diplomat described him later), ran away with their new-found potency and promised to sweep the Jewish State and its people from the area. The longer Israel waited the louder Shukeiry's voice might become and the more persuasive it might sound. Nasser's courage could grow, his resolve harden, as he watched Israel hesitate and hesitate and finally give up. Israel could not afford to admit a single weakness. But Eshkol's government was indecisive. The Alignment did not have the respect of the I.D.F., some of Eshkol's colleagues argued. Sectarian disputes could split the people. Israel needed to be absolutely united in this moment of supreme trial. Internal pressure mounted for Eshkol to vacate his Defence post and agree to form a National Government to counter an invasion threat and not just a blockade.

To many, Moshe Dayan, victor of 1956, seemed the logical choice for Minister of Defence. Eshkol absolutely rejected the idea (as did Golda Meir). He would approve a Government of National Unity, including members of Rafi and Gahal (Menachim Begin's rightist Herut–Liberal block). He would give up the Ministry of Defence to an agreed candidate (Yigal Allon was his preferred choice). He would even accept Dayan into the government. He would give him any post or make him chief of staff, but Defence was out. Dayan refused to compromise. The crisis deepened. Israeli public opinion (which is to say, media opinion) grew increasingly hawkish, but Eshkol could do nothing. The political crisis admitted no solution to the Arab threat – and the threat of war denied him an acceptable solution to the political crisis. The one weak link in the chain that held the unity of the Israeli people to its military foundation was Eshkol's stubborn refusal to subordinate the political to the military will. But the pressure continued to grow.

The Arabs felt the pressure growing, too. King Hussein of Jordan, the arch enemy of Syria and Egypt, felt it more than most. He had waited a week for Israel to attack Egypt. When no attack came he suspected that Israel might be weaker than he had supposed. On the morning of 31 March, having withdrawn his ambassador from Egypt only days before, Hussein climbed into the seat of a plane from the royal flight and took off from Amman, flying south and then east. Arriving in Cairo he made his way to a meeting with Nasser. The two men signed a mutual defence pact and Hussein flew back to Jordan. He had made, so he thought, an empty gesture of Arab solidarity. Stepping out of the plane he turned to an aide and remarked: 'Today I have taken out my life insurance.' The premium was a high one. Egypt, Syria and Jordan together were too great a threat to Israel. The next day Eshkol relented. Dayan became Minister of Defence and straight away opened up the campaign plans that the I.D.F. had refined and perfected in over ten years of only slightly disturbed peace.

Chapter 8

MIRAGE OVER BETHLEHEM

The Six Day War, June 1967

> With the closing of the Gulf of Aqaba, Israel is faced with two alternatives either of which will destroy it; it will either be strangled to death by the Arab military and economic boycott, or it will perish by the fire of the Arab forces encompassing it from the South, from the North and from the East.
>
> (Cairo Radio, 30 May 1967)

> Behind the frenzy and arrogance there lay Israel's suppressed sense of guilt towards the Arabs, the feeling that the Arabs would never forget or forgive the blows Israel had inflicted on them: the seizure of their land, the fate of a million or more refugees, and repeated military defeats and humiliations. Driven half-mad by fear of Arab revenge, the Israelis have, in their overwhelming majority, accepted the 'doctrine' inspiring their government's policy, the 'doctrine' that holds that Israel's security lies in periodic warfare which every few years must reduce the Arab states to impotence.
>
> (Isaac Deutscher, 'The Six Day War', in *The Non-Jewish Jew* (New York, O.U.P., 1968)

I

For many years Nasser had warned his fellow-Arabs that they must wait, that Egypt was not yet strong enough to avenge the débâcle of 1956 or reverse the shame of 1948–9. But through the escalation of the May 1967 crisis this voice of caution had grown dimmer, and had been finally silenced by the rising clamour of Arab hopes. Nasser, watching his army moving across the Canal and into Sinai, seems to have been hypnotised by the apparent strength at his and Egypt's disposal. Perhaps the years of waiting were over. Perhaps this was the moment.

It does not seem that he expected a military defeat of Israel.

Despite Shukheiry's barbaric statements about driving the Jews into the sea, few perceptive Arab statesmen and soldiers expected Israel to crumple up and die. But the Israeli Army, Nasser had begun to believe, could be held. And that in itself, since it implied the continuous closure of the Straits of Tiran, would be victory enough. The Egyptian Army, he wrongly and fatally surmised, was strong enough to achieve such a limited objective.

There were grounds for such hope. The paper-strength of the Army had been greatly increased in the eleven years since the Sinai Campaign. Over a billion dollars' worth of military equipment had been received from the Soviet Union, and Egypt now possessed a large margin of superiority in both tanks (1,100 to 800) and supersonic aircraft (205 to 92) over the enemy. Superiority in artillery, both towed and self-propelled, was of an even greater magnitude. Only, surprisingly, in manpower did the Egyptians lag behind. Some 100,000 men would fight in Sinai, forming forty per cent of the combined Arab total, itself roughly equivalent to Israel's quarter of a million troops.

The Egyptian Army's abundance of modern equipment was, it was hopefully assumed in Cairo, matched by a modern approach to warfare. The senior officers had, after all, been through 1948–9, 1956, the Yemeni War, and considerable Soviet instruction. They should have learned a great deal, and indeed some of them had. Unfortunately it was mostly in the conceptual field, and a large question-mark hovered over the Egyptian Army's ability to turn its new-found planning expertise into battlefield reality.

In the heady days of May 1967 it was more popular to assume that the bulk of the Army would rise to modernism, than to fear that the élite officer class would regress into feudalism. Even should things not go quite as smoothly as expected, the unambitious tasks set for the Army were surely well within reach. Two well-sited and heavily-held defensive positions (Rafah–El Arish and Umm Katef–Abu Aweigila) were to block the major trans-Sinai routes, while a minor attack was to be mounted into the virtually undefended southern Negev. If the Israelis should break through one, or even both, of the defensive positions they would be swiftly counter-attacked and thrown back by the cream of the

Egyptian Army, the 4th Armoured Division, and the powerful Egyptian Air Force. The possibility of disaster was almost non-existent.

All this, as events were soon to show, was illusion. Improvements in the Egyptian Army, like the improvements in Egyptian society which they reflected, had not as yet percolated far down the social hierarchy. This is not to criticise Nasser, or to belittle the strides taken since the ousting of Farouk and the British. Feudalism and colonialism do not disappear overnight; Egypt was, and still is, a deeply-splintered society. Communications between the various strata were extremely tenuous, in the Army as in the society.

The weaponry, though often more sophisticated than the Israeli counterparts, was not chosen for its ease of use, either as regards the men who would use it or the terrain in which it would be used. Most of it arrived in the two years immediately preceding the war, leaving far too little time for men from a basically pre-technological culture to familiarise themselves with its operation and maintenance. And without adequate maintenance the equipment grew less efficient, and hence even harder to operate.

The lack of social communication was even more crucial, and underlay all the Egyptian Army's failures in 1967. Imagine an army as a compartmentalised railway carriage. In the Israeli carriage, officers and men circulated freely, moving from compartment to compartment, speaking the same basic language, sharing the problems of fighting the war. In the Egyptian version the officers tended to lock themselves into their relatively luxurious compartment. There they sat drawing up detailed plans which they passed through a narrow slit in the wall to the next compartment, where the equally class-conscious junior officers and N.C.O.s were gathered. This group, largely recruited from the urban lower-middle class, and lacking the training or skills to interpret these orders in any meaningful fashion, simply passed them on, suitably divided up, to the other compartments full of *fellahin* wishing they were back at home. While this flow of orders persisted the Army resembled a mass of obedient but unimaginative minions controlled by a chair-bound mastermind. But stop the flow and there would be chaos. There was no group initiative in the Egyptian Army, there was only High Command initiative and personal initiative. The loss of the direction from on high would swiftly transform an army into a mass of individuals intent on personal survival.

And, as if to make absolutely certain that such a breakdown in the flow would occur, the communications equipment was either obsolete, misused, or both. The armour used crystal sets, which allowed a choice of any four frequencies from a possible hundred. In 1967 the Israelis discovered that the Egyptians were using the same four that they had used in 1956. The Army as a whole was supplied with radio telephones donated by the Soviets from stocks captured from the Germans in World War II. Understandably the Egyptians were reluctant to use such dated equipment; less understandably they relied instead on field telephones, and in the process turned Sinai into a gigantic cobweb of over-ground telephone lines. The fact that these lines were a sitting target for the I.A.F. seems to have occurred to no one.

All these problems became apparent only when the Army entered Sinai, before and during the battle. Nasser did not realise that the Army he had waved across the Canal in mid-May was already halfway to its knees before the Israelis attacked. Three weeks of communication failures, at all levels, had wreaked havoc. Kimche and Bawley recount one example:

A typical case was that of one of the battalions of a reserve brigade which had moved to El Arish at the end of May. Shortly after arrival they were given marching orders to Bir Hasana, although the brigade headquarters remained in El Arish. They bivouacked in the vicinity of Bir Hasana in an open area. They had neither food nor water – apart from their battle rations, which they were forbidden to touch. Communications did not function, and they had no ammunition. But they were told that the brigade headquarters would soon arrive and then all deficiencies would be rectified. For forty-eight hours the men waited impatiently for H.Q. and supplies to arrive, under the burning sun, with no orders and nothing to do. By that time many of the troops were already in a state of near-collapse and there was still no word or sign from brigade headquarters. The battalion commander gave the order to open battle rations and dig in. The following day, 5 June, the battalion was attacked from the air. The dug-outs were not ready and many, including the battalion commander, were killed. They had not even known that fighting had broken out.[1]

None of this was visible on the wall-maps in Cairo. There you could only see the divisions deployed as planned: 20th Palestine Division in the Gaza Strip; 7th Division holding the Rafah–El Arish axis; 2nd Division in Abu Aweigila and El Quseima; 6th Division holding the southern approaches at El Kuntilla, Nakhl and El Thamad; 3rd Division in reserve between Gebel Libni and Bir Hasana; 4th Armoured Division further back in the shadow of the Central Ridge. These formations were certainly where the maps said they were. But they were also often short of food, ammunition, working communications equipment, and vehicles in running order. The Egyptian High Command, far away down the telephone lines, was in for a surprise.

II

The Israelis too had been absorbing new weaponry through the eleven years of relative peace, but whereas the Egyptians had imported weapons and tactics as part of the same package deal, the Israelis had gone out looking for weaponry that suited their strategic intentions. The I.D.F. leadership had a clear picture of how it intended to fight a forthcoming war. Indeed it would have been difficult to have avoided such clarity, for Israel's geographic and military position left little room for choice. The limited size of the country, and its general configuration, ruled out a defensive war; the international situation, with both sides tied to superpower weaponry deliveries, ruled out a long one. Israel would have to attack, and at speed. The latter require-ment made a pre-emptive strike at Arab air-power essential.

Given this basic strategic intention, certain other decisions fitted neatly into place. The pre-emptive strike option required a certain kind of air force, the fast ground offensive a certain kind of army. The Sinai Campaign had pointed the way in both respects, and between 1956 and 1967 the cutting edges of the I.A.F. and Armour Corps were honed to a relative perfection.

It was fortunate that throughout this period the I.A.F. re-ceived fund priority, for both its commanders – Tolkowsky (1954–8), Weizmann (1958–66) – believed that in modern war-fare there was no substitute for the newest and finest planes. At first, availability appeared to be a problem, for only France would sell supersonic jets to Israel, and the French Mirage was a missile-firing plane and little else. The Israelis insisted on substantial modifications, and the version they purchased was also capable of cannon-fire and bomb-delivery. The one insurmountable problem remained the low bomb pay-load, a mere two tons of explosives. The number of planes Israel could afford, multiplied by the pay-load, was insufficient for the disabling pre-emptive strike that was the I.A.F.'s No. 1 priority.

Nothing more could be done with the plane, so the answer had to be sought elsewhere. It was found in speeding up, to an extraordinary degree, the turn-around period for refuelling, re-arming and target briefing. Whereas the E.A.F., like most other air forces, counted on anything up to two hours between touchdown and take-off, the I.A.F. ground crews, boosted by prestige campaigns and intensive training, brought the time required down to seven minutes. As the flight-time between Israel and inner Egypt was only 20–25 minutes this effectively multiplied the I.A.F., as regards the E.A.F., by three.

The pilots needed no prestige campaigns. To sit at the controls of an Israeli plane certified that they had passed through the stiffest selection test for pilots in the world. (The failure rate for applicants in the U.S.A.F. is twenty-five per cent, and in the I.A.F. is ninety per cent.) Each pilot entrusted with one of the 72 front-line Mirages knew that his performance at those controls was crucial to Israel. They were a small élite, rigorously trained; they spent almost as much time in the air as on the ground, and it showed. If the E.A.F. could be caught on the ground, then the I.A.F. was confident of destroying it on the ground. If not, then it would be destroyed in the air.

The Armour Corps, though not as liberally endowed as the I.A.F., had also been greatly expanded since 1956. It still possessed no new tanks, but large quantities of second-hand Centurions (from Britain) and U.S. Pattons (from West Germany) had been procured. Under the successive leaderships of Ben Ari, Bar Lev and Elazar the Armour Corps had become a distinctive part of the I.D.F., with its own uniform, a bizarre swearing-in-of-officers ceremony (in torchlight atop the Masada massif), and, on account of the complex technology involved, a higher level of formal discipline and specialisation than was usual in the Israeli Army.

Elazar was succeeded by Israel Tal in 1964, and it was he who pioneered the main operational innovations. The army of

1956 had allotted the Armour Corps only infantry-support and breakthrough-exploitation rôles; it was to be expected that Ben Ari's success would see a shift towards the familiar German panzer blueprint, of armour supported by mechanised infantry undertaking breakthroughs as well as their exploitation. But Tal went even further, dismissing the need for mechanised infantry. Tanks only required such support, he argued, when confronted by infantry-controlled anti-tank weapons, and since, in the cover-less desert, these would not be used in any numbers, Israel's limited resources would be better spent on new tanks than on superfluous armoured personnel carriers. This 'all-tank' concept became the central plank of Armour Corps' doctrine; it would be largely responsible for both the 1967 triumph and the relative failure in 1973.

Other innovations, and the streamlining of old practices, served to accentuate flexibility and so accelerate the armoured advance. Supply flexibility would be ensured by adoption of a 'push' system, in which fuel and ammunition were pushed forward to seek out customers, rather than the traditional 'pull' system, in which customers had to waste precious time searching for the goods. Formational flexibility would continue to rest on the 'ugdah' system's ad hoc grouping of brigades under freelance divisional H.Q.s; command flexibility was grounded in 'optional control', the system whereby commanders in the field took their own decisions, safe in the knowledge that the High Command would exercise its option to interfere should the general situation warrant it. Both the 'ugdah' and 'optional control' systems had their roots in the Palestine War; they represented a modern army's application of the guerrilla axiom that initiative should be the rule rather than the exception.

The Israeli strategic plan, drafted under Chief of Staff Rabin's direction, and approved by Defence Minister Dayan in early June, was basically simple. Fast-moving forces would break through the major Egyptian positions on the trans-Sinai routes and race for the Central Ridge passes, thus cutting off the bulk of the Egyptian Army from its bases and homeland. Jordan, it was hoped, would stay out of the war. There was little hope (or fear) of such Syrian reticence, but the Israelis believed they could conduct a holding operation in the north until such time as Egypt was accounted for. Then there would be a reckoning on Golan.

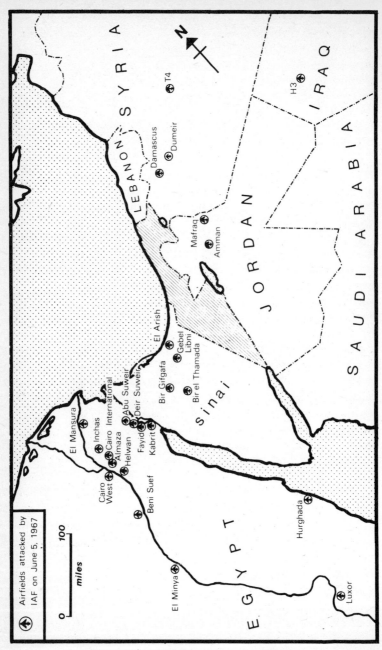

7. The Israeli air-strike, 5 June, 1967

The I.D.F., in contrast to its Arab opponents, represented an advanced culture's will to survival. As such its forces were both technically adept and possessed of the high morale that only comes from a high level of social cohesion. Israel believed it had to fight, and it believed it could win. On the morning of 5 June, as the columns of armour assembled on the Gaza Strip and Sinai frontiers, the planes of the I.A.F. sped down runways throughout Israel, took to the air, and swept out across the Mediterranean towards Egypt.

III

The early morning mists cleared to reveal a defenceless Egyptian Air Force. The traditional high alert status maintained in the hour following dawn had been relaxed, and much of the expensive-to-run radar equipment turned off. Many officers were on the road between their homes and their bases, temporarily incommunicado. The Egyptian C.-in-C., Field-Marshal Amer, was airborne, en route to inspect his troops in Sinai, and Egyptian A.A. units had been specifically ordered not to open fire without special authorisation. Three days earlier the War Minister had issued a new regulation prohibiting direct communication between the different Arab High Commands. Consequently a report from the Jordanian radar station at Ajlun, which had picked up the massed I.A.F. take-off, was lying on his desk throughout the day.

Most of this had been calculated by the Israeli Intelligence services; the pre-emptive strike had been planned to the last detail. The pilots moving in to attack the Egyptian air bases had practised the manoeuvre a hundred times on dummy bases in the Negev. First they put the runways out of action. Specially-designed bombs dropped from the aircraft to be stopped in mid-air by retro-rockets, and then driven vertically into the concrete by booster rockets. Next the Israeli planes turned, with cannons blazing, at the lines of Egyptian supersonic jets. And then the other combat aircraft, the transport aircraft, the hangars and installations.

Ten minutes after arriving they turned for home, and a second wave plunged down out of the sky to continue the destruction. By 9.30 nine airfields – El Arish, As Sirr, Bir Gifgafa,

Bir el Thamada, Abu Suweir, Fayid, Kabrit, Inshas, Cairo West – had been accounted for, and most of the E.A.F. with them. The Israeli strikes spread farther afield through the morning, to seven other Egyptian airfields, two Jordanian, five Syrian and one in Iraq. By early afternoon the Arab air forces had been largely destroyed, and the I.A.F. was master of the skies from the Nile to the Euphrates. Only one enemy runway had escaped unscathed, that at El Arish. The Israelis hoped to be using it themselves before the night was out.

IV

The Israeli force poised to cross the frontier comprised three divisions (or 'ugdahs') under Tal, Yoffe, and the famous Ariel Sharon. Tal's division, detailed to break through on the Rafah–El Arish coast road, was the strongest, with two armoured brigades (including the crack 7th under Gonen) and a mixed armour/paratroop force under Raful Eytan. All in all it contained three hundred tanks. Further south Yoffe's division, consisting of two armoured brigades (two hundred tanks), was to cross the 'impassable' sand-sea between the northern and central trans-Sinai routes, and to establish itself within range of the Bir Lahfan road junction. From this position it would offer assistance to the other two divisions, either directly or by intercepting any Egyptian counter-move from the interior of Sinai. Sharon's division contained only one armoured brigade, but was the strongest in terms of infantry and artillery. It was to mount a set-piece capture of the Egyptian positions at Abu Aweigila–Umm Katef, and thus force open the central route into Sinai.

7th Armoured Brigade crossed the frontier opposite Khan Yunis at 08.15, forty minutes before Eytan's force crossed it south of Kerem Shalom. Both forces were aimed obliquely at the Rafah crossroads defence complex, Gonen at the northern flank, Eytan at the southern. For 7th Armoured Brigade's approach Tal had decided to use the main Gaza–Rafah road, which he correctly guessed would not be mined. The two battalions – one of Pattons, one of Centurions – surged across the open space and into Khan Yunis, where they suffered heavy casualties and some confusion before turning south-west

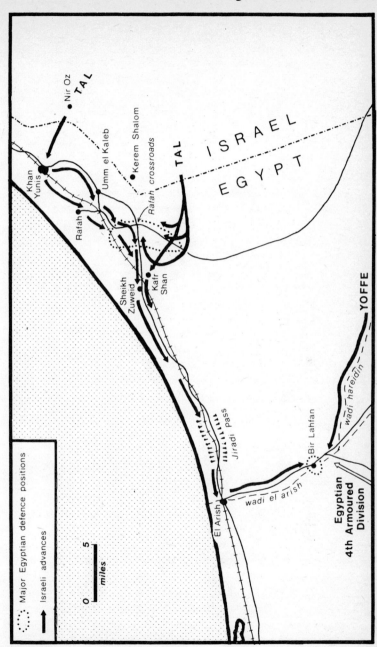

8. Rafah—El Arish, 1967

along the railway line towards Rafah. In the meantime the strong Brigade Battle Reserve (forty or so tanks), on the commander's own initiative, was moving on a more southerly course towards the small Egyptian position at Umm El Kaleb. Overrunning it with ease, the tanks rumbled on towards Rafah station and the Water Tower. Here they met up with the leading elements of the two major battalions, which had just driven through the sparsely defended Rafah camp area. Now all three formations were moving towards the north-eastern corner of the main defence zone.

The defences were laid out on classic Soviet lines. The attackers would be greeted with an artillery barrage, through which only the tanks could move with relative safety. These would next encounter extensive minefields. The sappers, called forward to clear a path, would be decimated by mortar and machine-gun fire from the trenches. Should any tanks be fortunate enough to break through the minefield unscathed they would run straight into concentrated anti-tank fire on the *pakfront* (groups of guns firing in coordinated salvoes) model. Behind this were even more anti-tank guns, tanks, and self-propelled artillery; even further back, the armoured reserve. An Israeli attack, the Soviet advisers doubtless told their Egyptian trainees, would be like a re-run of the German offensive at Kursk, a disaster.

It was not, however, 1943 any more. Neither did Sinai resemble the Central Russian Plain. And an Egyptian Zhukov was conspicuous by his absence. The minefields and artillery took their toll of the Israeli armour, but could not stop it. And once in among the defences Israeli tank gunnery quickly proved too much for the Egyptian guns. By midday the Brigade Battle Reserve and the Centurion Battalion had broken through on the El Arish road. Two kilometres to the north the Pattons were moving east alongside the railway line.

Eytan's attack in the south was a more confused affair, as the paratroopers and their supporting tank companies lost contact both with each other and with their grasp of the topography. One tank company, looking for Kafr Shan, found itself in Sheikh Zuweid in time to meet the 7th Armoured Brigade. Another fell into an Egyptian ambush, suffering severe losses. The paratroopers, bereft of tank support, found themselves in trouble, amidst a sea of Egyptian tanks and guns. But despite all these problems, and the disconcertingly high casualties suffered, Eytan's force gradually wrenched control of the area from the Egyptian defenders. By 16.00 the Rafah crossroads were cleared, and supply columns were allowed through for the still-advancing 7th Armoured Brigade.

Soon after noon the leading tanks of the Brigade Battle Reserve had reached the mouth of the Jiradi Pass. This was a formidable obstacle:

> Egyptian tanks in heavy concentrations on both sides of the roadway, in dug-out emplacements, their guns aimed at the narrow entrance to the pass. There were also batteries of anti-tank guns camouflaged under nets; mortars, with the range pre-set on the road, positioned in hidden locations in the hills; machine-gun positions and rifle pits spread out in the hills and fortified heights and invisible from the road; and mines laid along both sides of the road for the entire length of the fortified pass.[2]

The Brigade Battle Reserve simply drove through at speed, firing Rommel-fashion to port and starboard. Nobody had apparently informed the Egyptian defenders that an Israeli breakthrough had occurred at Rafah, and by the time they had recovered from the shock and returned to their guns, all but two of the Centurions had cleared the western exit. The column eventually reached the outskirts of El Arish at around 16.00. The pass, meanwhile, had been slammed shut behind them, and it was several hours before the rest of 7th Armoured Brigade, under cover of an artillery barrage and I.A.F. strikes, could break through to join its leading echelons.

At this juncture of the battle, according to Soviet/Egyptian doctrine, 4th Armoured Division should have been arriving to throw back the exposed Israeli spearhead. Most of the division had indeed left its Bir Gifgafa base shortly after dusk, and headed east with such intentions in mind. Unfortunately for the Egyptian Army, it was never to reach El Arish.

One of Yoffe's two armoured brigades had crossed the Sinai frontier at 09.00 and headed west along the dry Wadi Hareidin. After nine hours of painfully slow progress through the sand, and a short exchange of fire with an isolated Egyptian outpost, the brigade reached the El Arish–Abu Aweigila road two miles south of the Bir Lahfan defences and one mile south of the road junction. A long-range gun duel ensued between the Egyptian guns and Israeli tanks, which was only terminated by darkness. The brigade then settled down to wait.

At 23.00 one of the two tank battalions was sent south to assist Sharon's assault on Umm Katef. Soon afterwards, a long line of lights moving up the road from Gebel Libni signalled the expected arrival of 4th Armoured Division. The Israeli tanks opened fire, disabling three T-55s, and forcing the Egyptian column to douse its lights. Both sides fired blind across the darkness until an Egyptian fuel truck was hit, the explosion flooding the Egyptian positions with light. Their tanks scuttled back into the darkness, and for the rest of the night the two forces maintained a tacit ceasefire.

This was entirely to the Israelis' advantage. For several hours one battalion of tanks, aided by darkness and Egyptian timidity, was holding off two armoured brigades. And these were hours the Egyptians could ill afford to waste. By the time they did mount an attack, soon after dawn, the battalion on loan to Sharon's division had returned and the I.A.F. was ready and willing to intervene. The arrival of Yoffe's other brigade up the Abu Aweigila road clinched the issue. The 4th Armoured Division, which had moved east to punish the Israeli spearhead, now found itself the spearhead of an Egyptian retreat.

In the meantime Tal's tanks were moving south from El Arish against the other side of the Bir Lahfan defences. By 11.00 on 6 June his and Yoffe's divisions had made contact. The northern gate into Sinai was wide open.

V

Of all the Israeli commanders Ariel 'Arik' Sharon is by far the most interesting. Behind a rampant egomania that makes him almost 'impossible' to work with, there lurks a flair for the unorthodox that is unparalleled in recent military history. Sharon seems to personify the fundamental Israeli schizophrenia: the twinning of a bull-headedness that will forever ensure Arab hostility with an imaginative genius that continues to render that hostility impotent. His normal *modus operandi* has been to prepare a meticulously comprehensive plan, wait

Above: **David Ben-Gurion.**
(ISRAELI EMBASSY)

Left: **Moshe Dayan**
(ISRAELI EMBASSY)

Opposite page: **Giving blood for the war effort at the Egyptian Embassy in London, October 1973.** (VALERIE WILMER)

Top: **Israeli tanks in Sinai, June 1967.** (N. GUTMAN: CAMERA PRESS)

Above: **Israeli forces take Jerusalem, June 1967.** (POPPERFOTO)

Left: **King Hussein.**
(JORDANIAN EMBASSY)

Below: **Sinai, 1973**
(NEIL LIBBERT: CAMERA
PRESS)

Right: **Palestinian
guerilla on the Golan
Heights.** (CAMERA
PRESS)

Right below: **Israeli
Phantoms unloading
napalm.** (WERNER
BRAUN: CAMERA PRESS)

Above: **Golda Meir.** (ISRAELI EMBASSY)

Left: **President Sadat of Egypt.** (EGYPTIAN EMBASSY)

Right: **The Egyptians cross the Canal, October 1973.** (EGYPTIAN EMBASSY)

Below right: **Ariel Sharon, now Minister of Agriculture and Settlements in the Begin Government.** (ISRAELI EMBASSY)

Top: **A blazing tank, Sinai 1973.** (EGYPTIAN EMBASSY)

Above: **Palestinian refugee 'city' in Baqaa, Jordan.**
(BRIAN ARIS: CAMERA PRESS)

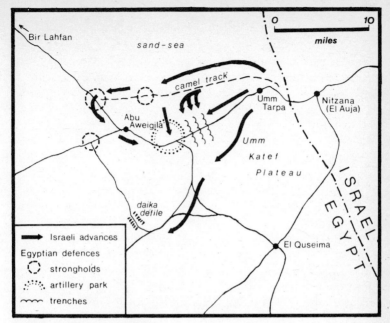

9. Umm Katef, 1967

for something to go wrong, and then cast the plan comprehensively aside in favour of an old-fashioned charge. Since this bizarre schemata, like a Salvador Dali painting, embraces both organisational finesse and a basic unpredictability, it is usually extremely effective.

In 1967 Sharon's orders were to take the strong Umm Katef position, some twelve miles west of Nitzana on the central Sinai route. Wedged between the cliffs of an eighty-foot plateau and a large sand-sea, the Umm Katef defences were, like those at Rafah, laid out on classic Soviet lines. A 300-yard minefield, three two-to-three-mile trenches manned by an infantry brigade, a 70-gun artillery park surrounded by its own trench, and a supporting force of 66 tanks and 22 self-propelled guns.

Sharon, believing the position to be held by a mere battalion, reversed his usual *modus operandi* and resorted to an immediate frontal attack on the morning of 5 June. But the minefields and Egyptian fire proved too much for the Israeli tanks, and the Centurion battalion was shifted along the camel track north of the road into flanking position. Another group of tanks was moved into an equivalent position south of the road, where it could keep watch on the track leading south to Quseima.

The extent of the Egyptian defences was now clear, and Sharon began planning for a night-attack of bewildering complexity. His intention was to hit the Egyptian defences from all sides simultaneously, a basically simple idea, the execution of which would require a great deal of movement and split-second timing, all in the darkness. The infantry brigade was moved up to Umm Tarpa in buses. From there it struggled across the dunes on foot for several hours, to a position north of the Egyptian trench lines. At the same time a small force of paratroopers was lifted by helicopter to a position in the desert just north of the artillery park, and the two tank forces north and south of the main road were moved west to, respectively, the Abu Aweigila–Bir Lahfan road and the Daika defile.

At 22.30 the attack began with a 100-gun artillery barrage. The three battalions of the infantry brigade moved in from the desert along the three Egyptian trenches, each battalion carrying lights of a particular colour. As they fought their way south the Israeli artillery laid down fire on the trenches immediately ahead of them. The Egyptian gunners should have been laying down similar support for their infantry, but instead found themselves fully occupied by the assaulting Israeli paratroopers. And the Egyptian armour, which should have been providing support for the artillery, found itself engaged by the Israeli armour moving round into its rear.

As the northern half of the trenches was cleared, sappers moved in to clear the minefield in preparation for the Sherman battalion's breakthrough. This was accomplished around dawn, and the Shermans met the eastward-moving Centurions in the Rouaffa Dam area at 06.00. By this time the Egyptian position had degenerated into a series of isolated pockets of resistance, and Yoffe's other armoured brigade could be fed along the main road towards its rendezvous with the Egyptian 4th Armoured Division at the Bir Lahfan crossroads.

So, by mid-morning of 6 June the Israelis had broken through the two main Egyptian shields and were poised to advance across Sinai. The only coherent force between them and the Suez Canal was the retreating 4th Armoured Division. Other formations that had not yet tasted combat – particularly Shazli's Armoured Group and 6th Infantry Division – were now effectively behind the lines, and so forced to devote all their attention to the business of escape. This disastrous situation was slowly becoming apparent to the Egyptian leadership. With the I.A.F., mostly absorbed through 5 June in counter-air force action, now able to fulfil a ground-support rôle with unmitigated vigour, this situation could only worsen. On the afternoon of 6 June the Egyptian High Command ordered a retreat to the line of the Central Ridge. Many units did not receive the order due to the prevailing chaos in communications. For those that did it was often too late.

VI

Despite the ideological hunger in most Israeli hearts for a united Jewish-controlled Jerusalem, and the less honourable hunger in many for the West Bank region of Jordan, Israeli attitudes towards war with Hussein were characterised by ambivalence. For one thing the I.D.F. was likely to be occupied fully in Sinai and on Golan, for another the Israelis did not wish to topple a reasonably amicable enemy, and find themselves saddled with another Nasser. The Jews had waited two thousand years for their state, as Golda Meir was fond of saying; they could wait a few more for Jerusalem. It was up to Hussein to make the decision.

Hussein was also, as usual, full of ambivalence, and he had no desire to take such decisions. But he really had no choice. Always regarded with deep suspicion by his fellow Arab rulers in the other front-line states, he could not afford at this juncture to appear anything less than whole-hearted in his devotion to Arab solidarity. Nor were his forces negligible. The power and reputation of the Arab Legion had been somewhat diluted by the years and the absorption of the Palestinian West Bank, and his Air Force consisted of only twenty-one subsonic jets, but there were 55,000 men under arms, and the two armoured brigades, equipped with Pattons and Centurions, were to put up the most creditable Arab performance of the war. Nothing too drastic was envisaged in the Jordanian strategic plan: a few gains in and around Jerusalem and Latrun, a limited offensive in the Gilboa range region in the north. At the outbreak of hostilities Hussein limited these still further, to the capture of the Mount Scopus enclave and the U.N. position in no-man's-land, both in Jerusalem.

The Israeli forces were much smaller, consisting of two infantry brigades on the coastal plain frontier, the large but second-string Etzioni Brigade in Jerusalem, and the Harel Mechanised Brigade (with one Sherman battalion) under 1956 hero, Ben Ari. Much of the fighting against Jordan would be done by last-minute reinforcements: a division under Peled from the northern front and a Paratroop Brigade under Motta Gur from Sinai.

Soon after the air-strike had been delivered against Egypt, the Israeli government sent a note to Hussein, via the U.N. chief in Jerusalem, promising that Jordan would not be attacked if she refrained from offensive action. Hussein's reply was the shelling of Jewish Jerusalem, the bombing of Tel Aviv suburbs, and long-range artillery fire at the Ramat David airfield. Around midday Jordanian forces took Government House in the U.N. zone, and appeared to be threatening Mount Scopus. All along the ceasefire line Jordanian troops opened fire.

While the Israeli infantry brigades held their ground and swopped fire with the enemy, Ben Ari's Mechanised Brigade was being ordered east from its Ramle base. Its original task was to relieve Mount Scopus, but this was soon widened to include the seizure of the high ground dominating the northern approaches to Jerusalem. Between 17.30 and 18.00 the division, in three battle-groups, advanced up the ridge north of the Jerusalem–Tel Aviv road between Maale Hamisha and Kastel. By 02.00 on 6 June they had wrested Biddu from the Jordanians and, advancing east, seized control of Nebi Samuel some two hours later. It was from this village that Richard the Lionheart had gained his solitary glimpse of the Holy City. The Israelis certainly had more than glimpses in mind by this time, and doubtless Ben Ari could perceive the flashes of battle in the city far below.

Gur's Paratroop Brigade had arrived in Jerusalem late the previous evening, and their attack went in at 02.20 on the 6th. The three battalions, each reinforced by a Sherman company from the Etzioni Brigade, charged across the wire-entangled minefields of no-man's-land to engage the Jordanians in hand-to-hand combat. Their general objective was the Mount Scopus ridge, their route lay through the built-up zone of north-east

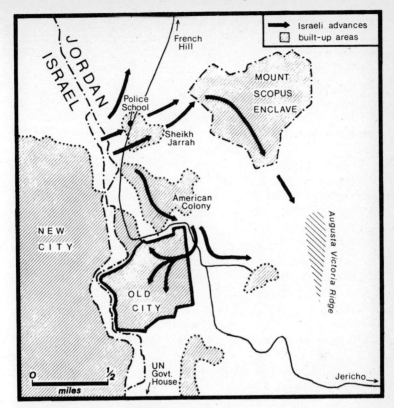

Israeli advances
built-up areas

JORDAN
ISRAEL

French
Hill

Police
School

Sheikh
Jarrah

MOUNT
SCOPUS
ENCLAVE

American
Colony

NEW
CITY

Augusta Victoria Ridge

OLD
CITY

UN
Govt.
House

Jericho

0   ½

miles

10. Jerusalem, 1967

Jerusalem. One major stronghold barred the way: the Police
School. Fiercely defended by the Arab Legion, its capture cost
the Israelis fifty dead, or seven per cent of their fatal casualties
for the entire June War. Nevertheless, by 07.00 the Israeli
forces had made contact with the Mount Scopus enclave, taken
the Sheikh Jarrah quarter and most of the so-called American
Colony. Of Jordanian Jerusalem little remained save the walled
Old City.

In northern Samaria the Israelis had also gone over to the
offensive. The previous evening (5 June) Peled had launched a
mechanised brigade across the border, and while a minor
column headed south for the main Nablus road the major force
worked its way to a position south-west of Jenin in the Dotan
valley. Brushing aside the local Jordanian armour, it moved
into the town from the south as an infantry brigade attacked

from the north. By 07.30 Jenin was securely in Israeli hands.

But not for long. Peled received news of sixty Jordanian Pattons moving north on the Tubas loop-road, and pulled his mechanised brigade out of Jenin to meet the threat. It reached the Qabatiya road-junction to find the Pattons well-ensconced, a situation that two armoured charges and I.A.F. strikes did nothing to reverse. In the meantime the minor column of armour had been halted by Jordanian forces at Arraba. The Israeli attack seemed to have stalled.

Such success, however, did not cut much ice at the Jordanian Command H.Q. There Hussein and General Riad, his Egyptian commander of the Jordanian Army, were finely balanced between apprehension and extreme apprehension. Since dawn the power of the I.A.F. had been making itself felt throughout Jordan. Jerusalem seemed about to fall. At 05.30 Riad had offered Hussein two alternatives: retreat to the East Bank or request a ceasefire. Neither appealed very much to Hussein. He very much doubted if he would get back an abandoned West Bank, he very much doubted if his dynasty would survive a unilateral ceasefire request. In either case he would need his army still intact. He could not decide. Twice in the next twenty-four hours he would issue and retract orders for a retreat across the Jordan, in the process causing untold confusion in the ranks of his hard-pressed army.

Jordanian problems were no more obvious to the Israelis than their own were to the Jordanians. Progress was extremely slow. In the north another brigade had crossed the frontier, this time east of Jenin, and advanced southwards through Deir Abu Da'if and Jalqamus to the Tubas loop-road near Zababida. There it was halted, like the mechanised force at the Qabatiya road-junction, by well dug-in Jordanian armour. From midday to midnight, despite intervention by the I.A.F., stalemate reigned. In Jerusalem the picture was the same. Three attempts to storm the Augusta Ridge were thrown back by the Jordanians, and until this dominating feature east of the city was taken the Israelis could not hope to launch an attack on the Old City.

Only Ben Ari's brigade was pushing the enemy back. By 06.00 it had reached the Jerusalem–Ramallah road at Tel el Fut, and after three violent encounters with the Jordanian 60th Armoured Brigade, secured the position. The brigade then moved

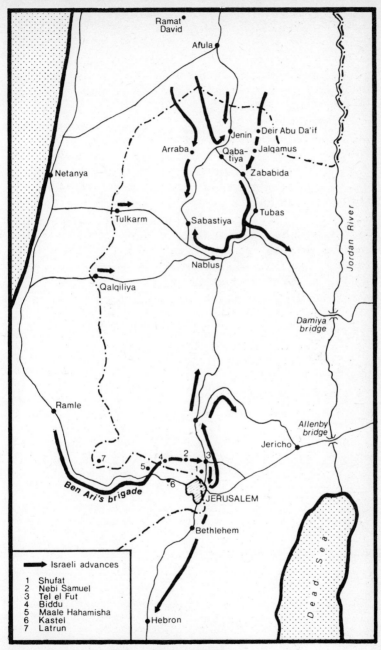

11. Jordan's West Bank, 1967

south towards Jerusalem, taking, after heavy fighting, the Shafat and French Hill strongpoints during the late morning and early afternoon. Seizure of the latter saw Ben Ari's brigade link up with Gur's paratroopers, so completing the Israeli chain around Jerusalem's northern perimeter. At 17.15 Ben Ari turned north once more, towards Ramallah. Slowly the noose was tightening around Hussein's army.

Sometime during the evening of 6 June the unfortunate King must have distinctly heard the trapdoor opening beneath him, as Nasser came through on the phone to inform him of the Egyptian Air Force's destruction the previous morning. For an hour or so Hussein's mind was made up. At 22.30 the Jordanian Army was ordered back over the Jordan river. The King had decided to save his Army and his throne at the expense of the West Bank. This was a sensible decision, but an hour or so later Hussein changed his mind once more. The possibility of a ceasefire – the U.N. was calling for one – had persuaded him to leave the Army where it was. After all, it would be galling to sacrifice the West Bank unnecessarily. But then the cease-fire call was rejected. Now both the Army, some of it retreating, some not, would be lost as well as the West Bank. There was one consolation: the King's dithering had saved him from an unambiguous retreat, and hence also from losing his throne.

Meanwhile his Army collapsed into confusion. The Israeli armour on the Tubas loop-road, on the night of 6–7 June, broke through the Jordanian road-block and motored swiftly south to Nablus. The townsfolk, mistaking them for Iraqis, were delirious. The Israeli armour motored on, turning north up the main Nablus–Jenin road. At Sabastiya they caught the Jordanian blocking forces on that road from the rear. Samaria had fallen.

Further south, at 08.00, a fourth attack was mounted against the Augusta Victoria ridge. It was empty, since the Jordanian forces, withdrawn during the night, had not returned. An hour or so later, Gur's paratroopers burst into the Old City. Resistance was minimal. The City of King David had been reclaimed, the City of Saladin lost once more to infidels.

By mid-afternoon on 7 June the West Bank was mostly in Israeli hands. Forces had reached the Damiya bridge on the Jordan and entered Jericho; elements of the Etzioni Brigade were entering Bethlehem and Hebron in the wake of the departing Jordanians.

VII

By the evening of 6 June the Egyptian leadership, like the Jordanian, was caught between the desire to save its army and the desire not to cede territory unnecessarily. To Field-Marshal Amer the breakthroughs at Rafah and Umm Katef signalled potential annihilation. He ordered a total withdrawal from Sinai. Nasser though was less prone to panic, and believed that the line of the Central Ridge could still be held. He countermanded Amer's orders, only for Amer to counter-countermand his own. This continual bombardment of contradictory orders – received by some units but not by others owing to the chronic breakdown of Egyptian communications – did nothing for the morale of the Egyptian forces. They merely bred uncertainty, and uncertainty bred panic, turning an already none-too-cohesive retreat into a headlong flight. Officers grabbed the first transport they could lay their hands on, leaving their men to abandon weapons and uniforms for the long cross-desert trudge to the Canal. The Egyptian Army slowly disintegrated.

In Gebel Libni that same evening, as their men rested after thirty-six hours' continuous activity, the Israeli divisional leaders talked with Gavish, the overall commander of the southern front. The objective – the destruction of the Egyptian Army – could now best be served, they decided, by a full-speed armoured advance to the Central Ridge passes. There the armour would adopt blocking positions against the slow-moving Egyptian forces retreating westwards. Tal's division was allocated the Ismailiya Pass, Yoffe's the Giddi and Mitla Passes.

The armour started west on the morning of the 7th, occasionally meeting minor resistance in the Egyptian camps strung at intervals along the desert roads. Tal's tanks blasted their way through Bir Hamma and Bir Rod Salim with assistance from the I.A.F., and by mid-afternoon had taken up positions covering the Bir Gifgafa road junction. Soon after arriving they spotted the bulk of 4th Armoured Division moving up the road from Bir el Thamada, intent on escape through the Ismailiya Pass. A tank battle raged through the evening, in which the

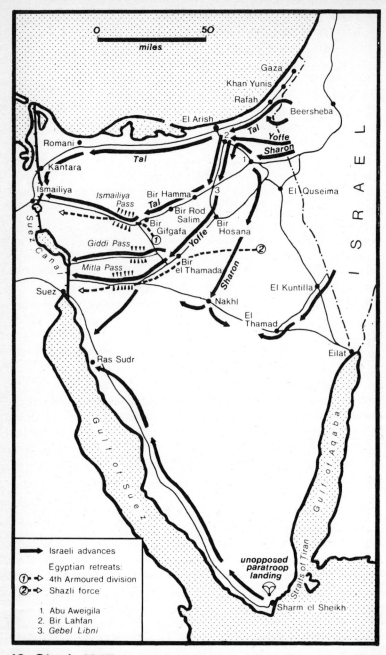

12. Sinai, 1967

Egyptian armour – whose commander had already retreated to Cairo – performed creditably. Most of the 4th Armoured Division managed to fight their way into and through the Pass before the Israeli armour established a strong enough blocking force at its eastern entrance.

Further south, Yoffe too was having problems. Having motored through Bir Hasana and Bir el Thamada to arrive one mile from the Mitla Pass entrance at 17.00, he discovered that his spearhead was down to a mere nine tanks, of which four were being towed. Not surprisingly, this small force found it impossible to block the entrance effectively, and one Egyptian force broke through before the Israelis managed to narrow the path with wrecked vehicles. During the night Yoffe took the risky but successful step of switching his two brigades (the fresh one for the worn-out one) in mid-action, and by dawn the Mitla Pass was definitely sealed.

There was no hope now for those Egyptian forces still east of the Central Ridge. While Tal and Yoffe held the passes, the I.A.F. took their toll of the retreating Egyptians. Each diving attack left a line of wrecked vehicles, and these lines acted as bottlenecks, slowing succeeding lines of still-moving vehicles, making them easier targets for the rocket-fire and napalm canisters of the darting silver vultures above.

Further east, the Israeli ground forces were mopping up. On the morning of 7 June the Gaza Strip had fallen after fierce urban fighting in Khan Yunis, and Sharm el-Sheikh had been found deserted. Sharon's division had spent the 6th clearing up Umm Katef, and the 7th motoring south across country towards Nakhl in search of the Shazli Force and 6th Infantry Division. The former retreated across Sharon's rear while the division slept on the night of 7–8 June, but 6th Infantry was not so fortunate. Retreating west along the 'Pilgrim's Way' towards Nakhl, it found itself trapped in a veritable 'valley of death' (Sharon's description), between the Israeli forces on its tail and Sharon's division in front.

Two days previously, at 22.30 on the 6th, a small force from Tal's division had left El Arish to follow the road west across northern Sinai. Through that night and the next day the unit cruised along, meeting minimal resistance. The following night was spent near Romani, and a clear run to the Canal was expected on the next day. But Egyptian resistance increased on the morning of the 8th, and the unit had to fight its way through two stiff engagements and the continuous attentions of the E.A.F., before eventually reaching the Canal bank near Kantara at 20.00.

In the interior both Tal and Yoffe's divisions had spent the day forcing and securing, with I.A.F. assistance, the Mitla, Giddi and Ismailiya Passes. Soon after nightfall, hearing that a ceasefire was imminent, both divisions sent forces across the remaining stretch of desert to the Canal, which they reached in the early hours of 9 June. Behind them the bulk of the Egyptian Army was scattered across Sinai, its weaponry and transport ruined or abandoned, its men succumbing in droves to the merciless desert.

VIII

Two of the three front-line armies were in ruins; only the Syrian remained intact. As international pressure for a ceasefire increased, the I.D.F. prepared to move against the Golan Heights.

The Syrian Army manning those heights was very similar to the Egyptian. It too had received substantial military aid from the Soviet Union in the preceding two years, effectively doubling its tank and A.P.C. strength. Approximately 60,000 men were permanently under arms, with some 40,000 trained reservists waiting in the wings. As in the Egyptian case, the new weapons had not been properly absorbed in the short space of time since their arrival, and they had suffered from inadequate maintenance. The Army as a whole reflected the deep divisions of Syrian society, divisions further sharpened by the chronic factionalism of Syrian politics.

The Syrians did have one great advantage. The west wall of the Golan Plateau constitutes a natural obstacle of the first order, stretching right along the frontier from the Hermonite massif to the Yarmak valley. From Israel it looks like 'a huge unbroken wall of rugged, cliff-like rock', and appearances, in this case, are not very deceptive. In the central section, between the B'not Yakov bridge and Koursi, the slope is slightly less steep; north and south of this section it is seemingly impassable and impregnable, the Heights 'present few openings; such that exist are mere slits of ravines let into the cliff faces and even the more gradual parts of the slopes are studded with huge basalt boulders'.[3] It was from atop these heights that the Syrians had periodically lobbed shells into the Israeli settlements in the valley below. Right along their length, and back across the plateau to a depth of ten miles, the Syrians had sought to improve nature's work with a formidable system of mutually supporting defences. The familiar Soviet defence patterns had been grafted on to the topography, the concrete grafted on to the rock. Gun emplacements in profusion glared down at the Israelis. There was no way around this Maginot Line; if the Israelis wished to engage the Syrian Army they would have to go up.

For, given this god-sent position, the Syrians were showing no desire to come down. While Jordan and Sinai burned, the Syrian Army was fiddling, launching derisory attacks on two nearby settlements (with heavy losses) and occasionally launching a lone aircraft or two on kamikaze missions into Israeli air-space. A strategic plan for the invasion of Israel did exist, but then so did one for the occupation of northern Jordan, and it seems that the Syrian government, piqued by Nasser's kissing of Hussein, would have preferred to implement the latter. But, Arab solidarity being the order of the day, it could not. The Syrian Army continued its peacetime hobby of lobbing shells at the Israeli settlements and waited. For a ceasefire, or for nemesis.

For four days, while their forces were fully engaged in Jordan and Sinai, the Israeli High Command maintained a defensive posture in the north. David Elazar, commander of the northern front and future Chief of Staff, wished to attack with the forces at his disposal, but his superiors, particularly Defence Minister Dayan, were loath to risk a possibly understrength assault against the known depth of the Syrian defences. By evening on the 7th success on the other fronts was freeing units for deployment in the north, but through the morning of the 8th thick mist veiled the Golan Plateau, making an attack inconceivable. By afternoon the imminence of a general ceasefire and heavy hints of Soviet intervention persuaded the Israelis to wait a while longer. They had no desire to suffer heavy losses, reach only halfway up the escarpment, and then be halted by superpower pressure. In the meantime the I.A.F. pounded the Syrian positions, and those units rushed north after several days' intensive activity were given a chance to rest and recuperate. If the Syrians, as yet virtually untouched, rejected the ceasefire, then the Israeli assault would be launched on the following morning.

At 03.20 on 9 June Syria accepted the U.N. call for a ceasefire, but it soon became apparent that neither side was observing it. In this case* it seems likely that the Israelis, unwilling to be deterred from a squaring of accounts with their most virulent enemy, were the guilty party. Either way the Israelis commenced their assault in mid-morning, after several preparatory strikes by the I.A.F. Elazar had chosen a narrow sector in the far north for the break-in. Here the escarpment was extremely steep, but the defences were relatively less dense and considerably less deep. Once atop the crest in this sector the Israelis would be ideally placed to motor south down the Banias–Butmiye road, thus unhinging the whole Syrian line and forcing a general withdrawal.

The two forces chosen to lead this major assault were a reserve armoured brigade and the Golani Mechanised Infantry Brigade. The former was to reach the fortified village of Qala astride the crest, the latter to clear its northern flank by seizure of the dominating hill of Tel Azzaziat.

As Syrian artillery fire whistled over and around them (some Syrian gunners, to the chagrin of their Soviet advisers, continued to aim at the Israeli settlements while the attack was in progress), the Israeli sappers worked to clear a path through the minefields on both sides of the border, and at 11.30 the leading tanks crossed and started to climb. Soon they were grinding up the winding tracks through a curtain of fire from artillery, anti-tank guns and dug-in tanks. The I.A.F. provided tactical support, drenching those Syrian positions in the line

---

* It should be stressed that throughout the Arab–Israeli conflict calls for ceasefire have been ignored, and those accepted subsequently violated, with amazing regularity by both sides, whenever a military advantage could thereby be secured. The Israelis broke the last two ceasefires in 1948-9 in order to evict the Egyptians from the Negev, and the 22 October ceasefire in 1973 in order to complete the encirclement of Egypt's 3rd Army. The Egyptians violated the 7 August 1970 ceasefire in order to advance their missile system into the Suez Canal Zone, and repeatedly ignored appeals for a ceasefire in the early stages of the October 1973 war when they appeared to hold an advantageous position.

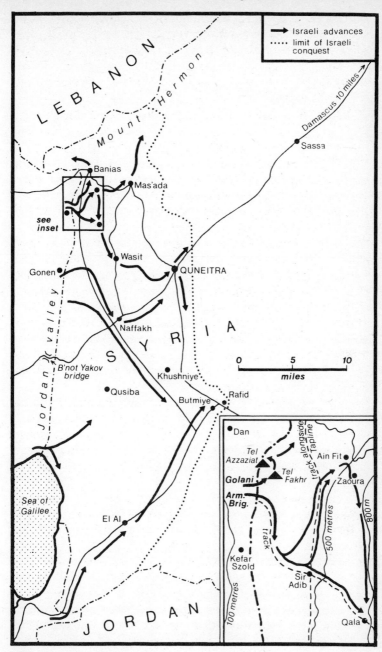

13. Golan, 1967

of advance with napalm and high explosive. The armour charged through two defensive positions, looking for the left turn to Zaoura on the intended route to Qala. The first combat-team missed it and, mistakenly taking a more direct route, climbed into the Sir Adib position's field of fire. The Israelis charged once more and overran the position. From here the road plunged downhill into a dip strewn with dragon's teeth and then wound sharply uphill again towards Qala. On one flank was a strong defensive position full of artillery and tanks, on the other a small plateau jammed with anti-tank guns. Not surprisingly, by the time the Israeli unit reached Qala it had lost all but two tanks and three successive commanding officers. In the village itself the remnants were pinned down by machine-gun fire and the arrival of a Syrian armoured unit.

The Golani Brigade was also engaged in a bitter struggle. Crossing the frontier at 14.00 it attempted to circle around behind Tel Azzaziat for an assault on the easier eastern slope. En route the brigade was halted by a strong defensive complex at Tel Fakhr, the fight for which proved almost as expensive as that for the Police School in Jerusalem. Thirty-seven Israelis died as the infantry stormed through minefields, barbed wire and trenches to engage the Syrian defenders with 'fists, knives, teeth and rifle-butts'.[4] An hour later, around 19.00, Tel Azzaziat was taken without much difficulty.

In the meantime the other two combat teams of the armoured brigade had reached Zaoura by different routes early in the afternoon. Having subdued the defences they turned south towards Qala, reaching the village at 18.30 and relieving the Israeli advance guard. In seven hours the Syrian line had been broken.

Other smaller breaches had also been opened in the Syrian line on the evening of 9 June, and on the following morning the Israelis went over to the attack along most of the Golan frontier. The Golani Brigade, which had been shelled from the Banias Ridge throughout the night, cleared the whole area north of its original break-in between Zaoura and the Lebanese frontier. The armoured brigade worked its way south from Qala through Wasit to Mansurah in the hours after dawn.

In Damascus there was an atmosphere of growing panic. The government, with the intention of hurrying a ceasefire and so retaining more territory, announced through Damascus Radio

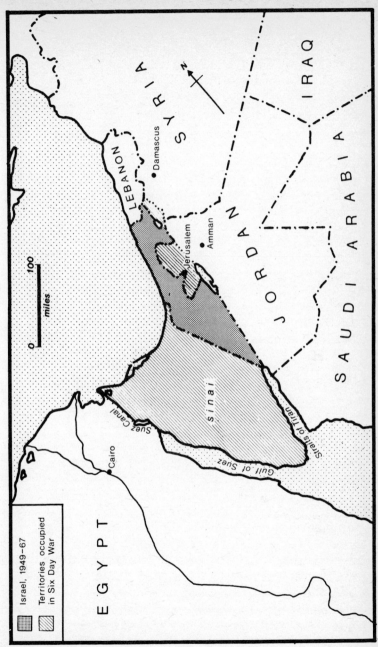

14. 10 June, 1967

that Quneitra had fallen at 08.45, some six hours before Israeli forces arrived to find it empty. The result of this premature broadcast was the opposite of that intended: the Syrian resistance in the field abruptly collapsed as the Army, led for once by its officers, sought to fight its way east through the non-existent Israeli encirclement. The Israelis then advanced, against negligible opposition, to a line Banias–Rafid along the centre of the plateau. By early evening the June War was over.

IX

Israeli troops stared out across the Suez Canal into the heart-land of Egypt, across the Jordan river at the mountains rising towards Amman, down the road to Damascus from the crest of the Golan Plateau. In six days they had won a magnificent victory. For a loss of 700 dead they had destroyed the armies of three Arab states.

But it was not a total victory. Nor could it be. There were no Israeli forces in Cairo, Damascus, Amman. The I.D.F. could kick the Arabs ever further from Palestine, but it could not hold them underfoot and force them to revoke their claim to the land. Even had there been no international pressure, no super-powers eager to see their ghoulish balance of terror mirrored in microcosm in the Middle East, the Israelis had not the power to occupy the Arab states and impose a peace of their choosing.

The subjugation of predominantly non-industrial states is not as easy as the subjugation of their armies. The Mongols were the finest practitioners of this ancient art; their methods were genocide and vandalism on a towering scale. Israel could not, would not, conceive of such means to their end.

Yet what were the alternatives? There was only one. To accept that the Arabs had not given up their claim to Palestine, that to them the June war was – as Nasser said it was – 'a setback' rather than a decision, and to wait, as the Soviet advisers and arms poured in to reorganise and re-equip the broken armies, for the next round. Politically, little had changed. There would be new diplomatic moves, of course, but no one would take them very seriously. The Arabs would per-haps move on to other levels of conflict – guerrilla warfare in

the newly occupied territories, oil diplomacy, international terrorism – while their armies were prepared for the next conventional war. This one had solved nothing. The Israeli victory,
set in motion by the Mirage force in two hours over Egypt, was
itself little more than a mirage.

PART TWO

Chapter 9

IN ANOTHER COUNTRY

The Struggle for Peace, 1967–1969

> Phlebas the Phoenician, a fortnight dead,
> Forgot the cry of gulls, and the deep sea swell
> And the profit and loss.
>   A current under sea
> Picked his bones in whispers. As he rose and fell
> He passed the stages of his age and youth
> Entering the whirlpool.
>   Gentile or Jew
> O you who turn the wheel and look to windward,
> Consider Phlebas, who was once handsome and tall as you.
>   (T. S. Eliot, 'Death by Water', *The Waste Land*)

I

> My home policy? I wage war. My foreign policy? I wage
> war. Always, everywhere I wage war – and I shall continue
> to wage war until the last quarter of an hour.
>   (Georges Clemenceau, 1918)

The United States and the Soviet Union had stood back from
the Sinai War, watching old-style imperialism kick out against
the relentless tide of history. Before the Six Day War they had
found themselves involved against their will. They tried to
pacify everybody concerned, while remaining aloof from the
action – but they gradually found themselves being thrust on to
centre stage despite valiant attempts to cling to the proscenium
arch. Oh, to stand in the wings and watch the action, taking
the stage only when the applause and cries of 'Authors,
authors!' became irresistible. Alas, it was not to be. The Arabs
did not like the lines they had been given; neither did the
Israelis like theirs and, as if to prove it, they had ad-libbed
their way into whole chunks of Egypt, Jordan and Syria. The

actors threatened to turn on the authors, the audience of nations threatened to join them, taking sides and beating each other's brains out in the U.N. auditorium. Something had to be done. The authors would have to put their heads together and come up with a totally different plot.

For the first time in almost twenty years, the Middle East situation had changed drastically. Israel had achieved a victory that had stunned not only the rest of the world, but had surprised and shaken victors and vanquished alike. It did not take the Israelis very long to recover from their shock. Assurances from before 5 June that Israel was not seeking territorial aggrandisement became transformed by the very scale of the conquest into demands that it should never withdraw. While Dayan had argued before the outbreak of the war that it was impossible to capture Sharm el-Sheikh without invading Sinai, only days after the ceasefire politicians, soldiers, political and military commentators and ordinary citizens were saying that it was impossible to *hold* Sharm el-Sheikh without *occupying* Sinai. The Israeli public had been told in the early days of June that their lives, and not just their state, were at stake. Inevitably, some lives had been at stake and some lives were lost. But mounting a successful operation to disarm the enemy was not enough. The military and political establishment proceeded to pick up the discarded weapons and turn them against their former owners.

Under the Eshkol Government, Israel had moved away from its militant Zionist stance. Eshkol's political defeat on 1 June was not itself a return to the militaristic conception of Israel. On the contrary, the acceptance of Dayan had been Eshkol's last, desperate measure to secure the unity of his Government. Israel could have fought, and won, a war under a Government in a state of chronic dispute with itself. But Eshkol doubted that Israeli democracy, as he saw it, could survive such an ulcerous condition. The Government would have been helpless to prevent militarism from growing ever closer to totalitarianism. And yet the scale of Israel's actual victory seemed to herald no more hopeful future. After the Six Day War three-quarters of the territory controlled by Israel was under military administration – a sort of state surrounding the state. The influence of the military and of the right wing who stood foursquare behind it increased accordingly.

Nothing is ever as simple as propagandists like to make out. Israel is not an expansionist state – although the net result of the 1948 and the 1967 wars has been an undeniable expansion of her territory. In 1948 one major motive for the capture of lands allocated to the Arabs under the United Nations Partition Plan was that the division of Palestine into Arab and Jewish zones as envisaged by the U.N. could only have worked had Arabs and Jews been prepared to accept some form of federation or, as the U.N. also envisaged, an economic union. Clearly, neither Arab nor Jew was able to accept such a high degree of integration. The two populations had been at each other's throats for decades – Palestinian Arab and Palestinian Jew both demanded autonomy, neither was about to give an inch. For the comparatively highly organised Jews it was a rock-bottom necessity to capture enough territory to turn their allocated zones into a viable geographical unit – without that there could not have been an autonomous State of Israel.

In 1967, victory created another territorial imperative. Many Israelis saw the 1956 U.N. settlement as a direct cause of Arab aggression. They saw that the post-1949 borders had encouraged constant harassment by guerrillas and other irregular soldiers of the Arab states and Palestinian people. They did their sums. 'The territory controlled by Israel since 10 June 1967 is four times its previous territory . . . ' wrote the Ben-Gurionite founder member of Rafi, Shimon Peres. 'While the length of her land borders has contracted to a quarter of what they were – 254 kms (and 1,000 kms of sea border).'[1] France, as Peres pointed out, has four metres of land border for every square kilometre of territory. The ratio was 50:1 for Israel before June 1967, and 7:1 after. Israel occupied the commanding heights of the Golan, the fertile West Bank up to the Jordan River's natural dividing line and the strategically vital and mineral-bearing Sinai Peninsula to within a stone's throw of the Suez Canal. Such positive advantages were a bonus since Israel felt there was a primary need for buffer zones which the United Nations had spectacularly failed to supply. But it was a highly attractive bonus. Once Israeli troops had occupied these territories *all* such considerations became justifications for continued occupation.

Granted that Israel felt threatened and even that the Israeli people found it hard to separate their fate from that of the state which ruled their lives, there was nonetheless a certain air of smug self-righteousness about much of what the leaders of Israeli opinion wrote and said in the heady days following the war. 'There is no return,' wrote Israeli author and playwright Moshe Shamir less than two weeks after the official ceasefire. 'The demand not to give anything back . . . is the most pacifist position today,' he argued in the pages of *Ma'ariv*, the Israeli evening newspaper, with a perverse kind of logic. 'It is the clearest expression of our aspiration towards peace and the assurance of peace. It is even more than that: the demand not to give up even a single foot of ground contains within itself not only a healthy sense of self-preservation and the sober political instinct of a people done with illusions once and for all. It is also the quintessence of thousands of never-expressed yearnings not to go back in a thousand other senses too; not to return to the recent past in any field, in any sense, in any fashion.'[2]

This feeling did not represent official policy, nor did many Israelis see the issues their victory had created in quite so sharply defined shades of black and white. And yet the fact that such opinions could be given the prominence they were reveals how little distance Israel had moved from militant Zionism. Shamir represented the war as one symptom of the resurgence of a 'raging torrent . . . sweeping all parts of the people along'. The Herzlian rhetoric is unmistakable. Israel may be isolated from the rest of the world, he says; Israel will have to continue the fight in the political world; Israel was united by the feeling that its very existence was threatened. Most of all, Shamir says, alluding to the biblical account of Moses' stutter: 'It was that torrent which compelled the leadership to stop stammering.'

It is tragically easy to find analogies to this position in recent political history. A crisis of leadership resolved by the creation of a strong 'Government of National Unity' with a heavy emphasis on militarism. The arguments of historic destiny, of Israel's right to impose its own terms on the areas it had conquered; even the twisted logic that equates pacifism with military might – all these are unhappily familiar. In the weeks following the end of the Six Day War it must have seemed all too possible to the defeated Arab States that Israel was no longer a country bent on mere survival but a state seeking to dominate the Middle East by military force.

From whichever side of the Suez Canal (or the Jordan River) you looked at it, the Six Day War irrevocably changed Israel's position in the Middle East. To leave the occupied territories, as Israel had left Sinai in 1956–7, would have been an admission of defeat; to remain was a proclamation of victory. But victory and defeat were not simply concerned with the status of a Jewish state on the disputed territory of the former mandatory Palestine. After 1967, victory or defeat were related to Israel's ability to control areas of territory by virtue of no other right than the right of conquest. International law, partition plans, U.N. resolutions did not come into it – Israel was in Golan, Sinai and the West Bank because it had *won* them in battle. And because they had been won that way, no amount of persuasion would get the occupiers to give them up.

A single decade had made all the difference in the world. By 1967 America was clearly losing its war in Vietnam and was quite prepared to let Israel do its military dirty work for it. American power, through Israel, was ready but unwilling to confront the Soviet Union in the Middle East.

The 1967 victory was decisive and crippling to all the Arab states threatening Israel. Thanks largely to the seizure of the West Bank, Israel's new borders were shorter and more easily defensible than its 1949 borders – which was not the case after the Sinai War. In the ten years to 1967, Israel had built up a well-equipped and highly trained army able to hold large areas with comparative ease. The Israelis had even developed a relatively large-scale and sophisticated domestic arms industry, and thus reduced their dependence on military aid. But the most important difference between the post-Sinai War and the post-Six-Day-War periods lay in the changes in Israeli official attitudes.

In 1957 Israel, weak and largely underpopulated, still nurtured a residue of faith in international diplomacy. As the years passed, this residue diminished as it became increasingly evident that diplomacy, negotiations and all the paraphernalia of international agreements were powerless to protect Israel from the hostility which its very existence engendered in the Arab states and the Palestinian refugees. From the first, Zionism had seized upon a practical approach that bypassed legalities and formalities. The birth and survival of the State of

Israel were living proof that a relatively small body of dedicated people could, by determined struggle, change those legalities and formalities. While Israel was yet an infant, it demanded official acknowledgement and international recognition as a child demands outward displays of love and affection. But in the end the Israelis realised that acknowledgement, recognition and the respect of international communities were all abstractions. Treaties were bits of paper, U.N. resolutions were just so many empty words, without the physical capacity to enforce them. Hence their reputation for arrogance and intransigence – it is nothing but a belief, firmly rooted in experience, that Israel had survived by its ability to win, by its power to impose its will on the world or, as Ben-Gurion has put it, by 'the *superior quality of the Hebrew nation*'.[3]

There is no cause for rejoicing in the essential correctness of this view. Israel is by no means the first nation and it will not be the last to comprehend its might as the revelation of an historic destiny and an innate superiority. If the British, the French, the Americans and, for that matter, the Arabs have scythed a passage across humanity in the abused names of civilisation, democracy, freedom or God – then why not Israel who only acts in the name of survival? And yet, it is a profoundly dehumanising truth whose only lesson has been death and endless misery. There is no solution to the Arab–Israeli conflict as long as both parties deny their common humanity. But humanity is not one of the 'reasons of state' which inform the actions of governments. Armed force might sustain a state where treaties and U.N. resolutions are powerless, armed force can secure the boundaries of a nation, but armed force has never been a good (as opposed to merely persuasive) argument for anything except continued hostility.

The Arab states confronted an Israel extended into their territory. The continued presence of Israeli troops was a perpetually repeated act of aggression as far as they were concerned. The Palestine question was not disregarded, but in contrast to its place in Nasser's exuberant proclamations of a few days earlier, it seemed so much further away now. The main thing was to get Israel out of the occupied territories.

The Russian revolutionary leader and military strategist, Leon Trotsky, had once commented: 'Ideas that enter the mind

under fire remain there securely and forever.' Under the fire of
June, the Arabs had learnt the bitter lesson of their own pitifully inadequate posturing. In some ways, Nasser's credit was
enhanced in the learning. He had, after all, warned against
hasty action and, in the weeks that followed the war he could
resort to attacks on 'Israeli treachery' to cover up the fool-
hardiness of his own actions. He offered to resign, but the
Egyptian people favoured no other possible leader. They demonstrated in his favour and he withdrew his resignation.
Nasser's analysis of Israel's rôle in the prevention of Arab
unity had been borne out by the events of June and, through a
perverse sort of mechanism, the impact of those events had
managed to bring the Arab states closer together than they
had ever been. Not for the first time, military defeat taught
many Arabs the value of diplomacy and tact. Not surprisingly,
this lesson was best learnt in Egypt and Jordan – the countries
that had suffered the largest losses. And in the end Nasser and
Hussein survived while Syria, Iraq and the P.L.O. suffered upheavals that toppled their leaderships.

An Arab Summit at Khartoum in September 1967, called by
King Hussein, was boycotted by the Syrians who totally
opposed a negotiated settlement of any kind. Shukeiry, representing the P.L.O., refused to attend the final session for similar
reasons. The Summit reiterated fundamental Arab positions:
no peace with Israel, no recognition and support for the
'national' struggle of the Palestinians. But in certain highly
significant respects the Summit decisions represented a real
change in Arab thinking. The Arabs still refused to accept the
possibility of direct negotiations with Israel since that would
have involved recognition. They stressed their determination
to arrive at a single multilateral settlement involving all the
front-line states. But there was a great deal of compromising
going on.

The Summit called for 'unified efforts at international and
diplomatic levels to eliminate the consequences of [Israeli]
aggression and to ensure the withdrawal of the aggressor
forces . . . from Arab lands'. A number of decisions were made
to help these efforts on the way – the lifting of a short-lived
oil embargo on pro-Israeli states; the creation of a fund,
financed by oil money, to compensate Egypt and Jordan and
to allow Egypt to keep the Suez Canal closed as a bargaining

counter; and the reconciliation of Egypt and Saudi Arabia over the Yemen. There is no doubt that the mood of the Summit was moderate, not to say conciliatory, and despite massive supplies of Soviet aid to Egypt in the weeks following the war, Nasser became increasingly aware of the need for a *rapprochement* with the Americans. The Summit indicated that Nasser and Hussein would be prepared to accept a settlement with Israel involving at least a partial withdrawal, the setting-up of demilitarised zones and internationally supervised discussions on the Palestine question.

The Israelis had heard it all before. Casting their minds back to 1956–7 they insisted on no withdrawal prior to a full peace settlement. Their concern over the implications of Arab unity led them to reject 'single party' negotiations with the Arabs in favour of separate talks with each concerned state, as had happened in 1949. Recalling those days, too, the Israelis insisted on direct negotiations aimed, in the first place, at the signing of a peace treaty. Their victory in June had demonstrated superior power yet again. They felt that they had no obligation whatsoever to make concessions to Arab demands or wounded Arab pride. Mediation would only weaken Israel's bargaining position. The Israelis considered their military strength and their presence in the occupied territories to be their only guarantees of security. Short of a successful military assault against Israel, nothing would persuade them to sacrifice either.

It was the old tradition of Zionist pragmatism once more, this time elevated to the position of a diplomatic *sine qua non*. But governments guided by pragmatic considerations tend to take foolhardy actions. Israel did not help the cause of Middle East peace by annexing the Old City of Jerusalem (not just a sentimental monument but, at one time, Jordan's major foreign currency earner). Nor was Israel's tendency to retitle certain occupied areas with Biblical Hebrew names (for example, the West Bank became Samaria and Judaea). It was as though Israel considered that time would sanction its occupations – and in anticipation the Israeli authorities were uncovering the ancient foundations of their disputed claims.

Despite the ceasefire and the Arab compromises, in the weeks following the Six Day War fighting continued along the borders, inland and at sea. Neither Arabs nor Israelis were prepared to accept peace on the other's terms and they could hold out as long as some great power kept them supplied with weapons and aid. It suited the U.S. and the U.S.S.R. to see that neither the Arabs nor the Israelis won total domination in the Middle East. Absolute victory was, therefore, ruled out. Aid continued to flow and the fighting simply carried on. The superpowers would have liked all the Middle East states to co-exist peacefully, if possible. But that was unlikely as long as the Arabs and the Israelis had unfinished business with each other. In the circumstances, the best that the U.S. and the U.S.S.R. could hope for was containment of the conflict – a state of limited war which never escalated to the nuclear level, never dragged in the superpowers themselves and never resulted in any major victories or defeats. But the fighting did escalate, as fighting is prone to do, and within weeks of the Six Day War it had become perfectly clear that the ceasefire existed in name only. Some sort of settlement which could at least define the limits of the conflict was becoming an extremely urgent need. The U.N. worked hard to draft the terms of such a settlement. Unfortunately, a proposed settlement is also a reason for fighting – especially when it is rejected by one or other party. The failure of a ceasefire is one thing. The failure of a proposed settlement adds even more fuel to the blazing fires of hostility.

II

A pleasant old buffer, nephew to a lord
Who believed that the bank was mightier than the sword
And that an umbrella might pacify barbarians abroad
Just like an old liberal
Between the wars.

(William Plomer, *Father and Son*)

The instrument of the intended settlement was U.N. Security Council Resolution No. 242. Its bearer was a Swedish diplomat and former ambassador to the U.N., Dr Gunnar Jarring.

Resolution 242 was the result of a compromise, initiated by the British, aimed at breaking a deadlock within the Security Council. Previous draft resolutions had been sponsored by the U.S. or the U.S.S.R. and introduced by pro-American or pro-Soviet member states. As a result, each had met with a veto issued by the opposing sponsor.

The ceasefire had, of course, cooled things down and the sense of urgency that had impelled the U.S. and the U.S.S.R. to cooperate in June 1967 had at first faded. But the continuing violent interchanges between Arab and Israeli forces risked opening a further act in this already interminable drama. The Khartoum Summit bent over backwards to arrive at a formula acceptable to America and the U.N. Some sort of U.N. intervention now seemed both urgent and possible.

The main obstacle to such intervention was America's fundamental agreement with Israel that Arab–Israeli affairs should be kept a regional matter even at diplomatic level. Indeed, America was prepared to avoid, at almost any cost, superpower intervention within the area. The Eisenhower Doctrine was a thing of the past and, notwithstanding the recent C.I.A.-manufactured coup in Greece, the American administration under Lyndon Johnson was not prepared to become embroiled in anything with even a faint whiff of Vietnam about it. The Middle East crisis was becoming ludicrously complicated. International opinion was becoming increasingly polarised: for example, African countries were vigorously opposed to 'Israeli aggression', Catholic countries objected to Israel's annexation of Jerusalem, and the West was disturbed by the massive injections of Soviet military equipment into Egypt. There was an election in 1968 for Johnson to ponder. And there was the problem of Arab oil supplies which were vital to the economic health of Britain, the E.E.C and Japan. There were a lot of angles for the Americans to consider. The result of all their deliberations was a draft resolution of unparalleled vagueness, whose only specific point was to propose the appointment of a U.N. mediator. It was vetoed.

The British subtly combined vague wording with specific reference and came up with a draft which managed to condemn Israel without committing anybody to anything apart from the appointment of a mediator. Resolution 242 is a worthy successor to the Balfour Declaration and since it has been the focus of negotiation since 1967 the relevant sections should be repeated and savoured by connoisseurs of diplomatic mumbo-jumbo:

'The Security Council
Expressing its continuing concern with the grave situation in the Middle East,
Emphasising the inadmissibility of the acquisition of territory by war and the need to work for a just and lasting peace in which every state in the area can live in security . . . ,
1. *Affirms* that the fulfilment of [U.N.] Charter principles requires the establishment of a just and lasting peace in the Middle East which should include the application of both the following principles:

  (i) Withdrawal of Israeli armed forces from territories of recent conflict;
  (ii) Termination of all claims or states of belligerency and respect for and acknowledgement of the sovereignty, territorial integrity and political independence of every state in the area and their right to live in peace within secure and recognised boundaries, free from threats or acts of force;

2. *Affirms* further the necessity

  (a) for guaranteeing freedom of navigation through international waterways in the area;
  (b) for achieving a just settlement of the refugee problem;
  (c) for guaranteeing the territorial inviolability and political independence of every state in the area, through measures including the establishment of demilitarised zones . . . '

(The resolution then requests the designation of a special representative with the job of mediating between Israel and the Arab States on the basis set out.)

Resolution 242 was passed unanimously by the Security Council. Syria immediately refused to accept it, but in early 1968 Jarring flew to the Middle East to begin talks with Israel, Egypt and Jordan.

The basic problem that he met has remained the bugbear of a negotiated peace ever since. Egypt and Jordan, concerned primarily for the return of the Sinai and the West Bank, argued that Israeli occupation should be terminated before any agreement could be discussed. To this end, Jarring's contacts informed him that they considered 242 to lay down specific guidelines for a peace settlement. In other words, that it was not negotiable and must, at the very least, be accepted by Israel as setting out the foundations of a peace settlement, involving a total withdrawal from *all* the occupied territories.

Israeli officials had a different interpretation. They told

Jarring that they considered 242 to lay down the terms within which some future settlement could be negotiated in direct talks between Israel and the Arab states. Such talks could only proceed after the Arab states had signed unconditional peace treaties with Israel. Israel would remain in the occupied territories.

The essential problem was whether acceptance of 242, however interpreted, should precede or follow the signing of a peace treaty or peace treaties. It was an insurmountable problem. Despite the Egyptian Foreign Minister's statement of 3 July 1968, that 'we accept the realities and one of these is Israel', there seemed no way round the impasse. Neither Egypt nor Jordan would accept peace before an Israeli withdrawal. Israel would not consider withdrawing before peace. Within a few short weeks, Jarring accepted defeat.

Egypt and Jordan continued to talk themselves into a corner. They were so desperate to remove Israeli troops from their territory that, one by one, they changed position on issues that had always been considered fundamental. Egypt dropped its inflexible anti-American guard. Refusal to recognise Israel was the next to go and, finally, by 1969 it seemed that the Palestinian issue had been completely forgotten. But there was still no progress.

In 1969 Richard Nixon assumed the American presidency. His special advisor on Foreign Affairs, Henry Kissinger, was a Harvard professor with a wide streak of the playboy in him. He combined historical erudition with Hollywood ballyhoo in the most unlikely of frames. His striving for self-publicity was caught up in a web of tired theories about the balance of power, spheres of influence and America's weakness as an 'island economy'. Frightened by the possibility of a superpower confrontation in the Middle East (especially since Israel was well on the road to producing its own nuclear weapon) and worried by the U.S.S.R.'s strength in the area, he calculated that it was crucial to improve relations with the Arabs while arming Israel against potential Arab hostility fuelled by modern Soviet weaponry.

In an effort to avoid Soviet involvement in the negotiating process, the Americans revived the Jarring mission. But the Arabs and the Israelis had come no closer to a settlement. The Americans were compelled to intervene directly but felt that they could only do so through bilateral talks with the U.S.S.R. or 'Big Four' meetings with the U.S.S.R., Britain and France. The Arabs welcomed the possibility of direct pressure from the great powers. But Israel remained totally opposed to any imposed settlement. Diplomacy had failed. Two years had gone by without a settlement seeming any the nearer. The Palestinian problem had not gone away, despite everyone else's most fervent wishes. In fact, the Palestinians had become something of a force to be reckoned with in international politics.

Syria had long supported guerrilla activity, and by late 1969 the guerrilla struggle, although militarily weak, had begun to attract approval and aid from other 'progressive' nations. The Islamic Summit, the non-aligned nations' conference, Russia, China and even the U.N. General Assembly declared their support for the Palestinian struggle and recognised the right of the Palestinians to self-determination. In the explosive Middle East the self-activity of guerrilla organisations was a detonator. It encouraged Nasser to rid himself of his debilitating belief in diplomacy, it threatened Hussein's oppressive moderation and it added a new force to the area's unstable equilibrium of forces. But if Egypt began to lose faith and Jordan began to lose confidence, the Israelis simply ran out of patience.

Chapter 10

FISH ON DRY LAND

The Palestinian Guerrilla Campaign, 1967–1972

> We reject the theory of quick victory, which is just idle talk
> and an effort to get things on the cheap.
>
> (Mao Tse-tung)

I

The Arabs had lost the third conventional phase of the struggle
with Israel as dismally as it was possible to lose. There could
be no hope of a fourth phase for several years. Yet, in the
absence of meaningful concessions from Israel as regards the
Palestinian issue, the struggle would continue.

There were several ways in which it would be expressed.
Naturally diplomacy would be attempted, and naturally it
would fail. On the so-called western front the Egyptians required a breathing-space to prepare their army for the 'War
of Attrition' (see following chapter), and a year or so's
abortive diplomacy would be relatively harmless. But on the
eastern front there was no need to wait. Here the emphasis
would be on guerrilla struggle. Jordan and Syria had no
stomach for a resumption of war; the Palestinians were dis-
enchanted anyway with what they considered the Arab states'
basic lack of commitment. The Palestinians themselves would
wage a 'national war of liberation', with varying degrees of
help and hindrance from the front-line states.

The guerrilla movements dated back to the late fifties, to
breeding grounds in the refugee camps and European univer-
sities, but it was not until 1965 that regular operations into
Israel began. Al Fatah was by far the largest organisation, and
in that year it conducted thirty-one such raids, twenty-seven
from Jordanian territory and four from Lebanese. In 1966
this total was greatly surpassed. The targets were mostly non-

military; Fatah had little desire to tangle with the Israeli Army. Rather, its intention was to stimulate tension in the area, provoke reprisals against the front-line states, and so foster another conventional war. It could be argued that Fatah was successful. Certainly the Israeli raid on Samu in October 1966 and the air battle with the Syrian Air Force in April 1967 – both essentially retaliatory moves against guerrilla activity – were important stepping-stones on the road to the June War.

The result of the war, however, was not the one Fatah was counting upon. But, perversely enough, the sweeping Israeli victory provided compensation for the Palestinians. The newly-occupied territories of the West Bank and the Gaza Strip seemingly offered ample scope for guerrilla warfare. The more 'progressive' Arab régimes agreed. The Syrian Ba'athist Party announced portentously that 'popular revolutionary war was the only way to counter the Zionist challenge . . . traditional wars exhausted the material resources of the Arabs, while popular war exhausts the enemy'. Syria took the lead in recruiting and training guerrillas, though naturally with no intention of allowing them to operate from Syrian territory. The reviled Hussein would carry that particular can.

So, through July, guerrillas began infiltrating the West Bank via Jordanian territory. Their initial aim was to organise popular support into a network of village cells. These would then provide supplies and information for the small fighting groups hidden in the hills. The Israelis would of course react by taking reprisals against the local population, so welding its loyalty to the guerrilla cause. And as this familiar spiral accelerated the guerrillas would increasingly resemble Mao's fish in the sea of the people.

Through August and September infiltration increased, and the guerrillas eagerly awaited the Israeli response. But to their surprise the Israelis refused to repeat the American mistakes in Vietnam. Their policy in the occupied territories was deliberately liberal. The local government structure was left intact, free speech allowed, the economy encouraged by judicious amounts of technical and financial aid. The local population, though discouraged from collaboration with the guerrillas, was not forced to collaborate with the Israelis. It was encouraged to remain neutral. For the guerrillas a neutral population was a disaster, in that it deprived them of necessary food supplies and information. In the open terrain of the West Bank, obtaining these essentials themselves would be suicidal. Rather than fish in the sea the guerrillas began to resemble fish left high and dry by the tide.

Needless to say the Israelis did not merely rely on the carrot of liberality. They also wielded an extremely efficient stick. Frequent Israeli patrols swept the area, making guerrilla movement difficult. Incidents were dealt with not by inflammatory action against the population, but by exhaustive searches for those responsible. Significantly it was the General Security Service, and not the Army, which was mainly responsible for counter-guerrilla activity. Its methods when dealing with individual suspects were probably none too pleasant, but this, from both the guerrilla and Israeli standpoints, was not important. What was important was the Israeli decision not to take counter-community action. With the contest restricted to only the Israeli security services and the guerrillas, the latter were doomed. By December sixty-three guerrillas had been killed and over 350 arrested. Fatah's skeleton network was in ruins. Some terrorist activity persisted, but no popular demonstrations of support accompanied it. The attempt to form a subversive base on the West Bank had definitively failed.

II

The conditions for creating a genuine subversive base on the West Bank had not been auspicious, but neither had they been completely absent. The Palestinian groups should now have come to terms with their initial failure, analysed its causes, changed their tactics, and sought to reverse it. But they chose otherwise:

> Instead of emulating the Vietcong in building local, self-sustaining, terrorist and guerrilla cells through a slow but solid process of subversion, the Fatah sacrificed its future for the sake of quick results. Lacking a genuine subversive base, it sent armed guerrillas from across the Jordan.[1]

This poor answer to a hard question had lasting consequences, in that it set in motion two mutually-supporting shifts in

Palestinian policy. The first involved a change in the nature of the struggle, from the building of a politico-military opposition within the occupied territories to the mounting of purely military raids into those territories. The failure of the latter would involve a further retreat, from action against Israel to action against Israelis. The Munich massacre of 1972 was implicit in the failure to secure a popular base in the West Bank in 1967–8.

The second shift involved a realignment of priorities, and a downgrading of the struggle with Israel in favour of a revolutionary rôle vis-à-vis their brother Arabs. After all, once deprived of bases in Palestine, the Palestinians were doomed to become cuckoos in other Arab nests. The progressive Arab régimes of Egypt and Syria, stronger for being relatively progressive, were both loath to allow rival progressive forces on their soil and strong enough to enforce such unwillingness. But the weaker régimes of Jordan and Lebanon, weaker for being more reactionary, were not only anathema to the revolutionary Palestinians, but also too weak to prevent the establishment of guerrilla bases on their soil. The scene was being set for an inter-Arab struggle that would dwarf both sides' apparent concern with the problem of Palestine.

As 1968 began, the culmination of this conflict was still two years and many heart-searchings away. For now the guerrillas began to raid across the Jordan river in earnest, slipping over by night to carry out diverse acts of terrorism and sabotage. The Israelis replied with artillery fire at the main camps close to the river, and occasionally found themselves exchanging fire with the regular Jordanian Army. This did little to deter the guerrillas, and as the raids continued the Israelis increased the scope of their reprisals, throwing artillery, mortar and tank shells across the river at guerrillas and Jordanian Army alike. Eventually the frustrated Israelis took the fatal decision to cross the river. On 21 March 1968 a sizeable force of tanks and motorised infantry attacked the large Palestinian camp at Karama (Karameh) for the second time.

The operation was a disaster. The Israeli force, harassed by guerrillas inside the sprawling camp, was pinned down by long-range Jordanian tank-fire. The pre-set limits of the operation prevented the Israelis from reaching and silencing the Jordanian tanks, and they had to withdraw, carrying twenty-

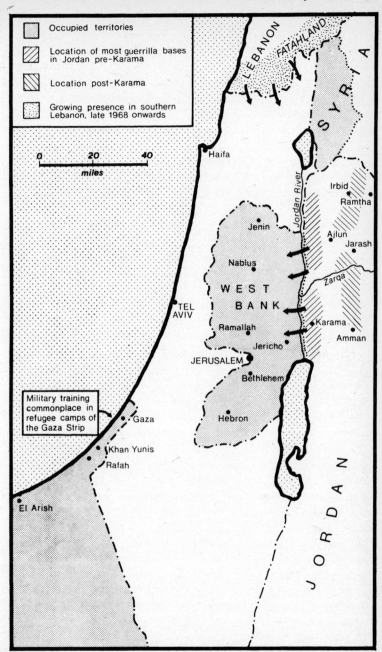

Legend:

- Occupied territories
- Location of most guerrilla bases in Jordan pre-Karama
- Location post-Karama
- Growing presence in southern Lebanon, late 1968 onwards

0   20   40
miles

Military training commonplace in refugee camps of the Gaza Strip

LEBANON
FATAHLAND
SYRIA
Haifa
Irbid
Ramtha
Jenin
Ajlun
Jarash
Nablus
Jordan River
Zarqa
WEST BANK
TEL AVIV
Ramallah
Karama
Amman
Jericho
JERUSALEM
Bethlehem
Hebron
Gaza
Khan Yunis
Rafah
El Arish
JORDAN

15. The guerrilla/terrorist war, 1967-70

three dead and over seventy wounded. To the Arabs, still half-stunned by the June 1967 débâcle, this looked like a glorious victory. Fatah, somewhat untruthfully, claimed the full credit.

But, as an Englishman said of Dunkirk: 'If this was a victory it's hard to imagine what a defeat would look like.' The 'Battle' of Karama was fought on Jordanian territory; it did nothing to shake the Israeli hold on the West Bank. Its main military end-product was the physical shifting of the guerrilla bases further east into Jordan; its real legacy was to exacerbate the political shift of Palestinian concern away from Israel.

This was not immediately apparent. Funds poured in for the Fatah 'victors', enabling them to train more guerrillas and buy more weapons. To some it may have seemed obvious that these new men and weapons could only be effectively used on Jordanian territory. King Hussein, doubtless with a large lump in his throat, was forced to acknowledge Fatah's glory. 'We are all *fedayeen* now,' he is reported to have said. For him the struggle to control the growing state-within-his-state was becoming more difficult by the day.

Across the Jordan river the Israelis were increasing Hussein's difficulties by making it ever harder for the guerrillas to leave Jordan. On the river's west bank two fences were erected, eight feet and five feet in height. The thirty-foot space in between was mined, and sensory devices and searchlights were mounted at intervals. Gaps were deliberately left in this barrier, and each morning Israeli patrols covered them, searching for footprints in the sand. The discovery of any such signs was swiftly followed by helicopter searches of the surrounding area. The effectiveness of these methods reduced the cross-river raids to an Arab version of kamikaze, and they continued only in small numbers. The primary guerrilla tactic through 1968 was the relatively impotent firing of 'Katyusha' rocket salvoes at empty territory. If the Palestinian guerrilla groups were to demonstrate a continuing virility, then they would have to demonstrate it somewhere else.

III

The three obvious targets for the Palestinian organisations were King Hussein, each other, and world opinion. By autumn 1968 the King's authority over his guerrilla guests was little more than nominal. 'They were strutting about arrogantly jostling Jordanian soldiers and police, who were mainly desert Bedu out of sympathy with the town-bred sophisticated *fedayeen* fighter.'[2] The kingdom of Jordan, itself based upon an uneasy truce between the original desert kingdom of Transjordan and the Palestinian West Bank, was fertile soil for this confrontation. The Jordanian Army was also sufficiently divided that Hussein could not be sure of its loyalties in a crisis. Even should the King choose to risk the reaction of his Arab neighbours, he could not move against the guerrillas with any certainty of success.

His most likely salvation from civil war in Jordan was an intensification of conflict between the various guerrilla groups. By late 1968 there were between twenty and twenty-five thousand *fedayeen* in the country. About half of them were living in the staging bases strung along the mountains bordering the Jordan valley, the rest scattered throughout the populated interior regions. The majority belonged to Fatah, led by Yasir Arafat, but there were three other major groups – the Palestine Liberation Army (P.L.A.) (the military arm of the then largely moribund Palestine Liberation Organisation), which was tightly controlled by its Egyptian and Syrian masters; the Syrian-backed and officered Saiqa; George Habash's Popular Front for the Liberation of Palestine (P.F.L.P.) – and eight or nine minor ones. Throughout 1968 these groups had made tentative moves in the direction of unity, both military and political, but with a notable lack of success. Arafat was busy taking over the empty P.L.O. structure, and filling it with his nominees, as a potential umbrella for the warring groups. He managed to oversee the creation of a Palestine National Council, which in July met to produce the Palestine National Covenant. This frail document aside, the meetings were not a very good advertisement for consensus politics, as the rich flavour of ideological differences was fully brought out by the spice of personal animosities.

While Arafat continued the endless search for common ground, the small but determined P.F.L.P. took to the air, hijacking an El Al airliner between Rome and Israel, and forcing the pilot to fly it to Algeria. After five weeks' bargaining the Israelis on board were exchanged for Palestinian prisoners in Israel. This whiff of success on the world stage encouraged the P.F.L.P. to strike again, and on 26 December two guerrillas attacked an El Al plane at Athens airport, killing a passenger. This time the Israeli reaction – some said over-reaction – was devastating. A commando force led by Raful Eytan descended on Beirut Airport, blew up thirteen Arab airliners, had a cup of coffee in the Airport bar, and returned home. Eytan paid for the coffee, but not for the planes. The damage was estimated at $70 million.

1969 began with the guerrilla forces in Jordan suspended between their inability to wage effective war against Israel and their unwillingness to risk a showdown with Hussein. The Katyushas continued to arc across the Jordan river; the Israelis continued to retaliate, usually against the Jordanians, as an incentive for them to restrain the guerrillas. The Palestine National Council met in Cairo in February, but was boycotted by the P.F.L.P., who preferred to continue their attacks on the world's air communications. In February the P.F.L.P. attacked an aircraft at Zurich Airport, killing two Israelis; in August a U.S. Boeing was hijacked. In September and November the El Al offices in Brussels and Athens were bombed. At the beginning of 1970 an airliner was blown up in mid-air shortly after leaving Zurich Airport, and the forty-seven people on board, only thirteen of whom were Israelis, were killed. At this point Arafat spoke out against P.F.L.P. policy, thus putting a seal on a year of disagreement between the various Palestinian groups. All that held them together was their shared animosity towards Hussein. This situation was rapidly becoming intolerable to both sides.

In the Lebanon a similar situation was evolving. The guerrillas had moved into the country in autumn 1968, and by March 1969 around three hundred were 'operating' in the Hasbani valley region. They conducted a few raids, but were mostly involved in the business of establishing their presence. The Lebanese government was not very anxious to have them, and the Army kept them penned tightly into a small area. This made it rather difficult to import supplies from Syria along the so-called 'Arafat Trail', and in October the guerrillas, with Syrian encouragement, attempted to break the stranglehold. They were promptly defeated by the Lebanese Army. Nasser intervened and the two sides signed the (Lebanese) Cairo

Agreement, which gave the guerrillas less freedom than they wanted but more than the Lebanese Army had been prepared to give them. This none-too-stable arrangement soon collapsed, creating a mini-civil war between the right-wing Lebanese Christians and the guerrillas. This too was eventually papered over, and the familiar cycle of guerrilla raids and Israeli retaliatory actions got under way along the frontier. The Israelis predictably built an efficient fence, and became singularly more adept at crossing the border than those on the other side.

Back in Jordan, in January 1970 Hussein made the mistake of trying to curb the guerrillas. Four days later eighty had been killed but the rest had seized control of half his capital. Hussein backed down; the guerrillas allowed him to. Neither side wanted a full confrontation, Hussein for fear of his Palestinian officers' loyalties, the guerrillas for fear of each other. But such a situation could not last indefinitely.

In August the spark was lit. Nasser decided to accept the Rogers Peace Initiative, and so end the 'War of Attrition'. When the Palestinians in Cairo objected, Nasser simply closed down their radio stations. Hussein was not in such an enviably powerful position, but he too now had to decide between the interests of his state and those of the Palestinians. He hesitated for two weeks and then, on 29 August, appeared on television to announce his decision. He accepted the Rogers Initiative. Furthermore he would not tolerate criticism of, or a challenge to, his government. Accordingly, the Jordanian Army was assuming its natural right to supreme military authority throughout Jordan. The fuse had been lit.

For three weeks it sparked merrily towards the powder-keg. Street disturbances broke out in most Jordanian towns; the Iraqis announced that any attempt on Hussein's part to crush the guerrilla movement would be opposed by the Iraqi Army. Hussein asked for international help. He received 'moral support'. An attempt on his life failed. The P.L.F.P. hijacked three international airliners on 6 September and flew them to Dawson's Field, an old British landing-strip in the desert north of Amman. The passengers were supposedly hostages to Hussein's good behaviour, but the hijackings merely alienated moderate Arab opinion and deepened the splits in the guerrilla ranks. In the meantime the guerrillas were taking over towns and territory in northern Jordan, and waiting for the expected Iraqis. The town of Irbid was proclaimed the 'First Arab Soviet'.

On 17 September Hussein officially opened the ten-day civil war by unleashing his Bedu élite on Amman. The Army wasted no time on subtleties, preferring to blast out the guerrillas with tanks, artillery and aircraft. House-to-house fighting continued for six days, the fall of the guerrilla-held Citadel area marking the end of Amman's 'pacification' by the Army.

In the north the war went less smoothly for Hussein. On the first day, fighting broke out in all the major towns, and by evening most of the kingdom north of the Zarqa river was in rebel hands. In the following days Syrian and P.L.A. tanks crossed the border and headed south towards Amman. But on 22 September they were forced back by the Jordanian 40th and 60th Armoured Brigades on the Irbid and Ramtha roads. Even had they broken through, Hussein would probably not have fallen. For, against such a disquieting eventuality, U.S. airborne divisions had been alerted in West Germany and the U.S. itself, and Israeli armour was massed on Golan for a possible strike into Syria.

On 25 September Hussein and Arafat agreed a ceasefire; it was ratified in the (Jordanian) Cairo Agreement two days later. The terms were similar to those of the Lebanese agreement: the guerrillas could remain, but under stricter supervision. This inconclusive compromise was followed, ominously for the guerrillas, by the appointment of rightist 'hard man', Wasfi al-Tal, to head the Jordanian government. Hussein was clearly determined that any further concessions would come from his opponents.

Through the winter and into the spring of 1971 clashes sporadically broke out between the Army and the guerrillas, culminating in bitter fighting at the end of May. The tension did not abate, and on 13 July Hussein finally moved to clear his kingdom of the guerrillas. Six days later some 2,300 had been captured, and many more had fled form Jordan. Significantly a fair number preferred Israeli to Jordanian captivity. One Israeli officer gratefully dubbed Wasfi al-Tal 'the man who killed more guerrillas in one year than we did in ten'. The guerrillas agreed. Later that year Wasfi al-Tal was gunned down by a new Palestinian group, whose name harked back to the 'Black September' of 1970.

Those guerrillas that had survived Hussein's clamp-down eventually arrived in Lebanon, now the sole base for raiding into Israel. This continued through 1971, but the same raid-reprisal cycle induced a new government campaign against the Palestinian presence. The Lebanese Army was no more kindly disposed to another military presence in its country than the Jordanian Army had been. The guerrillas survived on sufferance, their activity against Israel severely curtailed.

So, by the end of 1971 the Palestinian guerrilla groups had failed to achieve a secure base for the intended struggle against Israel. Thrown out of Jordan, completely controlled in Syria, restricted in the Lebanon, they had little to show for five years' endeavour save a growing recognition of their existence and the continued terrorist attacks on Israeli civilians by Black September. Hijackings multiplied in the early months of 1972. At the end of May several members of the self-styled 'Japanese Red Army' murdered twenty-six people at Lydda airport with grenades and machine-gun fire. Black September, not to be outdone, followed with the murder of several Israeli athletes at the Munich Olympics. These attacks, though bringing the Palestinian cause into the world spotlight, did so only to alienate many whose basic sympathies as regards the Arab–Israeli conflict lay with the plight of the dispossessed Palestinians. Further, rather than providing evidence of Palestinian strength they merely emphasised guerrilla impotence in regard to Israel itself. The latter retaliated by launching a hundred-plane raid into Syria and Lebanon, and a 36-hour invasion of southern Lebanon. Numerous refugees paid with their lives for the political naïveté – 'adventurism' is the marxist phrase – of the extremist Palestinian groups.

The attempt to sustain a basic threat to Israel's security through guerrilla and terroristic activity had utterly failed. The Palestinians, though they had become a political force which could not be ignored, had failed to become a military force of any significance. And, as long as Israel refused to negotiate, political power was of little relevance in the struggle for Palestine. By 1972 the continuation of that struggle was again dependent solely on the conventional military power of the Arab states.

Chapter 11

PHANTOMS OVER CAIRO
The War of Attrition, 1969–1970

> For to win one hundred victories in one hundred battles is not the acme of skill. To subdue the enemy without fighting is the acme of skill. Thus, what is of supreme importance in war is to attack the enemy's strategy. Next best is to disrupt his alliances. The next best is to attack his army. The worst policy is to attack cities. Attack cities only when there is no alternative.
>
> (Sun Tzu)

I

In the aftermath of the 1967 setback, Nasser accepted the three negative principles – no peace, no recognition, no negotiation – as the basis of Egypt's future relations with Israel. These negative principles were to be more than a concerted 'sulking' campaign, they were to be positively applied. In the case of the latter two, little more than active indifference was required, but 'no peace' seemed to imply a certain level of war. As there was no hope of resuming the full-scale activities of June 1967, the Egyptian Army was bound to seek a suitable variety of 'limited' war. But to what, or to where, would this war be limited?

The problem, Nasser decided, was not an urgent one. He waited vainly for international pressure to force the Israeli conquerors back, just as they, labouring under equally powerful delusions, waited vainly for their victory to settle into a satisfactory peace. In the meantime both sides periodically flexed their military muscles. The Egyptians sank the Israeli destroyer *Eilat*, and lost the use of the Suez oil refineries in the obligatory Israeli retaliation. But mostly Egyptian efforts were channelled into the diplomatic sphere, as recounted in Chapter 9. It was not until the autumn of 1968 that the obvious failure to break the diplomatic deadlock, and the emergence of a new

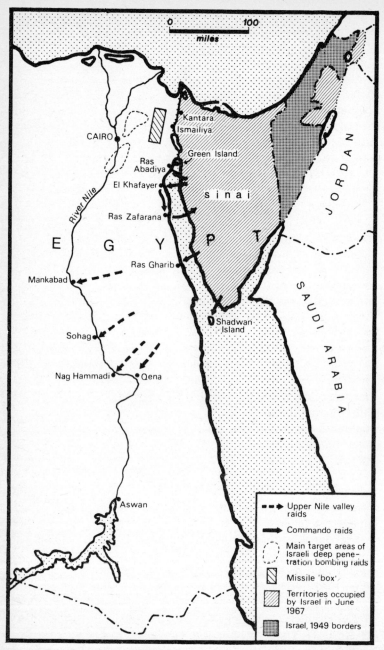

16. The war of attrition

Egyptian Army from the purges and re-organisations of the post-débâcle period, made it both necessary and possible to consider fully the military options. Then activity in the Canal Zone began to increase.

The Egyptians got off to a false start. In September and October ferocious artillery fire was directed on to the Israeli-held east bank, causing serious casualties. The Israelis, unable to reply in kind, retaliated with a heli-borne commando raid into the upper Nile valley. There they blew up the transformer and switching station at Nag Hammadi, and badly damaged the Nile bridges there and at Qena. This silenced the Egyptian artillery in the Canal Zone.

This was perhaps the most serious mistake made by the Egyptians before and during the 'War of Attrition'. O'Ballance believes that had they gritted their national teeth and 'taken a bolder course and continued to pound the largely unprotected Israelis on the east bank with heavy and continuous artillery barrages, they most probably would have forced them to withdraw back out of range'.[1] But instead, the Egyptians ceased fire, for several months, so giving the Israelis the time they needed to build the casualty-saving fortifications on the east bank known as the Bar Lev line.

By March 1969 events were pushing Nasser towards another try. The beginning of the Palestinian hijackings and Arafat's assumption of the P.L.O. leadership were threats to his leadership of the 'progressive' Arab world. They could only be countered by meaningful Egyptian action against Israel. President Johnson's apparent reluctance to sell Israel the new American 'Phantom' fighter-bombers had encouraged Nasser to believe that the enemy was more isolated than ever. Also there was a new Israeli premier, Golda Meir, to impress and intimidate. On 6 March the Egyptian gunners in the Canal Zone opened fire once more.

The Israelis threatened I.A.F. counter-action. This had apparently already been taken into account by Nasser. At the end of March he declared, somewhat superfluously, that the June 1967 ceasefire was 'null and void'. Some have taken this as the beginning of the 'War of Attrition'; others prefer Nasser's official proclamation on 23 June. Either way, by 22 April U Thant could announce with justification that 'a virtual state of war existed along the Suez Canal, and that U.N.

efforts [to end the hostilities] had been almost totally ineffective'. The Egyptian ball was gathering speed.

The primary Egyptian intention was to maximise their known advantages over the enemy – superior artillery and a higher tolerance of casualties – in order to maintain a continuous state of warfare in the Canal Zone. The Israeli forces on the Canal would be 'bled', the armistice line would not be allowed to solidify into a border, and international intervention to Egypt's benefit would ensue. So went the theory.

The Israelis could offer no more than passive defence – more fortifications – in the Canal Zone itself, but they would seek to maximise their own advantages – tactical ingenuity and command flexibility – in conducting de-stabilising raids outside this area. The Nag Hammadi raid had been successful in this respect, effectively freezing Egyptian triggers for five months. But, unfortunately for the Israelis, the second such raid late in April 1969 was a fiasco.

Through May and June the artillery barrages continued, and small Egyptian commando groups raided, somewhat ineffectually, into Sinai. The Israelis, too, launched commando raids, but mounting casualty figures in the Canal Zone – 700 since the June War – forced them to consider a more devastating response. In July the decision was taken to answer the Egyptian artillery with the 'flying artillery' of the I.A.F. On 19 July Israeli commandos attacked Green Island in the Gulf of Suez, and destroyed the controlling systems for the radar installations covering the southern sector of the Canal Zone. The next day, as the Americans walked on the moon and monopolised the world headlines, the I.A.F. flew through the blind Egyptian defences and into the attack.

The E.A.F., still frustrated from its enforced non-participation in the June War, took off, high on morale but low on tactical expertise, to meet the enemy. Though performing better than expected, the Egyptian pilots proved no match for the I.A.F. veterans, and by the end of the first week they had been temporarily grounded to avert further losses. The I.A.F., freed of an enemy in the air, proceeded to hammer the one on the ground. First the Egyptian A.A. guns and SAM-2 missile sites were attacked, and then the Egyptian forces on the Canal and their supply arteries.

These attacks continued through the summer and into

autumn. In early October Dayan somewhat retrospectively announced a 'limited air offensive' against the enemy's missile and early warning systems. The Army was also playing an active rôle. Two more raids into the upper Nile valley were mounted in June and August. On 9 September a sizeable force – six tanks and three A.P.C.s (all Soviet vehicles captured in 1967) with 150 commandos – was ferried across the Gulf of Suez to El Khafayer, whence it drove blithely down the coast for fifty miles, destroying an unsuspecting Egyptian troop convoy, several radar stations, and stealing a brand-new T-62 Soviet tank, before taking the ferry home to Sinai.

The net effect of these raids and the continuing I.A.F. offensive was a plummeting Egyptian morale. Though wishing to avenge the destruction of its missiles, radar installations, planes and troops, the Army could not launch an attack across the Canal for fear of the consequences. The sole legacy of the 'War of Attrition' seemed to be the half-million refugees created by the evacuation of the Canal Zone cities of Kantara, Ismailiya and Suez. Nasser had lost his war.

II

The Israelis, by re-imposing the military stalemate and thus the political deadlock, had won a significant victory. Had they now returned the initiative to the Egyptians, it is difficult to see what the latter could have done with it. But the Israeli leadership refused to cast its forces in such a passive rôle. Rather, they took the deeply mistaken decision to launch deep penetration raids into the Egyptian heartland.

This decision, opposed even within the Israeli Cabinet, was partly taken on military grounds – the raids would force a dispersion of the Egyptian A.A. forces and interrupt the flow of supplies reaching the Canal front. The primary motivation behind the deep penetration raids however seems to have been a desire to weaken or destroy Nasser's political standing in Egypt. This was foolish thinking. As anyone in Hanoi around this time could have told the Israeli leadership, the effect of such bombing raids is usually the strengthening of the political authority. More important still, Nasser was forced to demand from the Soviets a hitherto unknown level of intervention in Egyptian military affairs. This intervention – invoked to defend Egypt against the I.A.F. – would inevitably lead, given the nature of the ground and weapons involved, to the creation of an Egyptian offensive capability in the Canal Zone. As nothing else could have done, the deep penetration raids made the October 1973 war possible.

The responsibility can be shifted further back. The raids were only possible once the I.A.F. had received the new Phantom F-4 fighter-bombers from the U.S. The Phantom possessed not only the speed and acceleration necessary for air combat, but also a seven-ton weapon-load capacity and the ECM (electronic counter-measure) pods necessary for fooling the SAM-2s. Never before had the Israelis been capable of delivering such weights of explosives with such precision, and at such little risk to their precious pilots. The American sale of these planes had seriously altered the balance of strength between Israel and Egypt. The Soviets, fully aware of this fact, had tried to block the sale and failed. All they received from Nixon was the hypocritical offer of an arms freeze after the sale.

In the meantime Egypt was virtually defenceless. Through January and February the I.A.F. pounded targets in inner Egypt, some of them less than five miles from Cairo. 'All Egypt is our battlefield,' boasted Dayan. It certainly seemed so. On 12 February, close to a hundred Egyptian civilians were killed when the I.A.F. 'mistakenly' bombed a factory in Abu Zambal. Nasser, meanwhile, had already travelled to Moscow.

There, in two meetings entertainingly chronicled by Heikal in *The Road to Ramadan*, the Egyptian leader pressed the Soviets for some much-needed military assistance. First he asked for long-range bombers with which to retaliate, but these were refused. Second he demanded an effective defence against the Israeli Phantoms. The Soviets offered SAM-3s (more effective against low-flying aircraft), but there were insufficient Egyptian crews, and the training took six months. Nasser then demanded Soviet crews for the sites in the interior. When a temporising Brezhnev explained that effective missile defence systems also require aircraft, he demanded Soviet-piloted planes as well. The Soviet leaders, somewhat taken aback, muttered about international obligations, and so Nasser dropped his final bombshell. 'This means there is only one course open to me: I shall go back to Egypt and I shall tell the people the truth . . . that, whether they like it or not, the Americans are masters of the world. I am not going to be the one who surrenders to the

Americans. Someone else will come in my place who will have
to do it.' The Soviets agreed to meet the Egyptian demands.

Over Egypt the struggle continued, as the I.A.F. flew daily
raids. Then, in mid March the Israeli pilots noticed something
new. SAM-3 sites were under construction at many strategic
points in the interior, and an interlocking system of SAM-2s
and A.A. guns was under construction in a wide belt some
twenty miles west of the Canal. A few weeks later the Israelis
intercepted Russian speech on the airwaves. One hundred and
fifty Soviet pilots, flying Mig-21Js, had assumed responsibility
for the defence of the Nile valley and delta regions.

The Israelis now had another decision to make. Either they
ceased the deep penetration raids, leaving themselves worse off
than when they started, or they risked a direct confrontation
with the Soviet Union in Egyptian skies. They chose caution,
while making it known that they considered a line roughly
twenty-five miles west of the Canal to be the dividing-line
between the two forces. The Soviets tacitly accepted this new
'border' in the sky.

Nasser was exultant. On 1 May he announced, with more
than slight exaggeration, that 'our armed forces have regained
the initiative with bold military operations in the air and on
land.' The energy of the Egyptian Army at this time was mostly
being expended on the construction of their SAM box. Its successful completion would be awkward but not dangerous to
the I.A.F., so long as its ECMs proved capable of confusing
the missiles' directional instruments. But if the Soviets had more
advanced equipment up their sleeves – a likely prognosis – then
not only the sky above the box, but, given the 'slant range' of
the missiles, an area of the sky reaching almost to the Canal,
would be an effectively no-go area for the I.A.F. Through
May and June the Israelis prodigiously sought to prevent the
SAM box's completion.

Their attacks, though causing enormous Egyptian casualties,
proved ultimately unsuccessful, as the Israelis learnt to their
cost on 30 June. The previous night the Egyptians had moved
improved SAM-2s (or SAM-3s – there is some dispute) into
the box. The Israeli pilots found that their ECMs no longer
worked. Four Phantoms were shot down in the one day.

Israel called on the U.S. for help, and within days (perhaps
hours) American planes were arriving loaded with improved

ECM pods. The I.A.F. returned to the attack, making another determined effort through July to destroy the missile box, which now contained around six hundred missile launchers and over a thousand A.A. guns. High explosive and napalm rained down upon the sites, their workers and soldiers. But to the Israeli pilots it seemed that for every smoking ruin another brand-new missile site appeared. The I.A.F. could not neutralise the SAM box. Israeli options, apparently so numerous at the beginning of the year, were now reduced to three: all-out war, withdrawal from the Canal, or a ceasefire. Heavily pressured by the Americans, who were now panicking at the Soviet presence they had themselves induced, Israel chose the latter course.

The Egyptians were also willing. Their casualties had been running at over three hundred per day through July, and the Army was in dire need of a breathing-space. It would also be useful, to say the least, to finish the missile box under a friendly sky. Nasser confided to Brezhnev that he rated the Rogers Peace Initiative's chances at no more than half a per cent; it could not hurt to complete the comprehensive missile system in the space between the ceasefire and the Initiative's failure. Or, of course, to move the missile system forward. As soon as the guns fell silent on 7 August the Egyptians, in gross violation of the ceasefire terms, began easing the SAM box towards the Canal. Within a few days a fully integrated system of radar posts, SAM-2s, SAM-3s, and newly-delivered ZSU 23X4 A.A. guns was controlling the skies above the Canal.

This was a serious threat to the Israeli hold on the east bank. The I.D.F. plan for combating an Egyptian crossing of the Canal rested on the advanced warning and limited delaying capacities of the Bar Lev Line, the swift advance of the Israeli armour from inner Sinai to its pre-prepared ramps on the east bank, and the ability of the I.A.F. to support the fortifications and slow the crossing – by direct attacks on both the bridges and the Egyptian infantry – until first the armour, and second the reserve units, arrived. Take away the I.A.F.'s ability to operate almost with impunity above the Canal – as the advance of the SAM box now had – and Israel was left with a paper line of fortifications and armour that would advance to find its ramps already occupied by the enemy. The Egyptian Army now had the capability to mount a successful cross-Canal assault. Three years of futile diplomacy later, they would make use of it.

Chapter 12

THE END OF A ROAD

Negotiation and Re-alignment, 1970–1972

To govern is to choose.

(attributed to Pierre Mendès-France)

I

We shall not make Britain's mistake. Too wise to try to govern the world, we shall merely own it. Nothing can stop us.

(Ludwell Denny, *America Conquers Britain*)

A new decade introduced a new world. Great changes were being wrought across the planet – not least in that troublesome corner called the Middle East. Israel had met with embarrassing difficulties during the War of Attrition and there was no doubt that terrorist activities by and on behalf of the Palestinians had made their mark on the country's sense of security. It was in an uneasy sort of stasis, balanced between its newfound expanse and the traditional internal crises. To be sure, old political rifts had been healed in the wake of the June War: Ben-Gurion's Rafi had joined with the Alignment in 1968 to re-establish a once more secure ruling group. But on the other hand Menachim Begin's Gahal left the government three years after it had joined in 1967, over Israel's acceptance of the American-imposed ceasefire. Begin finally achieved power in 1977 when his Likud Party scraped through to victory on a small wave of popular disaffection at the continued Arab–Israeli stalemate combined with growing disquiet over Israel's economic prospects (the inflation-rate at that time ran at about thirty per cent).

It was also true that while the Israeli heartland remained fairly secure behind its substantial zones of military administration, the existence of those zones provided a number of critical problems. The more time that passed the greater was Israel's need to annex the territory. Popular pressure from the more Biblically-minded Isarelis combined with economic necessity to dictate a policy of eventual and, if possible, sly annexation. But how would Israel integrate over a million Arabs who still resided in the occupied territories? Immigration and the Jewish birth-rate alone could not be relied on to meet the likelihood of an eventual Arab majority. Israel could not institute a system of apartheid any more obvious than the one that effectively existed under military administration. In any case, such a move would finally put paid to any hopes of peace and would do nothing to help regain the ground Israel had lost among the countries of Africa and Asia whom it sought as trading partners. But the alternative to these options – to stand still and do nothing – was equally impossible. In the early seventies there were already plans to build a town of some 100,000 people at the port of Yamit in Sinai, west of the Gaza Strip. Throughout the seventies Jewish settlements were established in the occupied territories – sometimes with government permission but more often with only its tacit approval.

Despite all this, the old Zionist mixture of pragmatism and patience ensured that Israel made a few concessions, either to peace or to its internal problems. It was aided in this by the changed emphasis of American policy. Shedding their mask of non-involvement, the Americans became increasingly active in the search for a Middle East peace settlement. And yet, in line with the Nixon–Kissinger policy, while pursuing peace so selflessly they connived their way into a position of political dominance in the region. Israel was, of course, integral to this project, but so were Egypt, Jordan and Saudi Arabia. Saudi Arabia, with its vast oil reserves (twenty-five per cent of the world's known supplies), was perhaps the most important of all.

In 1969, at a time when the U.S.S.R. could still fairly be said to dominate a major part of the Arab world, U.S. Secretary of State William Rogers put forward his plan for a negotiated peace. He announced that henceforth U.S. policy would be a 'balanced one', and proceeded to make good his word by producing one of the most exquisitely balanced plans the Middle East had seen for a long time. The by now tediously familiar result was that Rogers' balancing act pleased no one and, therefore, offended everyone. It was rejected by Arabs and Israelis alike. The point, as Nasser's long-standing friend and confidant, Mohammed Heikal, has written, is that 'in the Middle East there are two local powers which could not make peace and two superpowers which could not make war'.[1] On the assumption of continuing superpower competition in the region there was little that could be done. And this was precisely the assumption that was to prove false.

By the end of the sixties, Egypt had proved itself to be little more than a liability to the U.S.S.R. The 1969 Libyan coup under the then violently anti-Soviet Muammar Gaddafi had further upset relations already strained by Nasser's *rapprochement* with the Saudis (and through them with the Americans). Gaddafi, too, had oil money and he professed a strong admiration for Nasser and an even stronger attachment to pan-Arab ideals. The common border between Libya and Egypt seemed to make them natural partners, and in October 1971 they were joined in an Arab Federation together with Syria (by then under the comparatively moderate leadership of Hafez Assad). The focus of Russian interest began to move south and east. They became especially concerned with affairs in the Horn of Africa and the Persian Gulf. No doubt one major reason for this development was Soviet expectation of the downfall of the arch-conservative Saudi régime. In particular, the U.S.S.R.'s interest may have been encouraged by leftist takeovers in the Yemen and South Yemen (formerly the Protectorate of Aden) towards the end of the sixties. Much of the Arabian Peninsula was in the throes of revolutionary upheaval and there can be little doubt that the U.S.S.R. had its eye on Saudi oil.

Egypt was having second thoughts about its relationship with the U.S.S.R., too. Egypt had become enormously indebted to its Soviet patrons and they would often insist on a course of action unpopular with the Egyptians. Apart from that, the U.S.S.R. had conspicuously failed to solve the pressing matter of Israel. In this light, Heikal's thesis about the two superpowers could only mean one thing: Egypt had to shed its Russian shackles. Indeed, when the War of Attrition started proving costly for Egypt in summer 1970, it was the Rogers' peace initiative that came to the rescue. American influence on Israel seemed a better bet to Nasser than to be cast deeper into perpetual Soviet bondage, even though he did hedge that bet by eliciting further Russian offers of personnel and weapons.

Of course, the Americans were not so guileless as to offer to put pressure on Israel simply for Egypt's benefit. On the other side of the Sinai, Rogers exchanged 500 million dollars of much needed military aid in return for Israel's agreement to abide by a ceasefire against its better judgement. America was moving in with alarming effectiveness.

Nasser's death, in September 1970, marked the turning-point in Soviet–Egyptian relations. His successor, the former Vice-President Anwar es-Sadat, was both a much more flexible and a more ruthless man. Within months of Nasser's death he had wiped the Egyptian leadership clean of all opposition. In particular, he attacked the pro-Soviets within the leadership, acting the day before William Rogers was due in Cairo for talks. Increasingly, economic, political and military circumstances pushed Sadat into America's embrace. The expulsion of Soviet military experts in July 1972 may have been interpreted simply as a neutralist gesture but it was, nonetheless, part of an inexorable slide away from Soviet influence culminating in the introduction of the 'open door' policy to encourage Western investment following the October War.

Egypt and Russia moved imperceptibly away from each other. In fact the October War was still fought with Soviet arms and assistance. But by the time that war was over and a new stalement had been reached, the switch was complete and once more Egypt looked westward for a solution to its problems.

II

From between the guns the merchants crept out.
(Bertolt Brecht, *On the News of the Tory Bloodbaths in Greece*)

Oil, of course, had been the greatest motivating factor in the struggle for the Middle East in recent years. America's main interests have been to secure its long-standing oil investments and to control the supply of oil to its major trading partners (and competitors) – the E.E.C. and Japan. In the late sixties

America became a net oil importer for the first time. Although the gap between imports and exports was only marginal American economic expansion would have inevitably involved a growing import bill at a time when domestic oil wells were passing their peak yields.

It's only necessary to look about you to see how vital oil is to a modern industrial economy. It doesn't just go into cars, it goes into plastics, paint, pharmaceuticals, animal feedstuffs and a multitude of everyday products whose absence would radically alter everybody's life. In Christopher Tugendhat's memorable phrase, oil is 'the biggest business'. It's the shaper of wars and the protector of empires, the maker of industry and the provisioner of nations. If one state could control the world's oil supplies, its position would be unassailable. As it is, five of the seven major oil companies in the world today are American – Esso, Mobil, Gulf, Socal and Texas (the other two are Shell and BP). All of them have extensive operations in the Middle East – an area which accounts for between sixty and seventy per cent of the world's known oil reserves.

America first moved into the Middle East in a systematic way in the late twenties, following an arrangement made among the French state-owned oil company, the entrepreneur Calouste Gulbenkian and four oil companies today known as Esso, Mobil, Shell and BP. The companies effectively carved up the former territory of the Ottoman Empire in their search for productive oil fields. The arrangement was know as the Red Line Agreement (see map 4) because the territory involved was marked off in red pencil on a small map. Until the Red Line Agreement, Britain had been the major oil power in the Middle East, controlling fields in Iraq and Persia. But the agreement effectively paved the way for American oil-imperialism to take over in the Middle East. This began to happen after the end of World War II when it became apparent that there were major oil fields within the Red Line area. As early as 1949, Saudi Arabia demanded and got a 50–50 agreement from an American company providing for equal shares in the profits on the sale of crude oil. This deal broke the Red Line Agreement and created the conditions for a radical restructuring of the Middle East oil industry. Moreover, it was made possible by the American government of the day agreeing to special tax arrangements for American oil companies.

In 1953, the Iranian government which had nationalised Iranian oil just over two years earlier was brought down by a C.I.A.-managed coup. In return, American companies received a forty per cent holding in a consortium extracting, refining and shipping Iranian oil. In these and similar ways the American oil companies acted as political agents in the Middle East and, conversely, the American government used its influence to benefit the oil companies.

Russia's interest in oil was, at first, confined largely to its rôle as an exporter. With a relatively under-developed economy and plentiful supplies of oil on its own territory, the U.S.S.R. was able to use oil exports as a means of obtaining foreign currency and as a political weapon. In particular, the U.S.S.R. would frequently supply cheap oil to states it was seeking to influence or pull into its orbit. Oil is a perfect export, being of more or less uniform quality, universally desired and easily transportable. In 1960 the U.S.S.R. promised the Indian government oil at a substantially reduced price. The American companies retaliated by cutting their price – thus reducing the income to producer countries. Oil is virtually the only export for most of the producer countries in the Middle East and, therefore, any sudden reduction in price can be disastrous to their economies. This fact, coupled with annoyance at not being consulted over the latest round of cuts, inspired the formation of O.P.E.C. (the Organisation of Petroleum Exporting Countries) at a conference called by the Iraqi leader, Abdul Kassem.

In many ways O.P.E.C. was a kind of counterpart of the nationalist movements that became active all over the Third World during the fifties. The relationship between O.P.E.C. and Arab nationalism is a particularly complex and significant one. The interests of oil-producing countries tend to cut across political, religious and cultural boundaries that are obstacles to unity elsewhere. However, for some years O.P.E.C. was little more than a protectionist grouping, striving to maintain oil prices at a given level. Towards the end of the sixties, partly in response to a growing demand for oil, partly in response to political pressures from inside and outside a number of Arab oil-producing states, and partly because of the need to fund Arab nationalism, the Arab states within O.P.E.C. moved rapidly to the offensive. Shortly after the June War the

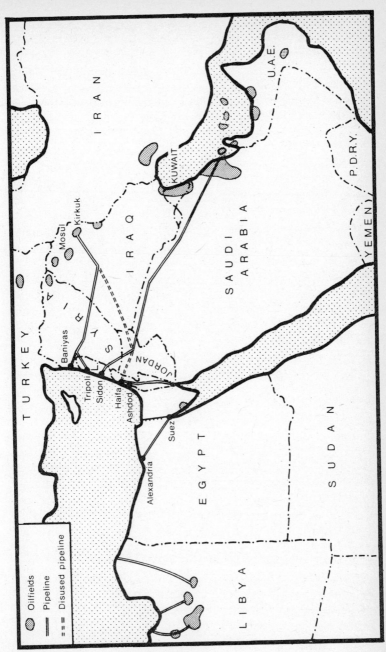

17. Oil in the Middle East

strengthening of the pan-Arab movement created the possibility of using what came to be known as 'the oil weapon'. However, it was not until the early seventies that important producer countries – notably Saudi Arabia – agreed to consider withdrawing oil supplies as a means of forcing America's hand over the Arab–Israeli issue. The Suez Canal (which had, in any case, been closed in 1967) had become largely irrelevant from this point of view, because most oil was by then being carried in super-tankers unable to pass through the Canal's narrow channel. Much of the rest was carried in pipelines – an Israeli one from Eilat to Haifa and the important TAP Line which cut across the Golan.

When the Arab O.P.E.C. members did impose an effective embargo in 1973, it was not an unqualified success, partly because there were alternative supplies of oil available from non-Arab producers, but mainly because it was a somewhat half-hearted gesture. For one thing, it came at a time when there was already general O.P.E.C. pressure for a substantial increase in oil prices, intended to offset inflationary rises in the cost of goods imported from the West and to make available investment capital. It was therefore a bargaining counter as much as a political weapon. For another thing, it suited American purposes as much as it clashed with them.

The Arab oil embargo hit America hard enough, convincing Nixon to introduce 'Project Energy Independence 1980'. But it has been suggested that America was less victim than perpetrator of the 'energy crisis'. The most serious repercussions were felt by the two greatest net oil-importing areas in the world – the E.E.C. (including Britain) and Japan – just when America was really beginning to suffer the consequences of relatively cheap production in these areas: high imports and low exports. The Arab oil embargo provided a timely setback to the E.E.C. and Japan – presumably much to America's relief.

Apart from all that, the oil companies' monopoly of refining and distribution facilities is cast-iron insurance against oil-producing states taking effective unilateral action. This was precisely the lesson of the Iranian oil crisis of 1951 to 1953. The main victim in that episode was Iran itself.

Nevertheless, there is some competition for the oil companies. It comes, not surprisingly, from the U.S.S.R. In recent years the Soviets have been pushing for an integrated world-wide energy delivery system, which they intend to head. Apart from that, the increasing trend towards a Western-style consumer economy in the U.S.S.R. has created a new demand for oil. There are considerable oil reserves in Eastern Siberia, but the U.S.S.R. has neither the capital nor the technology to build the necessary extraction and delivery systems. The solution the Russians have hit upon is stunningly simple. They import cheap Middle Eastern oil (mainly from nearby Iran and Iraq) and re-export some of it at a profit. The rest helps to meet domestic requirements. Acting rather like a giant oil company they earn themselves valuable foreign currency to help finance the development of their own oil fields and at the same time increase the availability of oil in Russia. Since the late sixties this system has been operating quite effectively, but as a would-be major oil-importer rather than an oil-exporter one major strand of Soviet foreign policy has changed. Growing interest in Saudi Arabia and the Persian Gulf sets the U.S.S.R. increasingly at odds with the U.S. For this reason America's continued support of Saudi Arabia has become crucial. As Soviet influence diminishes in the Arab world as a whole – thanks largely to Egypt and the Arab–Israeli conflict – the more it becomes a major aim of American foreign policy to secure Arab unity across a broad spectrum of political systems, from oil-rich conservative states like Saudi Arabia to poor, supposedly socialist states like Egypt. If the U.S. has learnt anything from Gamal Abdul Nasser, it's been that the achievement of Arab unity and a solution to the Arab–Israeli conflict are inseparable, and are likely to remain so.

America's efforts to own the world took another step towards realisation when, in the summer of 1970, William Rogers stepped into the Middle East arena in an attempt to secure 'a just and lasting peace'.

III

What they could do with round here is a good war. What else can you expect with peace running wild all over the place? You know what the trouble with peace is? No organisation.

(Bertolt Brecht, *Mother Courage*)

The 1970 Rogers cease-fire proposals, involving a 'stand-still' zone on each side of the Suez Canal (in the first instance, for three months) and a revival of the Jarring mission, were in principle acceptable to Egypt and Israel. Both had something to gain from them. Egypt wanted a halt to deep penetration raids and the chance to bring up reinforcements, while Israel sought aid and weapons to re-establish its superiority in the area. It is difficult to characterise either of these goals as peaceful, but for a moment peace reigned supreme on Israel's borders.

The Palestinians needed time to recover from the near-fatal blow dealt to them by Hussein's loyal Bedouin troops. Hussein himself, basking in the reflected glow of bloody victory, found his capacity for moderation vastly enlarged by the success of his repression. To the north lay Syria and the Lebanon. Assad's new régime still backed the Saiqa Palestinian guerrillas (whose number rapidly approached that of the largest group, Fatah). But Assad moved progressively closer to the 'moderate' position of Sadat. The Lebanon, quiet as ever, accepted the influx of refugees from Hussein's bloodbath silently and with equanimity. In fact, 'Black September' was not just more Arab sloganising – it was the mark of the avenger. The silence in Lebanon was ominous.

Meanwhile, the Iraqis were out on a limb, as usual, seemingly rejecting everything and everyone. There might never be any peace with them, but no matter – several scores of miles of other people's territory separated them from Israel.

Yet again, the chances of a general settlement seemed real enough. In February 1971 Jarring approached Israel and Egypt with a proposal for a separate peace. This was a substantial concession to Israel. But the proposal involved concessions on Israel's part, and now that the borders were quiet again the Israelis saw no need to give up anything. There would be no withdrawal to the pre-1967 Sinai border. In fact there would be no more than a ten-kilometre retreat from the Suez Canal, even though it was militarily unwise to maintain that position. Nor, of course, would there be any settlement of the refugee problem in accordance with Resolution 242.

The Egyptians, having announced their readiness to 'enter into a peace agreement with Israel', began to lose confidence in America's willingness to pressure their enemy. Israel refused to abide by any specific declaration of its intentions towards the occupied territories. Sadat continued to make definite proposals. In April 1971 he offered to reopen the Canal in return for a partial withdrawal by Israeli troops. He proposed that this be the first stage of a phased withdrawal from all occupied territories. The Americans picked up on the proposal and pressed for some sort of interim agreement. But the Israelis were not interested in the Canal (the Gulf of Aqaba being open) and they were even less interested in leaving the occupied territories. The possibility of a settlement floundered and sank.

The Israelis were gradually isolating themselves from the community of nations. Despite the growing Palestinian campaign of terror, Israel's intransigence undermined its declarations of peaceful intent. For a few months in 1971 America tried to pressure Israel by holding up the sale of planes. It was another half-hearted gesture. As 1972 dawned, and with it the run-up to American elections, Nixon relented and promised Israel more Phantoms and Skyhawks.

Sadat, meanwhile, had declared 1971 to be 'the year of decision'. But no decision was made and no action taken. Personal intervention by the new U.N. Secretary General failed to break the deadlock. Assad's formal declaration that Syria would at last accept 242 failed to move the Israelis or persuade the Americans of Arab good intentions. Sadat's expulsion of the Russians made no difference.

It was almost as though somebody high up in the American administration had decided to pursue the goal of stalemate in the Middle East. Despite Arab hostility towards Israel, Egypt had committed itself to the U.S. largely because Israel and America were such close allies But the more Sadat tried to please America, the more dependent he found himself on American good will. Unfortunately for Egypt, it was perfectly in line with the Nixon–Kissinger approach to strengthen Israel in an attempt to keep pushing Egypt closer to America. The Americans felt that a stalemate, as long as it remained a stalemate, was preferable to an imposed settlement against the will of either party. And Sadat found himself constantly making excuses for America – excuses whose feebleness could no longer be disguised once the 1972 U.S. elections were over and the re-elected Nixon continued to aid and abet Israel. Sadat ran out of reasons for not fighting.

It has been suggested that, when Kissinger became Secretary

of State in 1973, he calculated that a limited military defeat for the Israelis would make them more flexible than even the withdrawal of aid could do. If this is the case, the calculation was based on two assumptions: that Egypt's Soviet-supplied missile weapons could, if deployed in a surprise attack, impose just such a limited defeat on Israel; and that the U.S.S.R. would not become embroiled in an open-ended conflict with Israel. They were big assumptions to make, but not implausible. Past experience had shown that the Russians were as loath as the Americans to become involved in an uncontainable war in the Middle East. In addition, the early seventies saw moves towards détente which culminated in the Nixon–Brezhnev talks of June 1973. America and the Soviet Union clearly cast themselves in the rôle of the world's policemen. A little intelligence work, too, would have revealed the state of Egypt's arsenal and its true relations with Russia.

In any event, when Nixon and Brezhnev did meet they evinced an apparent lack of concern with the Middle East issue – if their joint communiqué is anything to go by. For Sadat it was the last straw, his final hope of a peaceful settlement shattered. With the astuteness of a man who knows the way the cards are stacked, he began to plan for a limited offensive against Israel. We have no way of knowing the real extent of Egypt's war aims, but for once it is clear that they did not include the annihilation of Israel. Sadat doubted whether he had the strength to drive Israel out of the Sinai – even with the aid of an inevitably forlorn Syrian stab at the Golan. Looking at the manner in which the operation was planned and executed, it seems more probable he intended to drive the Israeli front-line back to the Sinai passes in an attempt to persuade America of Egypt's determination and Israel of the need to negotiate. On 22 August 1973, in conditions of high secrecy, a group of Egyptian and Syrian officers met in Alexandria to discuss the final details of their plan for a simultaneous assault into Sinai and the Golan. 'No peace, no war' – no longer. It would be war.

Chapter 13

THE PEACOCK AND THE FOX

Prelude to War: November 1972 – October 1973

Pretend inferiority and encourage his arrogance.

(Sun Tzu)

I

Five years had now passed since the Arab defeat of 1967, five years in which little had changed at the heart of the Arab–Israeli conflict. The Palestinian refugees were still in their camps; Israel was still not recognised by the Arab states. The lands occupied in 1967 remained occupied. And, as would become apparent eleven months hence, Israel still had no secure borders. Despite contesting four wars, the Israeli leadership had still not realised that security in the Middle East could only rest on a political settlement, and not upon force of arms.

For two years since the official termination of the 'War of Attrition' the diplomatic circus had played to less than enthusiastic houses. As Nasser had noted succinctly in 1969: 'There can be no hope of any political solution unless the enemy realises that we are capable of forcing him to withdraw through fighting.'[1] Only then, the Arabs believed, would there be a change in Israeli notions of what was and was not acceptable.

Since 1967 the Arab High Commands, and particularly the Egyptian, had sought such a capability. Immediately after the June War, Nasser had locked himself away with tapes of the Israeli generals explaining the reasons behind their success. These were familiar enough: fast and flexible military operations made possible by the highly-trained and imaginative manpower typical of a united technological society.

The Egyptians could not hope to meet the Israelis on equal

terms in this sort of war. The social base was simply not there. But Egypt did have military advantages: a potentially higher number of men-in-arms, the capacity to endure a long war and higher casualties, and a military leadership with a penchant for the set-piece battle, in which every last action could be planned, prepared and directed from the top.

Nasser's 'War of Attrition' had attempted to mobilise these advantages on Egypt's behalf, and so strike at Israel's weaknesses: a low tolerance of casualties and the inability of the economy to withstand a long war. For a while it had worked, and might, given greater Egyptian nerve, have pushed the Israelis back into Sinai. But the construction of the Bar Lev line minimised Israeli casualties, and the I.A.F. had then to be played as a trump to which the Egyptians had no counter. Though the end of the war found the Egyptians, courtesy of the Soviets, acquiring a counter-trump in the form of an adequate missile defence system, the original objective – to 'bleed' Israeli manpower and the Israeli economy, had not been realised. The I.A.F. had borne the brunt of the fighting, and the I.A.F. was a regular force. No additional mobilisation had been required, no additional strain placed on the already over-stretched Israeli economy.

This was the situation inherited by Sadat in late 1970 after Nasser's sudden death in September. Sadat too knew that only military action was likely to break the diplomatic deadlock; he too had to decide what form this military action would take. At first he seems to have believed that spectacular gestures would prove adequate diplomatic midwives, and two such were planned. In December 1971 an Egyptian air attack on Sharm el-Sheikh was called off when the Indo–Pakistani war broke out and stole the hoped-for headlines; in October 1972 the planned establishment of a commando-held bridgehead in mid-Sinai was called off when the War Minister Sadeq refused to sanction such a suicidal waste of his best troops. He was replaced by General Ismail. Sadat resigned himself to the resumption of conventional war in the near future.

Here the primary legacy of the 'War of Attrition' – the moving forward of the missile system, and the effective A.A. defence over the Canal Zone now offered by its slant range – assumed critical importance. In denying the skies over the Canal to the I.A.F., an area had been created in which the

Egyptian Army could bring its advantages to bear against its enemy's weaknesses. An assault across the Canal offered a set-piece battle that could be planned and directed from the top, that could employ Egypt's superior numbers, and that would hopefully establish a new and bloodier stalemate. The super-powers would intervene, and Israel, suffering both militarily and economically, would be forced into making concessions.

The military scheme was also applicable on Golan, where the Syrian Army could mount a breakthrough to the western edge of the plateau under cover of a similar missile system. Once the Israelis were pushed back down the Golan escarp-ment, it was reckoned, the Israelis would find it both costly and time-consuming to fight their way back up. From the end of 1972 onwards, both Egypt and Syria were planning and pre-paring for a return to the conventional battlefield.

Their armies, for all the friction accruing from the swarm of Soviet advisers, were much improved: larger, better-equipped, better-trained. They had weaknesses certainly, but they were to fight according to their strengths; the Arab political and mili-tary leaderships had at last learnt to calculate ends according to means, and so to attempt the possible. Every facet of the forthcoming operation was meticulously analysed: the de-ployment of troops, the bridging operation, penetration of the sand rampart on the far bank, the destruction of the incoming Israeli armour. While carefully observing every Israeli move on the east bank, establishing the enemy's routine and planning accordingly, individual Egyptian units were ceaselessly trained in their individual rôles. The time needed to lay a bridge across the Canal was cut down from three days to five hours; the time needed to cut through the sand rampart halved by the ingenious employment of fire hoses. The incoming armour would be countered by the massed deployment of infantry equipped with wire-guided anti-tank missiles and rocket grenades, the I.A.F. by the relatively new SAM-7 individually operated anti-aircraft missile. Little was left to chance regarding this first phase of the battle-plan. If the Egyptians could not field a flexible fast-moving army, then they could field one capable of implementing a rigid and well-rehearsed operation.

The Egyptian High Command was confident, but naturally the greater the element of surprise, the longer Israel would wait to mobilise, and the easier the Egyptian consolidation on the east bank would be. To this end a deception plan of astonishing scope was dreamt up and implemented by the Egyptian Ministries of War, Information, and Foreign Affairs.

The increasing visibility of the preparations for attack made it essential that Israeli eyes were diverted. The Arabs adopted a reasonable, dove-like, diplomatic stance, and took every opportunity to encourage the Israeli obsession with the Palestinian groups. 6 October was the day chosen for the attack, specifically on account of the Canal tides, but also because it was Yom Kippur – the holiest day in the Judaic calendar. The Israelis would be fully absorbed in this and their election campaign. Further, they would not expect an Arab attack in the month of Ramadan.

Even more diverting to the Israelis, in the week leading up to war, was the Schonau affair. On 28 September two Arab gunmen held up a Prague–Vienna train at the Austrian border. Aboard the train were Soviet Jews en route to Israel via the Schonau Castle transit centre. The gunmen, styling themselves 'Eagles of the Palestinian Revolution', demanded that the Schonau centre be closed down. The Austrian government, to Israel's consternation, agreed to do so, and for several days the Israeli leadership's energies were directed towards reversing this decision. The 'Eagles', it later transpired, were controlled by Saiqa, the Syrian-controlled Palestinian organisation. It is hard to believe that the whole affair was merely fortuitous to the Arab deception plan.

For the benefit of those Israelis still watching their frontiers, great care was taken to present Arab activity as anything other than offensive in intention. Nothing was done to indicate a break with the normal routine. As this included grand manoeuvres every autumn, the large-scale movement of troops and equipment was not unusual. The Israelis did not notice that brigades driving forward to the Canal Zone during daylight hours only returned as battalions during the night. On the other hand, notices in the Egyptian press sanctioning leave for officers to take the 'little pilgrimage' during Ramadan, and deliberate leaks casting doubts on the efficacy of the Egyptian missile system, were probably eagerly noted by Israeli Intelligence.

A war was not expected. There did seem, it was true, to be a higher level of Arab activity than was normal, but this could

be explained as a typically paranoid reaction to the Israeli–
Syrian air battle of 13 September. The Arabs, the Israelis con-
fidently surmised, were half-expecting to be attacked. Which
explained their defensive deployment. Of course, they could be
offensively deployed without much trouble, but that had been
true at any moment during the last year. There was no need to
panic, and mobilise, as had been the case in May. That mobilisation had cost a great deal of money.

The Israelis were ready to be deceived.

II

In 1967 Israeli forces had occupied territory belonging to each
of the three front-line Arab states. In each case the new
'frontiers' offered greater strategic depth; in each case they
were also militarily superior in themselves. On Golan the
Israelis now looked down on the Syrians rather than vice
versa; on the Egyptian and Jordanian front-lines formidable
water-barriers separated the I.D.F. from its enemy. The
Egyptian Air Force had lost its Sinai bases, and Israeli notice
of an Egyptian air attack had been correspondingly lengthened.
Before 1967 Israel had been tied by geography to the pre-
emptive strike and the lightning attack. Now the I.D.F. could
wait for the enemy to make the first move without, it was
thought, incurring a crippling disadvantage. And the political
odium of 'aggression' would cling to the Arabs.

But the new 'frontiers' were far from an unmitigated blessing. They posed new and seemingly insoluble military problems.
Prior to 1967, the spectacle of an Egyptian Army moving
ponderously into Sinai had always provided advance notice of
an Arab attack. Syria would never dare to move against Israel
without such support, and Egypt could not, for obvious logistical reasons, deploy its army permanently in the desert. But
after 1967 the bulk of the Egyptian Army could be, and
frequently was, deployed in the Canal front-line. There would
henceforth be no clear-cut warning of an Arab ground offensive.

Yet Israel could not, for economic reasons, deploy a large
countervailing force on the east bank of the Suez Canal. And
the reserves, having farther to travel, would take longer to
arrive. Clearly a great deal rested on the calibre of the Israeli

Intelligence services. If they could divine Arab intentions at an early enough stage, then the reserves could be rushed forward in time to reinforce those few units permanently stationed in the vicinity of the Canal Zone.

The deployment of these latter units remained a matter of dispute within the I.D.F. leadership. The Bar Lev fortifications, built during the early stages of the 'War of Attrition', had been intended as a counter to Egyptian artillery fire, not as a counter to an attempted Canal crossing. Their enduring relevance was uncertain. Tal argued that they could be easily bypassed, and as such could function as no more than advance warning posts. The business of defence should be left to mobile armoured units. Gavish and Elazar, among others, counterargued that the Suez Canal only constituted a meaningful barrier so long as the Israelis maintained a physical presence on its eastern bank. The fortifications should constitute a defensive as well as a warning system.

In the immediate aftermath of the 'War of Attrition' no clear decision was taken. The Bar Lev line was strengthened, (through the construction of more tank ramps, roads, underground H.Q.s, water and communication systems) and heavily manned. Mobile armour patrolled the spaces between the forts. This failed to satisfy Tal. He continued to press for more mobile armour, and for a downgrading of the forts to the status of warning posts. Elazar, on becoming Chief of Staff in 1972, over-influenced by the lack of enemy activity in the Canal Zone, agreed to a downgrading of the forts without decreeing a corresponding step-up in the level of armoured patrols. The forts were now too strong for a warning rôle, and too weak for a defensive rôle. An Egyptian attack would simply trap the occupants.

On the Syrian front the same basic situation encompassed a greater danger. In 1967 Egypt had been both the strongest and the closest enemy; the Israelis had merely stood their ground in the north while securing a decision in the south. But now the Egyptian Army was way across the other side of Sinai, and the Syrian Army represented the immediate danger. This time the I.D.F. would first have to settle accounts on Golan.

The Israeli front-line now ran across the centre of the plateau, a flat plain broken by lone volcanic hills or 'tells'. A series of fortifications – emplacements protected by minefields,

wire and two or three tanks – had been constructed along the
line, and additional defensive positions sited on those hills
immediately behind it. High on the slopes of Mount Hermon,
an electronic observation post surveyed the entire plateau. Early
in 1973 the defensive system was further expanded. New roads
were built, and a deep anti-tank ditch, covered by new tank-
ramps, was dug out of the basalt.

Optimism was as evident on Golan as in Sinai. The ditch
would compensate for the lack of natural obstacles and *slow* a
Syrian attack. The armour in reserve, and the I.A.F., would
then *halt* it. The mobilised reserves would arrive and *throw it
back*. This was the expected scenario. Some had the sense to
doubt it. Tal noted his concern that the Syrian deployment of
an integrated SAM system would greatly impede the I.A.F.,
thus leaving the small fortifications and armoured units to bear
the entire brunt of a Syrian offensive. He was ignored. There
would be no war.

Elazar and Dayan thought war likely. The former expected
the Arabs to launch a new diplomatic offensive after the U.S.
Presidential elections in late 1972. They would of course be
frustrated in this effort, and would probably resort once more
to conventional war in 1973. This was the reasoning behind his
insistence, against Intelligence advice, on the expensive Israeli
mobilisation in May. But that crisis quickly passed. Elazar had
been proved wrong, and those who thought the Arabs unlikely
to fight were given further confidence in this mistaken belief.
Dayan, too, noted in May that 'a renewal of war in the second
half of the summer must be taken into account'.[2] He too was
ignored. Even should there be a war, the Israelis would win
without difficulty. There was no cause for concern.

In the last month of 'peace', as Arab preparations accelerated
and became ever more visible, the process of Israeli double-
think kept pace. The Arabs would not attack; the Israelis would
win. As in December 1971, December 1972 and May 1973, the
Egyptian and Syrian forces on the front-lines were growing
stronger by the day. Soon for the fourth time they would be
poised to unleash a full-scale offensive. The first three times
they had not done so. In what way did this crisis differ
from the others? Israel could not afford another unnecessary
mobilisation. The Schonau affair absorbed the nation's attention. The Arabs, poor fools, were preparing a defence against an

imaginary Israeli attack. Or they were bluffing. For each piece of evidence an answer was found to justify the prevailing tide of complacent optimism.

Fortunately for Israel, two decisions of crucial importance were taken, the first by Dayan and Elazar. Visiting the northern front in mid-September a concentration of Syrian medium artillery was brought to their attention. This was either a Syrian mistake or 'a clear indication to any military observer of an intention to attack'. Dayan and Elazar did not sound the general alarm, such was the weight of Israeli complacency. But their ordering of the crack 7th Armoured Brigade up on to the plateau was to prove of critical importance during the long night of 6–7 October.

In the meantime Israel waited for the crisis to pass, waited until 04.00 on the 6th, when Intelligence chief Ze'ira was woken with the news that the Arabs would attack that day. Two hours later Dayan and Elazar met to decide on mobilisation. Even at this late hour Dayan would agree only to a partial mobilisation, one sufficient for defensive purposes. He also rejected Elazar's plea for a pre-emptive air strike, a refusal reinforced by Golda Meir's 'kitchen cabinet' at 08.00. Mrs Meir had been warned by the American ambassador that U.S. arms deliveries were contingent on Israel not striking the first blow.

War was expected, wrongly as it turned out, at 18.00. After the 'war cabinet' meeting, Tal took the second decision of crucial importance. The rushing of reserves to the Golan front, he decided, could not afford to wait for the normal mobilisation by brigades. The reserves would have to be sent up in companies, platoons, ad-hoc groupings, however they arrived. The warning period had been lost. Now speed was everything.

On both fronts the Israeli defence plan rested on three conditions: twenty-four-hours' warning, a characteristically inept Arab attack, and full I.A.F. support for the heavily outnumbered ground forces in the front-line. None of these conditions obtained. The first had already been blown away. The others were soon to follow.

Chapter 14

A HOLY TIME, AN UNHOLY WAR

The October War, 1973

War, war, pointless war . . .   (Moshe Dayan)

We have fought and we shall go on fighting to liberate our
land which was seized by Israeli occupation in 1967, and to
find the means towards the restoration and respect of the
legitimate rights of the Palestinian people.

(Anwar Sadat, 16 October 1973)

I

At 14.00 on 6 October the Egyptian offensive began. The Air
Force struck deep into Sinai, attacking Israeli airfields, missile
batteries, artillery positions, radar and command installations.
On the west bank of the Canal two thousand Egyptian guns
opened fire on the Israeli positions across the water, and hundreds of Egyptian tanks moved into the pre-prepared ramps on
the high sand ramparts to pour fire into the forts of the Bar
Lev line. At 14.15 the first wave of infantry climbed into their
boats for the short Canal crossing. Minutes later they were
scrambling up the rampart on the far side. Some carried metal
tubes strung across their shoulders, some what looked like
holiday suitcases, some pulled little portable trailers. The tubes
were launchers for RPG 7 anti-tank rockets, the suitcases
contained the 'Sagger' wire-guided anti-tank missiles, the
trailers bore the hand-held SAM-7 anti-aircraft missiles. Reaching the crest of the Israeli rampart the Egyptian infantry
planted flags and began to unpack.

All around them the inferno of artillery fire raged. Behind
them successive boatloads of infantry were crossing the Canal.
As they reached the top of the ramparts the original wave
moved forward two hundred yards into the desert. Third and
fourth waves arrived to join the first and second, and the

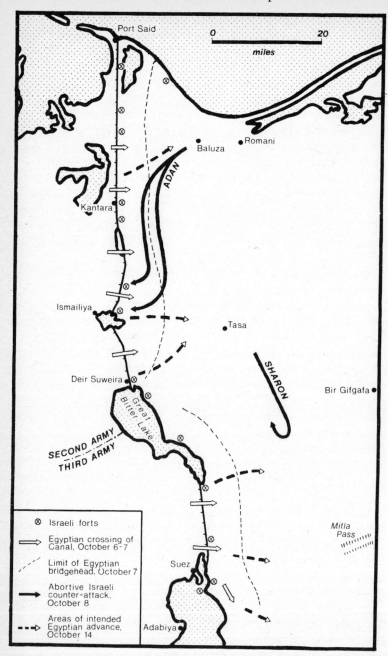

18. Egypt returns to Sinai, 6-14 October

various units leapfrogged forward into Sinai. By sundown the Egyptian infantry was firmly established between one and two miles from the Canal. On the following day it was intended that the bridgehead should be further deepened, and organised to withstand the inevitable Israeli counter-attack.

In their rear, on that first evening, the Egyptian engineers were blasting holes through the Israeli sand rampart with their fire hoses and clipping together the new Soviet bridges. On the section of the Canal south of the Great Bitter Lake the ramparts proved resistant to the hoses, and 3rd Army's armour was swiftly rerouted via a crossing-point near Ismailiya. The Israeli forts were under attack by specially-trained infantry units. Everything was going according to the master-plan. Only the feared losses had been grossly inflated. Two hundred and eight Egyptians died in the cross-Canal assault, as against an expected eight to ten thousand.

On the Israeli side of the Canal, facing this assault by something like 100,000 infantry and 600 tanks (the other 1,000 Egyptian tanks were kept on the west bank for some days), were 436 soldiers manning the forts, a handful of tanks and seven artillery batteries. Further back in Sinai were the three brigades of Mandler's armoured division, mustering 277 tanks. This was the intended counter-attack force.

The overall commander in Sinai was General Shmuel Gonen, who had led 7th Armoured Brigade with distinction in 1967. He had only recently reported to this post, and the improvements he immediately deemed necessary in the Israeli defensive system had not yet been implemented. Now, as the afternoon of 6 October passed, he was trying to identify the main Egyptian effort from the fragmentary intelligence reaching him in his Tasa H.Q. It was not until about 16.30 that it became apparent to him that the Egyptians were crossing in strength along the entire Canal front. There was no 'main effort'. At this point he was obliged, according to pre-war Israeli planning, to move forward Mandler's armour. He did so. It was not yet obvious that the scope of the Egyptian assault was beyond anything foreseen by the Israeli planners.

Early that evening the three tank brigades moved towards the Canal and into battle, disappearing, as far as Mandler and Gonen were concerned, into a veritable 'fog of war'. In fact they drove straight into the densest anti-tank barrage the world had ever seen. The Egyptian advanced infantry, scattered like 'specks dotted on the sand dunes' as one Israeli officer recalled, unleashed a hail of missiles and rocket-grenades from their 'Saggers' and RPG 7s. As Dayan was later to write: these weapons did not 'constitute a revolution, but rather an additional hazard on the battlefield, calling for greater care in the operation of armour. Tanks must resort to sniping and function less like galloping cavalry.'[1] But it would take the Israeli armoured commanders some days to learn this lesson. Weaned on the élan of Tal's armoured charge tactics, they galloped down to the Canal like a contemporary version of the Light Brigade.

By 01.00 on the 7th, or so it seemed to Gonen, the three brigades had reached the water's edge and relieved most of the beleaguered forts. This was an illusory assessment. The tanks were certainly rushing through the sand like water, but the sand was drying behind them and the water was slowly evaporating away. Through the night an ever-diminishing number of tanks rushed to and fro, on the horns of an ill-conceived defensive plan. The forts, too lightly manned to defend themselves and too heavily-manned to abandon, constantly distracted the Israeli armour from its primary function of stemming the Egyptian onslaught in the spaces between. Every cross-desert rush exposed the armour to anti-tank fire from the dunes and the high ramparts on each side of the Canal. By dawn the frightful truth was becoming apparent at Gonen's H.Q. Only about 50 tanks remained of the 277. The Egyptians were firmly established on the east bank. And worst of all, as Gonen was informed at 06.45, there would be no support from the I.A.F. The Syrian breakthrough on Golan had assumed crisis proportions, and no planes could be spared for the Canal Zone.

II

At 14.00 on the 6th, as the Egyptian bombardment began in Sinai, Syrian MiGs flew low over the Israeli positions on Golan, and the Syrian artillery opened up all along the ceasefire line. Behind that line, waiting for the word to move, were three infantry divisions (each containing 180 tanks) and two indepen-

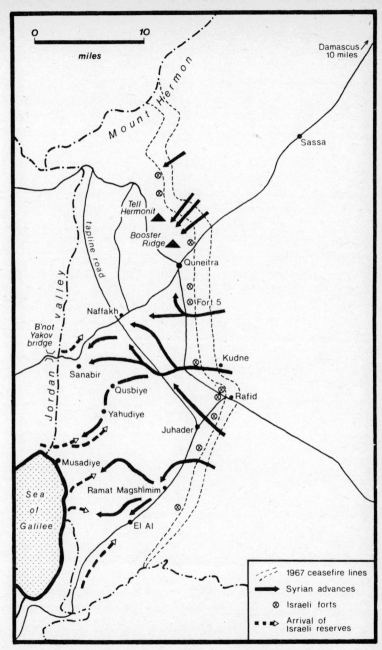

19. Golan: the Syrian attack, 6-8 October

dent tank brigades. This was the breakthrough force. In its rear, waiting for the breach to be opened for them, were the 460 tanks of the two Syrian armoured divisions.

On the Israeli side the forces in the front line consisted of two armoured brigades, the 7th and Barak, mustering 177 tanks between them, and the small garrisons of the eleven fortified strongpoints. The stronger and more experienced 7th Armoured Brigade was deployed to the north and west of Quneitra, where the main Syrian attack was expected. South of the Quneitra–B'not Yakov bridge road, covering a wider frontage with less armour, was the Barak Brigade. Three days earlier, the new commander of the forces on Golan, Raful Eytan, had wondered out loud as to the possible consequences of a major Syrian effort in this southern sector. He had received no answer from his staff.

The Syrians were about to provide him with one. Their attack plan envisaged three major breakthrough points: north of Quneitra, between Quneitra and Fort 5, and between Kudne and Juhader. But it was a flexible plan; the armour in reserve would be fed into the widest breach. And the widest breach would be the most southerly of the three.

Like the Egyptians, the Syrians had practised long and hard for this war: bridging anti-tank ditches, storming volcanic hills, familiarising themselves with the new Soviet missile systems. Now was the moment for putting it all to the test. Behind a rolling artillery barrage the mechanised infantry, with tank support, moved forward against the Israeli line. The tank brigades followed. By midnight, it was hoped, they would be looking down into Galilee from the crest of the Golan escarpment.

In the north events did not go as planned. The Syrian tanks, in groups of a dozen or less, and supported by two or three APCs, burst across the line in the spaces between the strongpoints and ran smack into the practised long-range fire of 7th Armoured Brigade. The tactics were hardly imaginative:

> The groups were often closely bunched together and appeared to ignore terrain features such as folds in the ground or defiles; instead the armoured groups rushed forward straight at the enemy. The only covering fire was that provided by the artillery barrage; the tanks themselves seldom followed a fire-and-movement tactical drill.[2]

Furthermore the Syrian infantry tended to stay on board the APCs, rather than getting off to deal with Israeli pockets of resistance. As a result, the lines of tanks and APCs hard on each other's heels proved ideal targets for the Israeli gunners. Soon the stretch of plateau between Booster Ridge and Tel Hermonit was littered with flaming wrecks.

In the north, Israeli experience and Syrian numbers tended to cancel each other out. For three days this battle would be fought and refought and fought again. But in the south the numerical imbalance proved too much for the less-experienced Barak Brigade. As the afternoon wore on, its commander, Ben Shoham, learnt of major breakthroughs south of Kudne, and north and south of Juhader. The information reaching him at his Naffakh H.Q. grew both less reliable and more alarming, so Ben Shoham decided to go and see for himself with a small ad hoc unit. But reaching the Juhader area the picture grew no clearer. At around this time, in the early evening, the southern sector swiftly degenerated into a disconnected series of local attempts to stem the Syrian tide. Unlike the 7th Armoured Brigade, which had managed to hold together and continue fighting as an integrated unit, the Barak Brigade was now dispersed over a wide area, its thirty or so remaining tanks facing the onslaught of well over 400.

Little support could be provided by the I.A.F. Though equipped with sufficient E.C.M. equipment to outwit the known danger of the SAM-2s and SAM-3s, the Israeli planes were virtually defenceless against the new, mobile SAM-6s. Over forty planes were downed on Golan that first afternoon, and for two hours air strikes were actually suspended while new tactics were urgently discussed. After dusk they resumed, the Israeli planes skimming.

in a low northward curve over Jordanian territory, hugging the contours until they rocketed up and over the Golan plateau to take the Syrian armour in the flank and then curve away west of Mount Hermon – hopefully without ever passing over the deadly SAM sites. It was partially successful: the loss rate dropped; but it was still worrying.[3]

It was indeed. The I.A.F. would have to accustom itself henceforward to a severely compromised mastery of the skies.

On the ground, as night fell, Syrian armoured units moved

up the Tapline route towards Naffakh and gingerly moved down the roads leading to the Sea of Galilee and the Jordan valley. The remnants of Ben Shoham's brigade could not stop the advance, but they could slow it down. They had to. If the Syrians reached the crest of the escarpment before the first Israeli reserves, then those reserves would find Syrian guns staring down at them. Through the night, small Israeli tank units heroically played cat-and-mouse with the Syrian columns, sometimes destroying five, even ten, times their own number of the enemy.

But at first light on 7 October the situation was still deteriorating from the Israeli point of view. The Syrians were feeding more tanks into the southern sector; there were now 600 operating against the ten to fifteen remaining to Ben Shoham's brigade. The leading Syrian echelons were in sight of the Sea of Galilee on the El Al road south of Ramat Magshimim, past Yahudiye on the road down to Musadiye, approaching the vital Naffakh crossroads and thereby threatening the flank and rear of the fully-engaged 7th Armoured Brigade.

The Israeli High Command acted with commendable resolution. Dayan, visiting the Golan front early that morning and realising the gravity of the situation, 'requested' of the I.A.F. that it concentrate its entire strength against the Syrian armour. And so, as Gonen lamented the withdrawal of planes from Sinai, the first of the day's many strikes went in on Golan. Simultaneously the first reserve units were being rushed up the escarpment from the Jordan valley. Eytan, trusting to the proven obstinacy of 7th Armoured Brigade, deployed the new units in the southern sector. Soon one reserve formation was in control of the Qusbiye crossroads; Syrian forces that had bypassed this position ran into another reserve unit moving up from the west. The other routes leading down to the Sea of Galilee were similarly blocked. The Syrian advance, in several places only a fifteen-minute drive from the Jordan, was halted in its tracks.

Yet as the advance was stemmed in the south, pressure increased in the centre and north. Naffakh Camp, the central Israeli H.Q. on Golan, came under attack around noon, the Syrian tanks actually breaching the perimeter fence as Eytan, cool as ever in his underground bunker, continued to control both the entire front and the flow of reserves moving up from the west. Naffakh was saved by the timely arrival of a reserve unit; in the north, 7th Armoured Brigade fought on without any hope of immediate assistance. From 08.00 on the morning of the 7th, for five hours, it withstood another massed attack in the area between Booster Ridge and Tel Hermonit, an area soon to be known variously as 'The Graveyard' and 'The Vale of Tears'. That night the Syrians would attack again, and the next day and the day after that, until by midday Tuesday, with seven of their original tanks still in action, the men of 7th Armoured Brigade would stare bleary-eyed at the wrecks of 260 Syrian tanks in the valley below.

This cheering sight was still two days in the future. As afternoon turned into evening on the 7th the Syrian tide was still flowing. Like a stream blocked at one point it merely sought a new course. At one stage the leading tanks of one formation were outside Sanabir, a mere three miles from the B'not Yakov bridge. The I.A.F., despite continuing high losses, mounted 'a supreme effort' around dusk. The planes switched their attention to the less heavily armoured supply convoys, reasoning that lack of fuel and ammunition would halt the Syrian armour. It worked. By nightfall the advance had been definitively halted.

The crisis was over, but not the battle. Pushing the Syrians back to the armistice line and beyond would take time and a significant portion of the I.D.F. For several days there could be no possibility of moving large forces south to face the Egyptians.

III

In Sinai they were badly needed. The Egyptian bridgehead was now a quasi-continuous belt of land several miles deep, held by five infantry divisions and around 800 tanks. Holding this force where it was required a major effort by the Israelis, throwing it back over the Canal would require more than what was available in Sinai on 7 October.

The Israeli reserve formations began to arrive that day, and Gonen divided his front between the three divisions now available. 'Bren' Adan commanded the northernmost division, hero-villain 'Arik' Sharon the central, and 'Albert' Mandler the division in the south. The success of the Egyptian crossing, not to mention already existing personal animosities, had already divided these commanders, and a unified sense of purpose was conspicuously lacking on the Sinai front. Two visits from Moshe Dayan during the day did little to improve matters. The first time he advocated a withdrawal to a line *east* of the Central Ridge passes, the second time, more optimistically, to the passes themselves. The Defence Minister's nerve seemed momentarily on the verge of cracking. So too did Sharon's, though in his case naturally in the opposite direction. He was all in favour of an immediate Israeli assault on the Canal. Gonen, his former subordinate but now his superior, thought this ludicrous and said so. Sharon consoled himself by insulting Gonen.

Fortunately, Chief of Staff Elazar was keeping a relatively cool head. He saw no immediate need for panic withdrawals, nor any immediate possibility of a counter-attack on the scale envisaged by Sharon. The I.A.F., still mostly engaged on Golan, had not as yet devised any satisfactory solution to the problems posed by the Egyptian missile system; the Israeli tanks were still almost exclusively equipped with armour-piercing shells, perfect for knocking out Egyptian tanks but next to useless against missile-firing infantry.

Despite these problems Elazar did order a limited counter-attack, to take place on the following day. He was apparently motivated by the time-factor. The Israelis knew that they could wage war for no more than thirty days without causing irreparable damage to their economy, and the longer the Egyptians were allowed to sun-bathe on the east bank the harder it would be to dislodge them. This reasoning was only superficially valid – two or so more days would have benefited the Israelis more than the Egyptians – and it is hard to believe that a lingering over-confidence was not primarily responsible for the decision.

The planning and execution of the attack proved less sound than the motivation. Adan's armour was to drive south at a distance of two miles from, and parallel to, the Canal, thus cutting through the Egyptian infantry without moving into range of the guns and missiles deployed on the Canal ramparts. If the Israeli armour succeeded in such a manner in rolling up the Egyptian bridgehead north of the Great Bitter Lake,

Sharon's armour was to undertake a similar manoeuvre south of the Lake. But if Adan's forces ran into trouble, then Sharon's division would move west to its rescue.

At first Adan's attack seemed to be going well, and Sharon was ordered south, but it soon transpired that the lack of Egyptian resistance stemmed from Adan's faulty line of march. Instead of moving south two miles from the Canal, it was five miles away. Adan's armour was simply driving across the front of the Egyptian bridgehead, rather than through it. When Adan realised the error and turned his armour westwards it quickly ran into the terrifying missile barrage of the Egyptian infantry. Tank losses were severe. Adan, asking one of his commanders why he was withdrawing, received the reply: 'If you continue to ask me questions there will be nobody left to answer in a few minutes.' Sharon, who had been ordered by Gonen to reverse his southward move and come to Adan's assistance, proved reluctant to do so. An enraged Gonen accused him of disobeying orders and asked that he be removed from his command. Sharon replied that the orders were confused! And while these two poured oil on to the metaphorical flames of their mutual animosity, Adan's tanks were sprouting real flames out in the desert.

That evening Dayan and Elazar arrived to sort things out. Militarily, it was obvious that the Israeli Army's attachment to Tal's all-armour doctrine had outlasted its usefulness. The potency of 1967 had become the death-ride of 1973. The two decided that the Israeli forces in Sinai would have to assume a strategic defensive posture until such time as Syria was fully accounted for. As regards the personal squabbling, Elazar and Dayan tried to persuade Gonen and Sharon to patch things up.

The extent of their failure in this endeavour was soon apparent. Gonen, following orders, decreed a policy of strength conservation. This decision obviously cut as much ice with Sharon as a cardboard sword; the next day, 9 October, he mounted a major attack in the central sector. It was a disaster. The spearhead force under Colonel Yagouri ran into an Egyptian ambush.

Tanks and other missile groups were carefully dispersed astride the road in concealed positions . . . a force [Yagouri's] of 100–110 tanks charged south on a front of 1–1½ kilometres astride the road. The missile screen in depth held fire according to plan, as did the rest of the troops, until the leading enemy tanks reached the line of the lateral road . . . the whole area churned up into a mass of exploding shells.[4]

The Israelis lost at least thirty-five tanks and Yagouri, to his disgust, got prime time on Egyptian television.

Astonishingly, and fortunately for Israel, the deviant Sharon was not dismissed on the spot. Dayan in fact recommended that he exchange posts with Gonen, but Golda Meir refused to countenance this. Israel was not only in the middle of a war. She was also in the middle of an election campaign, and Sharon was the leader of an opposition party. It was Elazar who came up with a solution, appointing Haim Bar Lev to the new post of 'the Chief of Staff's representative in Sinai'. Bar Lev would be the power behind Gonen's weaker throne; he would look after Sharon, or so it was hoped. Days later, like Gonen before him, Bar Lev would be unsuccessfully pushing for Sharon's removal.

While this group were behaving like German generals in front of Moscow, the rather less chaotic northern command was carrying the war back to the Syrian armistice line. On Golan a counter-attack had been launched on 8 October. A new division under Peled moved up the Gamla Rise and El Al roads towards Rafid, while another new division under Laner forced back the Syrians on the Yahudiye, Tapline and Sindiana roads. Through that day and the next the Israelis battled forward against heavy resistance, until by the morning of the 10th the two forces converged to trap the Syrians in a large pocket around their Khushniye concentration area. By noon the Syrians were back over their 6 October start-line, 850 tanks the poorer.

The Syrian losses, though enormous, were not decisive. The Syrian Army was far from beaten. More than 500 tanks remained for use, and the missile system continued to claim Israeli planes. The defence system on the ground, laid out with typical depth and thoroughness, stretched back down the road to Damascus. And a massive Soviet air-lift of spare parts and replacements was already under way. The Israeli objective – the 'silencing' of the Syrian front – was some days away from attainment. It was still impossible to undertake a large-scale transfer of forces from Golan to Sinai.

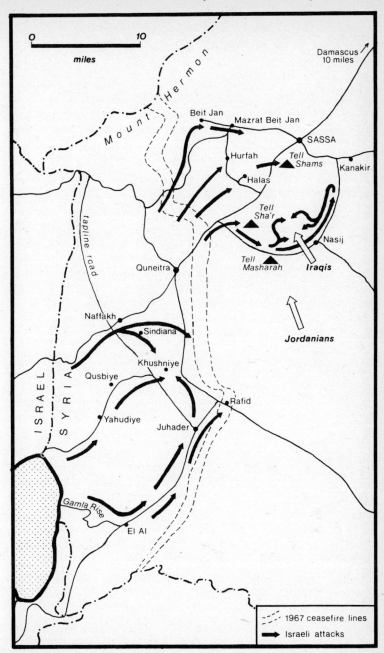

20. Golan: the Israeli counter-attack, 8–13 October

This was one of the three factors holding up an Israeli offensive against the Egyptian bridgehead in Sinai. The second was the deployment of the two Egyptian armoured divisions on the *west* bank of the Canal. Until those 700 or so tanks crossed over to lead the expected Egyptian attack into inner Sinai, any Israeli attempt to establish a cross-Canal presence would be suicidal. Accordingly, Sharon's repeated requests for permission to launch such an attack were repeatedly turned down. Elazar and Bar Lev were prepared to wait. For the Egyptian armour to cross, for the Army as a whole to leave the relative safety of its missile cover. Then the enemy would bear the burden of attacking, the Israelis would throw them back, and an invasion of the west bank would have every chance of success.

The third factor prohibiting an Israeli attack was the strongest of the three. A matter of hours after the war began, the Israeli government had formally asked for a military supply air-lift from the United States. It expected reasonably swift compliance, but instead got Henry Kissinger. The U.S. Secretary of State was determined to preserve détente with the Soviets, and it was clearly endangered by the present situation in the Middle East. Furthermore the *new* situation provoked by Arab success in the first days of the war – in effect, a limited Israeli defeat – promised to provide a permanent solution to the aggravatingly eternal Arab–Israeli problem. If Israel could be forced to accept a ceasefire *in situ,* thus legitimising the Arab gains, the path to an overall settlement might suddenly appear a little less overgrown. And the only way Israel could be bludgeoned into accepting such humiliation was by means of withholding arms supplies. Kissinger at first refused arms deliveries outright and, once pressured into agreeing them in principle, did his best to obstruct their delivery.

It almost worked. By the end of the week the I.D.F. was running dangerously low on tank and artillery shells and air-craft. The Israeli government, its back to the wall, was ready to accept a ceasefire along the lines proposed by Kissinger. The shortages made an offensive in Sinai out of the question. Israel, it seemed, would not get the chance to hit back at the Egyptians.

IV

In Cairo the situation was judged differently. President Sadat
had started this war with one aim in mind: to break the deadlock by forcing the two superpowers to impose a settlement on
the reluctant Israelis. Compared to this a few miles of desert
meant very little. He would not accept any ceasefire proposals
that did not include cast-iron guarantees of a general political
settlement. It would be that or nothing. With his troops poised,
so he thought, for a triumphal march into Sinai, Sadat found it
hard to believe that it might be nothing. He rejected Kissinger's
terms.

The Israelis gratefully withdrew their acceptance. The U.S.
government, lacking meaningful alternatives, began to match
the Soviet air-lift to the Arabs with one of their own to Israel.
The I.D.F. could breathe again.

The other two prerequisites of an Israeli attack across the
Canal were also becoming available. On the morning of 11
October the Israeli forces on Golan moved across the 1967
ceasefire line. 7th Armoured Brigade attacked north of the
main Damascus road, fighting its way into Beit Jan, Hurfah
and Halas that afternoon. The next day the brigade took
Mazrat Beit Jan and advanced to the outskirts of Sassa, but
an attempt to take the Tell Shams feature was thrown back
with heavy Israeli losses. The Syrians were conducting an
orderly retreat; there was no repeat of the panic flights of
1967.

The main problem confronting the Syrian Army was a growing gap between the two divisions retreating north-eastwards
and the one division retreating eastwards and south-eastwards.
On 11 October, Laner's armoured brigades poured through this
gap to take Tell Sha'r. On the following day a swift drive
through Nasij and up the Kanakir road threatened the Syrian
position at Sassa from the east. This key-point on the main
road was now under attack from both sides.

The situation was saved by the timely arrival of the Iraqi
3rd Armoured Division south-east of Nasij. The arrival of
this formation was the high-point of its endeavours, for
Laner, drawing back the armour on the Kanakir road, quickly
constructed a trap for this new threat on his flank. The
Iraqis duly obliged by driving their 180 tanks straight into

it, losing 80 of them in the process.

From this date – the evening of 12 October – the front settled down into a noisy stability, with the Israelis holding a large new bulge of Syrian territory. The arrival of Jordanian armour to bolster the Arab forces had little impact, offset as it was by the deporable lack of coordination between the different Arab commands. On one occasion the Jordanian armour launched a pre-arranged attack on the Israeli positions around Tell Masharah, but before reaching the enemy the Jordanian tanks had been pummelled by supposedly supporting fire from the Iraqis and strafed by the Syrian Air Force. The Israelis had already started shifting units south to Sinai.

The Egyptians were also preparing to move. Their original plan had envisaged a major armoured offensive, aimed at Bir Gifgafa (Refidim), between 11 and 15 October. This third phase, unlike the crossing and establishment phases, had not been planned in any detail, and as the first week went by it seemed that Ismail was reluctant to take the obvious risks involved. He suspected, quite correctly as it turned out, that once beyond their missile cover his tanks would once again prove less than a match for their Israeli counterparts.

But events and people were pushing Ismail into the great gamble. It was clear that the military success so far achieved was insufficient for the political results intended; moreover the situation on the Syrian front would probably soon release Israeli forces for action in Sinai. The Syrians, who for a week had been bearing the brunt of Israeli strength, were not surprisingly demanding that the Egyptians do something in Sinai to relieve the pressure. By 11 October Ismail had little room left for manoeuvre. On that day the two Egyptian armoured divisions west of the Canal emerged from their lairs, and began crossing into Sinai.

Through 13 October the Egyptian forces mounted probing attacks all along the line, and on the following day they began the full-scale offensive, launching close to a thousand tanks against a similar number in the Israeli line. The attack, though reasonably well conceived, was distinguished by a doleful lack of tactical imagination. The Egyptian tanks, like the Israeli tanks a week before, charged headlong against well-positioned anti-tank guns, anti-tank missiles and hull-down tanks. Outside the missile umbrella the I.A.F. and E.A.F. met on equal terms with equally predictable results. By afternoon the Egyptian armour was withdrawing westwards, leaving over 250 tanks scattered across the sands. The Egyptian Army had shot its bolt. Now Sharon would have his glory.

V

For several years the Israeli High Command had been considering the problems involved in mounting a cross-Canal operation, and certain preparations had already been made. A mile or so north of where the Suez Canal enters the Great Bitter Lake, opposite Deir Suweir, the Israeli sand rampart had been hollowed-out, re-covered and marked with red bricks. Nearby in the desert a walled vehicle park had been constructed for the protection of a crossing force.

By the second week of the war the Egyptians were firmly in control of the east bank, and the Israelis might have expected a certain amount of difficulty in reaching this proposed cross-

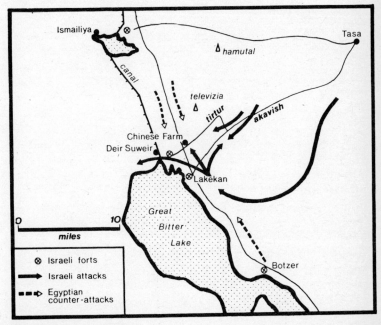

21. Chinese Farm

ing-site. But here they had a stroke of fortune. During the unauthorised and abortive attack of 9 October one of Sharon's armoured brigades had uncovered a priceless piece of intelligence. Between the northern flank of the Egyptian Third Army, close to the Botzer fort, and the southern flank of the Second Army, *opposite Deir Suweir*, was a gap twenty-five kilometres wide. The way seemed clear.

To Sharon, of course, it had been clear since the war began. The failure of his earlier attacks had been caused not by the Egyptians but by inadequate support from his own side. This nonsense aside, it was generally agreed that only on the west bank were conditions ideal for the classic Israeli armoured drive, only there could the deadlock be broken. Until 14 October Sharon had been restrained by his superiors, but in the aftermath of the Egyptian armoured débâcle on that day, the promise of success at last came to outweigh the risks involved. Late that evening Elazar gave Sharon the green light. He was to seize a bridgehead on the far bank and funnel Adan's division through to the plains beyond.

At 17.00 on the next day, 15 October, one of Sharon's armoured brigades attacked the Egyptian positions on the 'Televizia' and 'Hamutal'* features with the aim of drawing Egyptian forces away from the crossing area. Two hours later the main force struck across country towards the Great Bitter Lake. The leading armoured brigade under Reshef was to seize the crossroads near Chinese Farm** and move north-eastwards along the Akavish and Tirtur roads, clearing them of Egyptian forces. Behind Reshef were a paratroop brigade and a unit of tanks from another of Sharon's armoured brigades; these were to cross the Canal by boat and raft, and establish a three-mile-deep bridgehead on the western bank. Through this corridor – along Tirtur and Akavish, through the Chinese Farm crossroads, over the Canal, and into 'Africa' (as Sharon insisted on calling it) – Adan's division would drive with a pre-constructed bridge. All in the one night.

From the beginning the operation fell behind Sharon's grossly optimistic schedule. The paratroopers and tanks got

* These names, and those of the roads mentioned below, are Israeli military designations.
** Chinese Farm was so-named by Israeli soldiers who, in overrunning the area in 1967, discovered ideographic documents. The area had in fact been used by Japanese agronomists for irrigation experiments.

across the Canal before dawn, but only by dashing through a minute gap between the Lake and the spreading battle around Chinese Farm. Reshef had run into real trouble, finding his force 'suddenly in the midst of a vast army, with as far as they could see concentrations of hundreds of trucks, guns, tanks, missiles, radar units and thousands of troops milling around'.[5]

The Israelis had unwittingly driven straight into the administrative H.Q. of the Egyptian 16th Infantry Division, which the day before had also taken in the battered 21st Armoured Division. As Reshef's force arrived at the crossroads 'thousands of weapons of all types opened fire in all directions and the whole area as far as the eye could see went up in flames'.[6] The force sent up Akavish broke through, only for the Egyptians to reseal the road in its wake. As dawn broke the Israelis were suffering heavy and mounting casualties around Chinese Farm, the roads were still closed to Adan and the pre-constructed bridge, and across the Canal a small force of paratroopers and 28 tanks were apprehensively awaiting an Egyptian counter-attack.

Was Sharon deterred? A foolish question. He wanted to push on into 'Africa'. It was too quiet for him in the as-yet-unnoticed bridgehead, like 'Acapulco' as one of his troops commented. Gonen was far from amused. He furiously ordered Sharon to stay put and organise the bridgehead. Sharon refused, arguing with a brilliance bordering on lunacy that to dig in on the west bank would render his force more conspicuous, and so invite counter-action. After ending the conversation as abusively as possible Sharon hung up, split his tank force up into raiding parties, and sent them out into Africa. A few hours later he had the nerve to ask Gonen and Bar Lev for reinforcements for his half-empty bridgehead. They replied that their hands were full doing Sharon's job of opening the corridor on the east bank.

Doubtless Gonen and Bar Lev were right to refuse Sharon reinforcements, but Sharon was right to send out his raiding parties. The Egyptians had been severely unbalanced by the drive on Chinese Farm; it was important that they remained so. Thirty-three years before, Guderian had been blissfully driving his tanks across northern France when ordered to halt by his High Command. 'I neither would nor could agree to these orders, which involved the sacrifice of the element of surprise we had gained,"[7] he later wrote. Subtract the Prussian stiffness, and the tone is identical to Sharon's. The rationale is also the same. Surprise, speed, keep the enemy guessing. Particularly an enemy like the Egyptian Army, proverbially rigid, far easier to break than to bend.

The Egyptian command structure was little better equipped to deal with Sharon than it had been in 1956. The difference between this army and previous Egyptian armies lay in Ismail's acknowledgement of the lack of initiative at the lower levels, and the framing of his strategy accordingly. The plan for the Egyptian crossing had required precious little initiative from anyone, it had almost unrolled itself. But once the Israelis seized the initiative, Ismail swiftly inherited all the consequences of the traditional Egyptian lack of it in the field. It was odds-on that accurate information would take an endless time reaching his underground bunker outside Cairo, but until it did so, and a new flow of orders worked their way down the hierarchy, the Egyptian Army was virtually paralysed.

Sharon knew all this in his bones. He did not know that the west shore of the Great Bitter Lake was held by Palestinian and Kuwaiti units, thus further complicating the Egyptian command channels, or that when Ismail did get news, on the *afternoon* of 16 October, it would be of five amphibious tanks crossing the Lake. But he could have guessed something of this nature would occur. He knew instinctively that the Egyptians would not, could not, react speedily to a barely visible threat.

When attacked, of course the Egyptians fought back hard. Hence the three days of bloody battle around Chinese Farm as Bar Lev, Gonen and Adan sought to secure the corridor through to Sharon's 'Acapulco' on the west bank. Here the threat to the Egyptians was visible in the extreme, and by evening on the 16th C.-in-C. Shazli himself had arrived to take charge.

Through the day the Israelis had been slowly working their way through the dense lay-out of minefields and anti-tank positions, seeking to avoid the hail of rockets and missiles zooming around them. That night, with infantry support, Adan's division tried once again to open the Tirtur and Akavish roads. The former stayed shut, but with an Israeli paratroop brigade desperately holding the ground between the two roads, the bridge was safely transported down Akavish before dawn. Early the next morning the Egyptians finally mounted counter-attacks, from both north and south, against the corridor. Unfortunately these attacks were ill-timed; the Israelis had time to repulse 21st Armoured Division's thrust from the north while the southern Egyptian force – the 96 tanks of the 25th Armoured Brigade – was still moving up the shore of the Great Bitter Lake. Reaching the vicinity of the Lakekan fort this force suddenly found itself under attack from three separate directions. 86 Egyptian tanks went up in smoke.

The corridor was now secure, if hardly peaceful. On the far side of the Canal Sharon's raiding parties were destroying SAM sites on the ground, and so opening up the sky for the I.A.F. At noon on 17 October Adan's armour began moving across the newly-laid bridge to consolidate the African bridgehead. Late the following day a disgraced Shazli would bury his head in his hands and say: 'The war is over. A catastrophe has occurred.' Indeed it had.

VI

Through the next three days, as Adan's tanks rolled south towards the Gineifa hills, the pressures for a ceasefire were growing on the government in Israel. Yet again the I.D.F. was struggling to complete the final act before the superpowers dropped the safety curtain.

Sadat was daily more ready for an end to the adventure, provided the conditions were not too humiliating. Two days earlier Kosygin had stepped off a plane at Cairo airport; in his briefcase were satellite pictures of the Egyptian armoured débâcle on the 14th. Soon he was closeted with a rapidly sobering Egyptian president and new pictures of Sharon's African bridgehead. Somehow the Americans would have to be persuaded to halt the rampant Israelis, or the Soviets themselves would have no alternative but outright intervention to save Egypt.

As it turned out, the Americans would need little persuasion. In Washington the drift towards superpower confrontation had not gone unnoticed, despite the thick dark clouds of

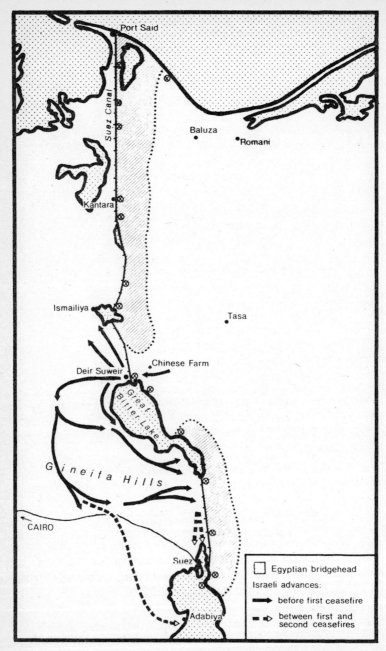

22. Israel crosses into Africa, 19-24 October

Watergate. But this was not all. On 17 October the O.P.E.C.
oil ministers had met in Kuwait, and a five per cent cutback
in production had been agreed, until such time as United
Nations resolutions were 'implemented' in the Middle East.
It was the Saudis who had kept the figure down to a moderate
level, for during talks in Washington that same day they had
received personal assurances from Nixon of a positive American response. They were all the more chagrined, therefore,
when on the following day Nixon, without apparently considering how such behaviour would be construed, sought
formal Congress approval for the military air-lift to Israel. The
Saudis naturally construed it as a slap in the face and Feisal,
in true desert style, slapped back twice as hard. The daily
delivery of 650,000 barrels of oil to the U.S. was abruptly
discontinued.

This was a serious matter. When a flustered Brezhnev came
in over the hot line on the evening of the 19th, Kissinger was
ready. Early the next morning he took off for Moscow.

And while he stared down at the frozen Arctic, seeking
inspiration for mutually agreeable ceasefire proposals, the
Israelis were pressing south towards the Cairo–Suez road, lifeline of the Egyptian Third Army. An Israeli presence on the
west bank was insufficient; it would merely provide a counter
to the Egyptian presence on the east bank. The Israelis were
not thinking in terms of symmetry. They intended to reach the
Gulf of Suez, and comprehensively cut off the Third Army.
That would be victory. But would there be time?

By late evening on the 21st, Kissinger and Brezhnev had
agreed the details of a classically vague ceasefire resolution.
The two parties would cease firing, and then simultaneously
implement Resolution 242 and begin direct negotiations. This
was to come into effect twelve hours after its acceptance by
the Security Council that night – 06.53 Israeli time on
Monday, 22 October. Golda Meir begged Nixon for an extension – for a 'tidying of positions' – and was turned down flat.
Perhaps the American president brought to her notice the lack
of proposals for *enforcing* the ceasefire.

Perhaps he did not. It made little difference. The Israelis
were not to be stopped. At 18.53 they had only advanced units
on the Cairo–Suez road, and the war went on. Through the
23rd Israeli forces pushed south to reach the Gulf of Suez at

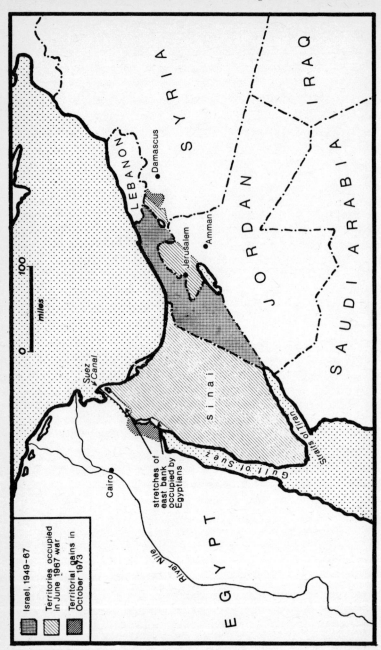

23. 24 October, 1973

Adabiya. The Egyptians, whether the superpowers liked it or not, had been defeated.

They did not like it. The Soviets accused the Americans of betrayal, and threatened unilateral intervention. Kissinger and Nixon responded with an American nuclear alert. The Soviets said it had been a misunderstanding. Third Army remained trapped, and the war was over. Close to 20,000 Arabs, and 2,500 Israelis, had died. Israel, having won yet another war, prepared to lose yet another peace.

Chapter 15

THE WHEEL TURNS FULL CIRCLE

Developments 1973–1978

> As war continues, both sides come more and more to resemble each other. The uroborus eats its own tail. The wheel turns full circle. Shall we realise that We and They are shadows of each other? We are Them to Them as They are Them to Us. When will the veil be lifted? When will the charade turn to Carnival? Saints may still be kissing lepers. It is high time that the leper kissed the saint.
>
> (R. D. Laing, *The Politics of Experience*)

I

On Friday 21 December, some eight weeks after the war's conclusion, representatives of Egypt, Jordan and Israel met at Geneva. Beneath a sepia fresco depicting 'man's advance from barbarism' Israel accused the Arabs of the 'mentality and ideology that produced the gas chambers' and the Arabs accused Israel of 'aggression, mass murder and terror'.[1] At least they were talking.

This rather shoddy miracle was largely the work of Henry Kissinger. The American Secretary of State had been determined that this time the warring parties would at least reach the peace table. For one thing, there was the personal kudos involved in solving the insoluble; for another, this time American interests were at stake. The détente with the Soviet Union, which formed the basis of the Nixon–Kissinger foreign policy, had been visibly shaken by the October war. A shared desire to avoid confrontation had somehow produced an American nuclear alert. And if this boded ill for future crises, the Arab oil embargo was already taking its toll on the western economies, and Feisal was showing no inclination to slacken the pressure. Peace, or at least visible progress towards peace, was the order of the day.

The Arabs were relatively willing. Egypt and Syria had both fought hard against the hitherto invincible Israelis. They might have lost, but military honour and national pride were reasonably satisfied. Now, after two decades of crippling their economies to maintain swollen war machines, the front-line states were ready to talk. With the oil weapon and justice on their side, the Arabs were hopeful that the U.S. would drag a reluctant Israel to Geneva.

Israel was an angry and confused nation. The cost of the war had been high, both in casualties sustained and in the level of damage done to the already fragile economy. Furthermore, the obvious unpreparedness of the political and military establishment to face the Arab attack raised grave questions as to that establishment's continuing vitality. But the war had at least been won. Why could not this military triumph be translated into political gains? In fact the reverse was happening. Israel's diplomatic isolation was growing as European and African governments, for reasons of oil and Third World solidarity respectively, deserted the still-floating Zionist ship. This perhaps could be coped with; it was to the United States, and to her alone, that Israel was irreversibly beholden. But the continuing potency of the I.D.F. rested, as the recent war had all too clearly demonstrated, on continuing U.S. military deliveries. The economy was equally dependent on U.S. government aid and the continuing flow of contributions from the American Jewish community. And the U.S. wanted peace. Israel, expecting to be as ill-served by peace as by war, went to Geneva.

Kissinger had got most of the parties involved to the conference table, but he could not extend public negotiations beyond the mutual mud-slinging of the opening speeches. It is doubtful whether he expected to. The positions of the two sides were clearly too far apart for successful negotiations towards an overall settlement. King Feisal had made it quite clear that the oil embargo would not be lifted until Israel withdrew behind her pre-1967 boundaries or, more specifically, until the King himself was able to pray in an Arab-controlled east Jerusalem. The Israelis were obviously not about to make such a withdrawal overnight, if ever. Kissinger was therefore more interested in providing the semblance of progress towards peace. The problem should be tackled step by step, starting with the easier issues – Sinai and Golan – and moving gradually, in an atmosphere of growing mutual trust, towards the core of the problem: the West Bank and the Palestinians. If Kissinger could just take one step, he was convinced that Feisal could be persuaded to moderate his stance. By playing on the Saudi régime's fear of radical, and particularly Soviet, influence in the area, and by promising continued American pressure on Israel, Kissinger hoped both to diffuse the oil crisis and secure moderate Arab support for a slower, American-inspired progress towards peace.

Accordingly, his behind-the-scenes efforts at Geneva were devoted to securing an agreement between Israel and Egypt for a limited military disengagement in Sinai. Since this was clearly in both sides' interest – Egypt would have her October gains legitimised, Israel would be able to withdraw her troops from an increasingly untenable position on the west bank – only mutual suspicion and the Israeli election held up the signing until mid-January.

This Sinai disengagement, and the similar Golan agreement in May, certainly reduced the risk of a renewed outbreak of fighting; the Saudis lifted the embargo in March. So far, so good. But did it bring an overall settlement any nearer? Or perhaps obviate the need for one? It possibly occurred to Kissinger – as it doubtless did to the Israelis – that one or two 'steps' might remove the need for more. If Egypt and Syria could be bought off, then who would wield a sword on behalf of the Palestinians?

The answer, of course, was that Egypt and Syria could not be bought off, and that any such hopes rested in a remarkable ignorance of Arab realities. There are three traditional ways of dividing the Arab world into two: in terms of ideology, wealth, and proximity to Israel. These divisions tend to coincide. The richest, most reactionary states have been furthest from the fighting; the poorest, most radical, right in the front line. But this has not meant that the former group have all the advantages. In the Middle East power is measured not only in wealth, but in ideological dreams and commitment to the Arab cause vis-à-vis Israel. If few revolutionary groups can ignore the constraints imposed by host governments and the need for financial support, few régimes to the right of centre can ignore the radical call to arms without risking the wrath of their neighbours or their own populace.

This cross-cutting web of wealth and dreams has imposed a formidable series of political checks and balances on the Middle Eastern states and movements. If Egypt's leaders can only swing as far to the left as the Saudis and Americans will allow, without falling once more into dependence on the Soviets and a new war with Israel, then they can only swing as far to the right as pan-Arab sympathies – largely the prerogative of the leftist groups – will allow, without losing both their position in the Arab world and the support of their own people. For most other Arab states the situation is similar. Syria balances uneasily between the need for Egyptian and Saudi support in the confrontation with Israel, and the ideological pull of Iraq and the Palestinians. The Saudis need peace to lessen the influence of extremists, and they need the extremists to legitimise the pan-Arab acceptability of the peace. The end-result of all this is a narrow Arab consensus, which any Arab state or movement ignores at its peril. Just as the P.L.O. could expect no support from this consensus for the dream of a secular socialist Palestine, so any Egyptian or Syrian leadership seeking a separate peace with Israel would find itself an Arab pariah. Rather, everyone would have to stick together, and make sacrifices. The Egyptians and the Syrians would have to carry on bearing their military burden, the Saudis to help them pay for it. The Palestinians would have to sacrifice their sweetest dreams for the easy sleep of the Sheikhs. It was the only way. Kissinger's notion of separating the Arabs, and dealing with them piecemeal, was a fool's dream. The following eighteen months would prove as much.

II

In Egypt, Sadat was pursuing internal policies appropriate to his new international friendships, shifting the country away from the Nasserite vision of Arab socialism in the direction of a more liberalised economy and society which would be fuelled by Saudi wealth and, hopefully, American investment. Soviet–Egyptian relations, which had begun to deteriorate in 1970, were further damaged by Soviet behaviour during the war – most notably the Soviet pressure for a ceasefire as early as

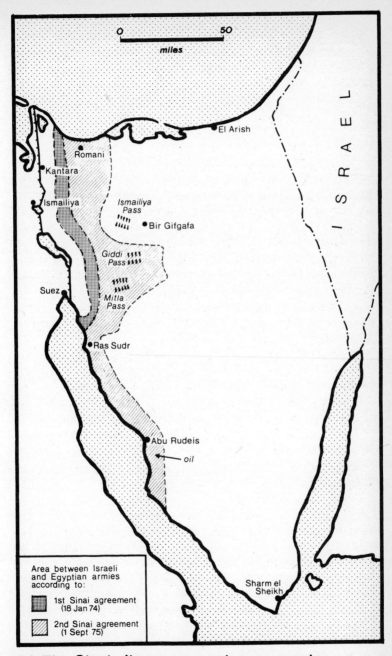

Area between Israeli
and Egyptian armies
according to:

1st Sinai agreement
(18 Jan 74)

2nd Sinai agreement
(1 Sept 75)

24. The Sinai disengagement agreements

6 October – and by Sadat's ever-growing admiration for the
Americans. The Soviets responded to the latter with a go-slow
on arms shipments; Sadat replied with thinly-veiled insults.
Internally the Egyptian leader strengthened his position by removing the influential Nasserite, Mohammed Heikal, from the
editorship of *al Ahram*. He demonstrated his desire for peace
by commencing the clearing of the Suez Canal. All this
naturally pleased his friends in Washington and Riyadh, and
if his fellow-Arabs were less effusive, for the moment they
were prepared to suspend judgement.

Israel had no such sense of direction. At the end of 1973 the
general election had returned Labour – and Golda Meir – to
power, but with a barely workable majority. The nation was
feeling indecisive, and proportional representation insured that
the government would reflect it. In April the Agranat Commission reported its findings on the October crisis, and though
Golda Meir herself was exonerated, the level of recrimination
was sufficient for her to call it a day. The weaker figure of
former Chief of Staff Rabin took over the business of shuffling
majorities in the Knesset.

On the international front Israel was receiving conflicting
messages. Through March and April, as the Egyptians made
soothing noises to the west, the Syrians were conducting a
low-level battle of attrition in the north. And while the Americans were putting continuous diplomatic pressure on Israel for
a moderate stance, the hard-line Palestinian groups were eliciting only anger and defiance with their anti-civilian raids of
the early summer.

The Israeli government tried to keep pace. Rabin persuaded
his colleagues to accept a disengagement agreement for Golan,
and even to evict some squatters from the West Bank area of
Nablus. But, just in case anyone might mistakenly view the
latter decision as a sign of impending concessions vis-à-vis the
West Bank, the squatters were told to squat elsewhere in
the occupied region. Further, Israeli plans for the future of
Jerusalem, released later in the year, featured a vast conurbation
stretching from Bethlehem to Ramallah, and east as far as the
new Red Heights settlement on the road to Jericho. Meanwhile the I.A.F. pounded the refugee camps in southern
Lebanon.

In October Kissinger conducted another four-capitals-a-day

tour, but to little apparent effect. Sadat was all for a second
Sinai deal, and the Israelis expressed guarded interest, but no
one else was very keen. The Saudis cautiously refused to commit themselves; the Syrians could only conceive of such a deal
if it were linked to another one on Golan. But on Golan there
was little ground to trade; the I.D.F. could make no more
than a token retreat without falling back into the Jordan
valley. The Israelis refused. The Syrians, with equal logic,
decided that there was no future in bilateral dealing, and that
there would have to be an overall settlement – including the
Palestinians – or nothing. The Palestinians naturally agreed
with them. After a year of vicious internal squabbling the
P.L.O. was ready to reappear on the world stage. At the Rabat
summit in October 1974 the P.L.O. was decreed to be the 'sole
legal representative of the Palestinian people', and armed with
such credentials Arafat had triumphantly appeared before the
U.N. General Assembly.

All this doubtless gave Sadat cause for thought. Two impera-
tives guided his policy: the need to keep the peace ball rolling,
and the need to keep his fellow Arab leaders happy. For the
moment he decided that the former was more important. He
was still having trouble with the Soviets. A projected visit by
Brezhnev was cancelled at short notice; the Soviets continued
to refuse either a moratorium on Egyptian debts or further
arms deliveries. The Egyptian economy appeared to be sinking
beneath the weight of military expenditure and the top-heavy
bureaucracy inherited from the Nasserite age. Sadat needed his
friendship with America. He needed pressure on Israel for
peace, and investment for the economy. He would risk the
wrath of his fellow Arabs for a second deal in Sinai. But it
would have to be a good one.

Through 1975 the bargaining continued. A Kissinger tour in
March failed to produce any miracles – the Israelis wanted too
much for too little, four years' non-belligerence from Egypt for
a retreat to the middle of the Sinai passes. The familiar American stick and carrot were produced soon after; Ford
mentioned the dreaded word 'Geneva' and promised a huge
arms bonanza. Israel, by midsummer, had agreed to a line
behind the passes. Sadat looked warily over his shoulder, saw
that Syria was fully involved in confronting Iraq and the
growing crisis in Lebanon, received a very discreet 'yes' from

King Khaled (Feisal had been assassinated in March), cut the non-belligerency period in two, and signed.

Syria was furious, the P.L.O. likewise. Sadat was obliged to close down the latter's Cairo radio station. But this was only a temporary measure. Without the P.L.O.'s agreement there could be no peace, and Sadat had now to woo them back to the fold. One thing was clear. He had stretched the limits of the Arab consensus as far as it could be safely stretched. This had been the last step for the 'step by step' approach. Now there would have to be a leap. But only those at the centre of the conflict – Israel and the P.L.O. – could now make meaningful concessions. America would have to pressure the former, the Arab world the latter. The wheel had come full circle since 1947. Once again the rival claimants for Palestine would have to meet face to face.

III

The prospect of a U.S. presidential election year offered the Israelis a respite from Kissinger's sticks and carrots. There were no votes to be had from antagonising America's large and influential Jewish population. Neither would the Arab states cause much trouble. Egypt was still busily moving away from 'Nasserism', waiting on American promises, and attempting to justify its pan-Arab integrity to the rest of the Arab world. This itself was in some disarray. The Syrian régime was fighting a two-front ideological campaign against Egyptian moderation and Iraqi extremism, and seeking a compensating two-front friendship with King Hussein and the P.L.O. In the Lebanon, class, communal and national allegiances had finally sorted themselves into a civil war of growing ferocity, which fully absorbed the military energies of the Palestinians.

But if Israel expected a breathing-space she was sadly mistaken. The weak Rabin government found itself subject to growing economic and political pressures. The burden of defence expenditure continued to weaken the economy; the Israeli pound was devalued ten times between August 1975 and August 1976. Only the flow of U.S. aid prevented an economic catastrophe. As regards military supplies the situation was the same. Although Israel was making progress in the development of a domestic arms industry – building its own Kfir planes, Ben-Gurion tanks, helicopters and missile boats – the source of the necessary capital remained the U.S. By 1976, American aid accounted for thirty-five per cent of the I.D.F. budget. This growing dependence implied a growing vulnerability to U.S. pressure, should any incoming president choose to exert it.

As has been seen, there now remained only one area in which such pressure could be exerted, that of the Palestinian question. And through 1976 the Palestinians living under Israeli rule were at last beginning to raise their national voice. A schoolchildren's riot on 13 March led, two weeks later, to the first sustained demonstrations on the occupied West Bank. Mayors resigned, curfews were imposed, numerous arrests were made. A general strike was called for 30 March, and half the Arab work force stayed at home. In the accompanying violence six Arab villagers were killed and over three hundred arrested. The Israelis, with that endearing madness which informs so many of their actions, went ahead with the scheduled local elections; the results were a triumph for the nationalist cause in general and the P.L.O. in particular. Ominously for Israel's future, there were echoes of the West Bank disturbances inside Israel 'proper'. And a hostile Arab populace posed greater dangers to Israel than the Arab armies ever had. Either there would have to be an overall settlement, or a tightening of 'security measures' in the occupied areas.

The Rabin government continued to pursue its vacillatory course. New restrictions were imposed, but hardly with an iron hand. The Israeli failure to agree an overall policy with regard to the illegal Jewish settlements in the occupied territories merely reflected a failure to agree on the eventual fate of those territories. This political weakness went hand-in-hand with Israel's continuing military strength. The lengthening reach of the I.D.F.'s potency was well demonstrated by the Entebbe raid of early July 1976. The hostages were brought home. But, in the long term, what use was such military potency when the primary problems were political? And what use was a lengthening reach when they lay on Israel's own doorstep?

On the other side of the great divide, the P.L.O. was not without problems of its own. The Arab world had accepted it as the 'sole legitimate voice of the Palestinian people', and the U.N. had effectively legitimised this claim by allowing the

P.L.O. to participate in the Security Council debate on Palestine in early 1976. But this did not imply an acceptance of either the possibility or desirability of implementing official P.L.O. policy. This still centred on the rights of the Palestinians to their homes in Palestine, to the consequent destruction of the Zionist state, and to the creation of a multi-national secular state in its stead. In private, moderates like Arafat would concede their willingness to establish, as a first step, a Palestinian state in the occupied territories of the West Bank and the Gaza Strip. If the price of such a state was a recognition of Israel, then perhaps it would have to be paid. And if this mini-state proved too small, then, as Arafat said on more than one occasion, there was always Hussein's Jordan.

But there were many Palestinians who disagreed. Some were still members of the P.L.O., others had joined the Rejection Front. Led by Habash's P.F.L.P. – now outside the P.L.O. – and supported by Iraq and Libya, the Rejection Front was opposed to any recognition of Israel, to any abandonment of maximalist goals. They were determined on a path of struggle, and peace was not one of their objectives. Their power would have to be severely limited before the 'acceptance front' – Egypt, Syria (usually), the Saudis, most of the P.L.O. – could present to Israel and the world its public devotion to a minimalist programme. Fortunately for Sadat and his friends, the Lebanese civil war provided the opportunity for bringing the P.L.O. as a whole reluctantly to heel.

The roots of the Lebanese conflict are outside the bounds of this study, and can only be briefly summarised. Basically, the apportioning of political power according to an outdated communal census gave the Lebanese Christians an undeserved predominance in the political structure. This would doubtless have proved less explosive had the Christians not also secured a lion's share of the country's economic bounties. Communal and class lines coincided. And as a result the sporadic communal violence of early summer 1975 quickly escalated into virulent class conflict. The Muslim 'left' faced the Christian 'right'.

The 'rejectionist' Palestinians were soon involved militarily, but the moderates, though obviously in sympathy with the Lebanese Muslim 'left', chose not to commit themselves directly. Lebanon was a sanctuary the P.L.O. could not afford

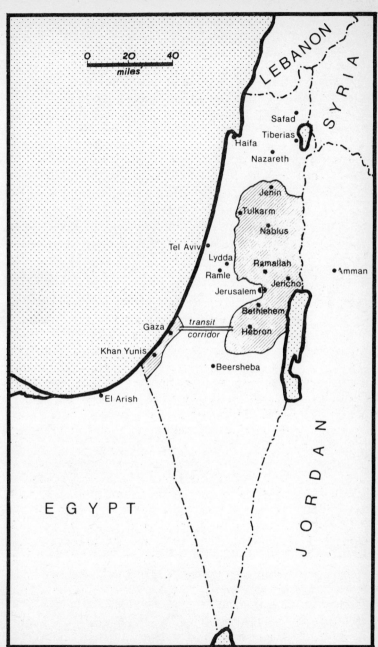

25. The projected Palestinian state

to lose, and most of its leaders were reluctant to take the risk of outright intervention. Rather, they supplied covert aid whilst publicly playing the rôle of mediators.

Such a low-profile Palestinian rôle was not in the interests of the more aggressive Christian groups. They were eager to portray the Lebanese conflict as one between the Lebanese and the Palestinians, and so shroud the socio-economic factors that divided the Lebanese community itself. At the end of the year the Christians attacked the refugee camps in Beirut, and the moderate Palestinian groups were drawn into the war in earnest. Their military training and weaponry quickly earned them the senior rôle in the radical Muslim alliance, and from this point the war started to turn against the Christian groups. The Lebanese Army, hamstrung by the same divisions which divided the country, finally fell apart in January 1976. The political alternatives now seemed reduced to two, either partition or a total 'leftist' victory.

Neither of these prospects excited Lebanon's neighbours: Israel and Syria. The former was loath to intervene too overtly at this stage, fearing the possibility of a full-scale Middle East war. But Syria, once apprised via the U.S. that Israel would accept her intervention, was not so reluctant.

The reasons for the Syrian intervention were complex, but certain obvious interests were involved. Clearly a state controlled by the Muslim 'left' and the Palestinians, perhaps allied to the rival Ba'athists in Iraq, would pose an ideological threat to Assad's régime in Syria. Further, since such a state would inevitably take an extremist line vis-à-vis Israel, Syria would lose her leadership of the 'eastern front', and might well be dragged into a new conflict with Israel, at a time of somebody else's choosing, with probably disastrous consequences.

Assad's first move, in January, was to send large detachments of the Syrian-controlled Palestinian groups, the P.L.A. and Saiqa, into Lebanon. This attempt to assert Syrian control over the 'left' forces failed dismally, as many of the P.L.A.–Saiqa members defected to rival groups. The only remaining alternative was a full-blooded invasion by the Syrian Army, and this duly took place at the end of May. Its rôle was to impose a settlement, which in the prevailing military circumstances meant saving the Christian 'right' from a Muslim 'left' victory. The latter naturally objected, forcibly. The Syrians, with Christian support, turned their guns against their erstwhile allies.

The moderate Arab leaders – Sadat, Hussein, Khaled – were as keen as ever to demonstrate their solidarity with the Palestinians in public, and equally keen in private to see a lessening of their radical influence. The Syrian 'peacekeeping' force was converted into a pan-Arab force by the simple expedient of painting new insignia on the Syrian tanks. Through the summer the Palestinian resistance was slowly ground down.

By September the job had largely been done, and everyone was looking for a settlement. Assad had gained effective control over the Lebanon; in the southern border region the Israeli Army was making its presence felt. The Palestinians were eager to preserve what strength remained to them. The other Arab leaders considered the P.L.O. sufficiently cowed to make it more amenable to a Middle East peace settlement, and sufficiently alive to preserve the romantic fiction of Arab solidarity. Doubtless they observed with satisfaction that Arafat's Fatah, which had borne most of the fighting, had strengthened its leadership within the P.L.O.

All the parties to the Lebanese conflict were summoned to Riyadh and told to patch things up. Sadat forgave Assad for intervening, and Assad forgave Sadat for the second Sinai deal. Khaled wrote some handsome cheques. In November a reluctantly acquiescent P.L.O. watched the (Syrian) tanks of the Arab peacekeeping force roll into Beirut. The Arab consensus had been re-established. All the righteous noise emanating from Libya and Iraq was of little account, for the military power of the front-line states, the ideological power of the P.L.O., and the financial power of the Saudis were all walking a moderate path towards peace with Israel. Or so they hoped.

IV

The inauguration of Jimmy Carter as President of the United States encouraged the Arabs to believe that 1977 was to be the year. Carter had repeatedly stated that a Middle East peace settlement was high on his list of priorities, and his vision of its likely shape was closer to the Arabs' own than that of any previous president. It had to be. Kissinger's deals had removed the wrappings, and beneath the layers of Arab–Israeli enmity, hidden but never transcended, lay the struggle for that stretch of land between the Jordan and the sea. For the first time since Truman's day, American energies would have to be devoted to the problem of Palestine. Sinai and Golan were secondary issues, the residues of Arab nationalism's sense of pride and duty, of Israel's struggle for security in a hostile world. A solution to the territorial issue of Palestine would not satisfy duty or security, but it would certainly make them less a matter of life and death.

Palestine had to be shared. There was, and is, no way around this conclusion short of eternal war. If the Palestinian Jews – now irrevocably Israelis – must concede the justice of the Palestinian Arab cause, then the latter must accept the enduring reality, within pre-1967 borders, of Israel's existence. In 1977 American policy openly recognised the obvious. There had to be a Palestinian state created in the occupied territories of the West Bank and the Gaza Strip.

A settlement built around this proposed state could, many thought, herald a new era of peace, stability and development in the Middle East. Nearly everyone would benefit, not least the settlement's Western and pro-Western backers. The front-line Arab states, free of crippling defence expenditures and fuelled by Western capital, could perhaps halt their economic slide and stabilise their political situations. The oil-rich régimes could say goodbye to their love-hate relationship with the U.S. – love of their 'free world' ally, hatred of their pro-Zionist enemy – and would never again be tempted to interfere with the Western world's energy supplies. Israel would not be abandoned; she would be pressured, by whatever means proved necessary, into a position of the greatest security she had ever known. The Palestinians would have a homeland, albeit a truncated one, and would hopefully expend their radical energies domestically. The Soviet Union would have no future rôle to play in the area.

But, despite the convenience accorded to western interests, such a settlement does seem to offer the optimal solution to the short-term problems of the Middle East. A Palestinian home-land, of any size or dimension, would see an amelioration of their long tragedy, and at least the chance to determine a national future, freed from the pressures of confronting Israel, freed from the need to beg a living from a reluctant and

suspicious Arab world. A slow regularisation of relations between Israel and its Arab neighbours would lessen the risk of
nuclear conflict, both between the states involved and between
their superpower friends. A secure Israel might feel free to
encourage the development of that positive aspect of Zionism's
historical schizophrenia: the collectivism enshrined in the kib-
butzim settlements and many of the old institutions of the
Yishuv's pioneering days. Such a trend within Israel would
certainly mean more, in the long term, for Habash's vision of
a socialist Palestine than the decades of bloody struggle at
present envisaged by the P.F.L.P.

Most important of all, in the absence of any immediate prospect for radical social change in the Middle East, such a settlement represents the only possibility of averting a further war.

Of this, the Arab leaders were fully aware. Peace was in
the interests of their régimes; they were willing to make the
necessary concessions. The Palestinians were in no position,
after Lebanon, to gainsay a 'reasonable settlement'. Differences
remained within the ranks of the P.L.O.; most were prepared
to go to Geneva, but differed as to what they were prepared to
accept. Hints were dropped that Israel would be recognised –
either directly or through acceptance of a revised Resolution
242 – if Israel would herself recognise the P.L.O.'s right to
represent the Palestinian 'nation'. The Arabs waited for
Israel, under pressure from the U.S., to demonstrate a willingness to make concessions.

They were disappointed. Israeli obduracy, far from decreas-
ing, became more brazen with Begin's accession. Reinforced by
a renegade Dayan at the foreign ministry, and by the appointment of the zealous Sharon to oversee the settlement programme, the new prime minister was opposed to concessions of
any kind. The occupied West Bank was blandly denoted a
'liberated area', the P.L.O. characterised as terrorists and
nothing more. Israel, it seemed, would again trust to time and
some fancy footwork to legitimise its 1967 gains. For, in the
last analysis, no one in Jerusalem believed an American administration would really tighten the military and economic screws
in the name of an anti-American Palestinian independence.

At first Carter seemed to have such unbelievable intentions
in mind. He went out of his way to reciprocate Sadat's over-
tures, and encouraged Palestinian hopes by speaking openly of

a national homeland in the occupied territories of the West Bank and Gaza Strip. But as 1977 unrolled it became apparent that Carter saw a *gradual* process, involving both superpowers, as the only guarantee of a stable and lasting peace. He would not pressure Israel into a premature, and thus dangerous, settlement.

For Sadat this was a disaster. He wanted action. But if the bread riots earlier that year had eloquently argued Egypt's need for peace, no one else seemed too interested. The economy continued to decline, the Armed Forces were under-equipped, the Soviets spurned all offers of reconciliation. Sadat needed to pull something out of the bag that would help to quieten popular unrest, whilst simultaneously forcing somebody (preferably Carter) to pay attention to his demands. Unwilling and unable to make war, Sadat tried seduction instead. He went to Jerusalem, addressed the Knesset, even kissed Golda Meir. Though he conceded nothing save the principle of direct negotiation and the recognition implicit in such a visit, the other parties to the dispute were confounded. Assad and the moderate Palestinians hurried to Tripoli for a meeting with the rejectionist states and groups. Sadat was roundly condemned, but there was a conspicuous failure to agree on anything more positive. In the erstwhile 'moderate' camp, Hussein, the Saudis and Carter each in their own way tried to cope with this profoundly unsettling experience. Hussein flew hither and thither, promising everyone that he agreed with them in private but couldn't yet say so publicly. The Saudis, who can more easily afford to practise aloofness, expressed their surprise and nothing else. Carter's views usually coincided with those of the last person to whom he had spoken. Everyone waited for an Israeli response – either negative or positive enough to let them off this new-found hook.

They waited in vain. Begin was at least prepared to talk about substantive issues, and accordingly Israeli–Egyptian discussions were held and committees formed. But the most Israel seemed inclined to offer the Palestinians was a form of *bantustan* on the West Bank, an 'autonomous' region ringed by Israeli guns.

This was less than even Sadat had hoped for. He was now left with two equally perilous alternatives. He could accept Israel's position, or at least ignore it, and push on with a

separate peace, claiming all the while that his fellow Arabs
had left him no choice. But to do so would not only forfeit
Egypt's long-held claim to leadership of the Arab world, it
would also place Sadat's own position in great jeopardy.

It now seems more likely that he will return, cap in hand, to
the wreckage of the Arab consensus, his own room for
manoeuvre severely circumscribed by the enormity of his
aberration. If so, peace in the near future is out of the question.
Rather the stage will be set for another war. It is unlikely that
Israel will wait as she did in 1973. A pre-emptive Israeli strike
on the Golan front will probably open the next war, to be
followed by a comprehensive slaughter in Sinai. Either before
or after this happens, Sadat and Assad will be replaced by more
radical figures, probably of the right and left respectively. The
Soviet Union will re-enter the Middle Eastern arena, and on
terms of her own choosing. Israel might, if pressured, resort to
nuclear weapons, with consequences difficult to foresee. The
Gulf States will cut the flow of oil, with consequences only too
easy to foresee. And inside Israel and the P.L.O. the moderates
will go to the wall, and the notion of an Arab Palestine side
by side with Israel will disappear into historical oblivion.

V

No one should belittle the intensity of Israel's fears. The
obscene growth of anti-Semitism in Europe between the wars,
and its horrific consummation, will not be soon forgotten.
Those who survived, those who reached the shores of Palestine
on the broken-down boats of the post-war exodus, remember
what they escaped. The black-and-white evidence of the Nazi
obscenity has perhaps flickered across our Western television
screens once too often. The pictures are now historical clichés,
leaving us chilled but essentially indifferent, an echo from
another age. But for those, like Begin, who were related to,
those humans who once fleshed out the hideous piles of skele-
tons, it is still the same age. They know what one people can
do to another. And the Arabs, trapped within their own communal anger, have done little to assuage their enemy's fears.

But fear, and guilt, do strange things to the collective mind.
Many Israelis today seem to believe that Palestine was 'empty'

when they arrived, that the Palestinian Arabs were brought in from elsewhere to work on Jewish farms. This is purest fantasy, but fantasies are not without importance. More reasonably, Israelis will claim that the Arabs living inside Israel have both a higher standard of living and greater democratic freedoms than those living in the neighbouring Arab states. This is not too far from the truth, but neither are the similar arguments put forward by the men who rule South Africa. The granting of economic and political rights is of severely limited relevance when the more basic right of self-determination is so flagrantly denied. A Jewish state does not exist to serve Arabs.

The Jews do not have a monopoly on collective tragedy. In fact, in escaping from their own the Jews created one for another people, the Arabs of Palestine. The refusal of Israel to come to terms with, or even recognise, this fact, lies at the heart of the present conflict. The Palestinians cannot be ignored, bought off, or expected to settle somewhere more convenient. In the words of the Cherokee Memorial:

> Were the country to which we are urged much better than it is represented to be, and were it free from the objections we have made to it, still it is not the land of our birth, nor of our affections. It contains neither the scenes of our childhood nor the graves of our fathers . . . What must be the circumstances of a removal when a whole community embracing persons of all classes and every description, from the infant to the man of extreme old age, the sick, the blind, the lame, the improvident, the reckless, the desperate, as well as the prudent, the considerate, the industrious, are compelled to remove by intolerable vexations and persecutions brought upon them in the forms of law?[2]

The Cherokees were driven west. In a recent film a chief described how he went to Washington seeking redress, and was told to 'endeavour to persevere'. 'I thought about that for a long time . . . and then I declared war on the United States.'[3] It is small wonder that the Palestinians have declared war on Israel, and have fought, as the Jews did against the British, with the crude and cruel weapons of the weak.

Two tragedies confront each other in Palestine. Each must make room for the other. It is high time that the leper kissed the saint.

CHRONOLOGY

Section I

1881–2   Modern Jewish migration to Palestine begins.

1882   Great Britain assumes control of Egypt.

1897   First Zionist Congress in Basle.

1904–5   First organised land-purchases by Zionists in Palestine.

1915   McMahon Letter 'promises' British support for eventual Arab independence.

1916   Arab Revolt begins against Ottoman rule. Sykes-Picot Agreement divides the Middle East into British, French and Russian spheres of influence.

1917   Balfour Declaration speaks of the establishment in Palestine of a national home for the Jews.

1918   End of First World War sees dissolution of the Ottoman Empire.

1920   Great Britain granted mandate to administer Palestine. Major Zionist organisations – Histradut, Haganah, Va-ad Leumi – established in Palestine.

1922   Churchill White Paper on future of Palestine.

1929   Serious outbreaks of anti-Zionist Arab rioting, followed by Passfield White Paper advocating restrictions on Jewish immigration and land purchases.

1931   First pan-Arab Congress held in Jerusalem.

1933–6   Rise of anti-Semitism in Europe produces sharp increase in Jewish emigration to Palestine.

1936   Arab General Strike in Palestine; British send in more troops. Egypt becomes nominally independent.

1939   New British White Paper proposes independent Palestine based on then-existing population balance (2 Arabs to 1 Jew), to come into effect in ten years.

1941   Haganah takes part in British invasion of Syria.

1942   Zionists adopt Biltmore Programme.

1944   Irgun resumes terrorist campaign against British occupation.

1945   Formation of Arab League.

1946   Transjordan granted independence.

1947   Britain refers Palestine problem to United Nations, which, in November, decides to partition the territory along communal lines. Civil war begins.

1948   Arab Liberation Army infiltrates into Palestine (January onwards). Jewish community fully mobilised in February.
Jews secure Tiberias, Safad, Haifa and Jaffa in late April and early May.
British mandate ends 14 May. State of Israel proclaimed same day.

Section II

1948

15 May	Five Arab armies invade Palestine
11 June	First ceasefire.
8–18 July	Israelis take the offensive, capturing western Galilee, Nazareth, Lydda and Ramle.
17–18 July	Second ceasefire.
17 September	U.N. mediator Count Bernadotte assassinated in Jerusalem.
15–22 October	First battle for Negev. Israelis take Beersheba.
22 December	Second battle for Negev begins.

1949

January	Israeli advance into Sinai stopped by British ultimatum.
	Armistice talks begin on Rhodes.
March	Israelis seize southern Negev and secure future site of Eilat on Gulf of Aqaba coastline.
	Last armistice (with Transjordan) signed.

1950

May	U.S., Britain and France agree to limit arms sales to Middle East.
July	Israeli Government promulgates Law of Return.

1951

July	Gulf of Aqaba closed to Israeli shipping.
	King Abdullah of Jordan assassinated.

1952

July	King Farouk of Egypt overthrown by officers' coup.
August	Hussein proclaimed King of Jordan.

1953

August	C.I.A.-organised coup overthrows anti-western Mossadeq in Iran.
September	Israel begins diversion of Jordan waters.
December	Ben-Gurion resigns as Prime Minister of Israel.

1954

July	Israeli sabotage operation in Cairo (source of later Lavon Affair).
August	Franco–Israeli arms deal, financed by U.S.
October	*Bat Galim* incident.
	Anglo-Egyptian agreement on evacuation of Suez Canal base.
November	Algerian War of Independence begins.

1955

February	Lavon resigns.
	Ben-Gurion returns as Minister of Defence.
	Israelis launch Gaza Raid.
	Baghdad Pact formed.
April	Bandung Conference.
May	Soviet Union agrees to sell arms to Egypt.
August	*Fedayeen* raids begin from Egypt.
September	Egypt secures Czech Arms Deal.
November	Israel occupies El Auja demilitarised zone.
December	U.S. and Britain offer to finance Aswan Dam.

1956

July	U.S. withdraws offer to finance Aswan Dam.
	Nasser announces nationalisation of Suez Canal.
23 October	Britain, France and Israel agree to coordinated aggression against Egypt in secret Treaty of Sèvres.
29 October	Sinai Campaign begins with paratroop drop near Mitla Pass.
30–31 October	Israelis force their way into Sinai.
5 November	Israelis take Sharm el-Sheikh.
	Anglo-French attack on Port Said.
7 November	Ceasefire.
15 November	U.N.E.F. force arrives to patrol Israeli–Egyptian frontier.

1957

January	Intensive U.S. pressure forces Israeli withdrawal from Sinai (completed in March).
March	Jordan terminates alliance with Britain.
April	Suez Canal re-opened.

1958

February	Egypt and Syria joined in United Arab Republic.
June	Coup in Baghdad topples Iraq's pro-western rulers.
July	Crisis in Lebanon. U.S. marines intervene. British forces in Jordan.
December	Soviet Union agrees to build Aswan Dam.

1959

March	Iraq withdraws from Baghdad Pact.

1961

January	Organisation of Petroleum Exporting Countries (O.P.E.C.) constituted.
September	Syria secedes from U.A.R.

1962

July	Algeria wins independence from France.
September	Republic proclaimed in Yemen.
October	Egypt sends troops to Yemen.

1963

February	Kassem overthrown in Iraq.
March	Ba'ath comes to power in Syria.
June	Eshkol becomes Prime Minister of Israel.
December	Israeli 'National Water Carrier' completed.

1964

January	First Arab 'summit' in Cairo.
May	Shukeiry elected president of newly-formed Palestine Liberation Organisation (P.L.O.)

1965   Fatah begins raids into Israel.

1966

February	Pro-Soviet coup in Syria.
November	Egypt and Syria sign mutual defence pact.
	Israelis conduct Samu Raid into Jordan.

1967

7 April	Major Israeli–Syrian air clash – Syrians invoke defence pact with Egypt.
13 May	Reports of Israeli troop concentration on Syrian border (unconfirmed).
16 May	Nasser asks U.N.E.F. to vacate Sharm el-Sheikh.
23 May	Nasser closes Straits of Tiran.
31 May	Nasser and Hussein bury differences in Cairo.
1 June	Dayan becomes Israeli Minister of Defence.
5 June	Six Day War begins with Israeli air attacks on Arab Air Forces.
5–6 June	Israelis break through into Sinai.
7 June	Old City of Jerusalem falls to Israelis.
9 June	Israeli forces reach Suez Canal in south, and storm Golan Heights in north.
10 June	Six Day War ends.
July	Guerrilla infiltration of occupied West Bank begins.
August	Arab summits in Khartoum. Oil Ministers meet in Baghdad.
November	Resolution 242 adopted by U.N. Security Council. Gunnar Jarring named U.N. Special Representative in the Middle East.

1968

January	Jarring visits Egypt, Jordan and Israel.
21 March	Israelis attack Palestinian camp at Karama.
July	Palestine National Covenant agreed.

	September	Palestinians moving into southern Lebanon.
	October	Israelis begin construction of Bar Lev fortifications on the east bank of the Suez Canal. Israeli forces raid Upper Nile valley.
26	December	P.F.L.P. attack El Al airliner at Athens airport.
28	December	Israeli commandos attack Beirut airport.

1969

	March	Golda Meir succeeds Eshkol as Israeli premier. Nasser declares 1967 ceasefire 'null and void'. War of Attrition begins.
	April–May	Artillery duels across Suez Canal.
19	July	Israeli Air Force attacks Egyptian forces in and immediately behind Canal Zone (raids continuing for the rest of the year).
1	September	Coup in Libya brings Gaddafi to power.
	October	(Lebanese) Cairo Agreement between Lebanese government and Palestinians. Rogers Peace Initiative (made public in December).

1970

	January	Hussein attempts to curb Palestinians, but is forced to back down. Israeli Air Force begins 'deep penetration raids' into Egyptian heartland.
	February	Nasser goes to Moscow for military assistance.
	March	SAM-3s appear in Egyptian defence system.
	April	Soviet pilots defending Egyptian heartland.
	May–July	The battle of the 'missile box'.

August	Ceasefire follows Israel and Egypt accepting Rogers proposals.
6 September	P.F.L.P. hijacks three airliners, and takes them to Dawson's Field near Amman.
17–27 September	Jordanian Civil War.
27 September	(Jordanian) Cairo Agreement between Hussein and Palestinians.
28 September	Nasser dies. Sadat takes over as President (at first as acting President).

1971

February	Jarring submits proposals to Egypt and Israel – rejected.
April	Sadat offers opening of Suez Canal for phased Israeli withdrawal – rejected.
13–20 July	Second Jordanian Civil War. Palestinian guerrillas ejected from Jordan.

1972

May	Japanese Red Army attacks Lod Airport.
September	Black September group kills Israeli athletes at Munich Olympics.

1973

April	Arab military commanders agree plan of attack against Israel.
May	Israel mobilises on basis of false intelligence.
13 September	Major Syrian–Israeli air battle.
28 September	Schonau Affair begins.
6 October	Egyptians attack across Suez Canal, Syrians on Golan.
6–7 October	Arab successes in pushing Israeli forces back.
8 October	Israeli counter-attack in Sinai fails; Syrians halted on Golan.
9–12 October	Israelis recover initiative on Golan.
14 October	Egyptian offensive defeated.

16 October	Israelis cross Suez Canal.
18 October	Saudis impose oil embargo on U.S.
22 October	First ceasefire.
23 October	Israelis complete encirclement of Egyptian Third Army.
24 October	Second ceasefire.
December	Egypt, Israel and Jordan meet (briefly) at Geneva.

1974

January	First Sinai Disengagement Agreement.
February	Egyptians begin clearance of Suez Canal.
March	Saudis lift oil embargo.
April	Rabin succeeds Golda Meir as Israeli Prime Minister.
May	Golan Disengagement Agreement.

1975

| May onwards | Communal conflict in Lebanon escalates into civil war. |
| September | Second Sinai Disengagement Agreement. |

1976

January	Syrian-controlled Palestinian groups intervene in Lebanon.
March–April	Widespread disturbances in occupied West Bank.
May	Syrian Army invades Lebanon.
July	The Entebbe raid.
September	Riyadh Conference temporarily defuses situation in Lebanon.

1977

| January | Jimmy Carter inaugurated as U.S. President and (February) Secretary of State Vance tours Middle East. Food price riots in Egypt. |
| March | Hussein and Arafat reconciled at Afro–Arab Summit in Cairo. Carter calls for Palestinian homeland, |

under Jordanian tutelage.
Rabin at the centre of second major
scandal to hit his party in months.
Palestine National Council, meeting in
Cairo, agrees on possibility of negotiating
with Israel.

April — Trouble flares up in Lebanon leading to a
virtual 'proxy' war between Israel and
Syria.

May — Widespread disturbances in West Bank.
Menachim Begin's Likud Party wins
Israeli elections and forms coalition.
U.S. and U.S.S.R. issue joint statement on
Middle East, calling for reconvening of
Geneva Conference.

June — Egypt and U.S.S.R. in unsuccessful talks
aimed at reconciliation.

July — Talks between Begin and Carter, and
between Sadat and Hussein.
Israel announces policy of settling West
Bank and (November) establishes Jordan
River as new border.

October — U.S.S.R. steps up support for P.L.O.

November — Israeli bombing raids against Lebanon.
Begin appeals to Sadat for peace.
Sadat agrees to address Knesset (does so
on 21st).

November–
January: — Series of bilateral talks involving Egypt,
Israel, U.S. and Britain culminate in
Begin's visit to Egypt and establishment
of Israeli–Egyptian political and military
committees.
Sadat closes P.L.O. offices in Cairo and
sacks pro-Soviet ministers in his
government.

December — Tripoli conference attended by Syria,
Libya, Algeria, Iraq, and P.L.O. rejects
Sadat initiative.
Begin rejects P.L.O.s right to represent
Palestinians.

1978
     January   Carter talks with Hussein and Sadat
during world tour.
Israeli–Egyptian political and military
committees meet in Jerusalem and Cairo.

REFERENCES

Chapter 1:

1. Kurzman, *Genesis*, p. 505.
2. ibid., p. 556.

Chapter 2:

1. Hobsbawn, *Age of Revolution*, p. 131.
2. Cited in Mansfield, *The British in Egypt*, p. 4.
3. Cited in Wilson (ed.), *The Political Diaries of C. P. Scott*, p. 255.

Chapter 3:

1. Cited in Gilbert, *The Arab–Israeli Conflict*, p. 10.
2. Cited in ibid., p. 14.
3. Cited in Ben-Gurion, *Israel*, p. 54.
4. Cited in Mansfield, op. cit., p. 287.

Chapter 4:

1. From Pinsker, *Auto-emancipation*, cited in Rodinson, *Israel – a Colonial Settler State?*, p. 40.
2. From Herzl, *The Jewish State*, cited in Rodinson, op. cit., p. 42.
3. From Pinsker, *Auto-emancipation*, cited in Rodinson, op. cit., p.41.
4. This remarkable letter is quoted in full in Vital, *Zionism*, p. 295.

5. From Herzl's diaries, cited in Ghilan, *How Israel Lost Its Soul*, pp. 29–30.
6. Ben-Gurion, *Israel*, p. 827.
7. ibid., p. 839.
8. Cited in Luttwak and Horowitz, *Israeli Army*, p. 79.
9. Cited in Ben-Gurion, op. cit., p. 386.
10. Cited in Stephens, *Nasser*, pp. 112–13.
11. ibid., p. 133.
12. ibid., p. 163.
13. Eden, *Full Circle*, p. 352.
14. ibid., p. 353.
15. The comment was directed at Anthony Nutting, who later resigned over Suez. The incident is cited in Mansfield, op. cit., p. 312.

Chapter 5:

1. O'Ballance, *Sinai Campaign*, p. 16.
2. Luttwak and Horowitz, op. cit., pp. 114–16.
3. ibid., p. 140.
4. Dayan, *Story of My Life*, p. 194.

Chapter 6:

1. Cited in Draper, *Israel and World Politics*, p. 20.
2. ibid., p. 22.

Chapter 7:

1. Ismael, *The Arab Left*, p. 87.
2. Cited in Ben-Gurion, op. cit., p. 752.
3. Cited in Draper, op. cit., p. 32.
4. ibid., p. 33.

Chapter 8:

1. Kimche and Bawley, *Sandstorm*, pp. 163–4.
2. Teveth, *Tanks of Tammuz*, p. 189.
3. O'Ballance, *Third Arab–Israeli War*, pp. 230–31.
4. Churchill and Churchill, *Six-Day War*, p. 186.

Chapter 9:

1. Peres, *David's Sling*, p. 13.
2. Reprinted from *Ma'ariv* in Bondy, etc., *Mission Survival*, pp. 487–91.
3. Ben-Gurion, op. cit., p. 843 (Ben-Gurion's emphasis).

Chapter 10:

1. Luttwak and Horowitz, op. cit., p. 307.
2. O'Ballance, *Arab Guerrilla Power*, p. 61.

Chapter 11:

1. O'Ballance, *Electronic War*, p. 43.

Chapter 12:

1. Heikal, *Road to Ramadan*, p. 165.

Chapter 13:

1. Cited in Herzog, *War of Atonement*, p. 15.
2. ibid., p. 43.

Chapter 14:

1. Dayan, op. cit., p. 418.
2. Palit, *Return to Sinai*, pp. 95–6.
3. *Sunday Times* 'Insight' Team, *Yom Kippur War*, p. 161.
4. Palit, op. cit., pp. 84–6.
5. Herzog, op. cit., p. 212.
6. ibid.
7. Guderian, *Panzer Leader*, p. 107.

Chapter 15:

1. *Sunday Times* 'Insight' Team, op. cit., pp. 484–5.
2. Gloria Jahoda, *The Trail of Tears* (Allen and Unwin, 1976), p. 22.
3. *The Outlaw Josey Wales*.

SELECT BIBLIOGRAPHY

Abir, M. *Sharm el-Sheikh–Bab el-Mandeb: The Strategic Balance and Israel's Southern Approaches* (Hebrew University, Jerusalem, 1974).

Allon, Y. *The Making of Israel's Army* (Vallentine Mitchell, 1970).

Bell, J. B. *The Long War* (Prentice-Hall, Englewood Cliffs, N.J., 1969).

Berger, E. *The Covenant and the Sword* (Routledge and Kegan Paul, 1965).

Ben-Gurion, D. *Israel – A Personal History* (New English Library, 1972).

Bondy, R., Zmora, O. and Bashan, R. (eds.) *Mission Survival* (W. H. Allen, 1967).

Calvocoressi, P. *World Politics Since 1945* (Longmans, 1968).

Cameron, J. *The Making of Israel* (Secker and Warburg, 1976).

Chaliand, G. *The Palestinian Resistance* (Pelican, 1972).

Childers, E. *Common Sense About the Arab World* (Gollancz, 1960).

Chomsky, N. *Peace in the Middle East?* (Fontana, 1975).

Churchill, R. S. and Churchill, W. S. *The Six-Day War* (Heinemann, 1967).

Cole, G. D. H. *The Intelligent Man's Guide to the Post-War World* (Gollancz, 1948).

Davis, U., Mack, A. and Yuval-Davis, N. (eds.) *Israel and the Palestinians* (Ithaca Press, 1975).

Dayan, M. *Diary of the Sinai Campaign* (Weidenfeld and Nicolson, 1966).

Dayan, M. *Story of My Life* (Weidenfeld and Nicolson, 1976).

Dekmejian, R. H. *Egypt Under Nasser* (University of London, 1972).

Draper, T. *Israel and World Politics* (Secker and Warburg, 1968).

Eden, A. *Full Circle* (Cassell, 1960).

Gathorne-Hardy, G. M. *A Short History of International Affairs 1920–39* (O.U.P., 1950).

Ghilan, M. *How Israel Lost Its Soul* (Pelican, 1974).

Gilbert, M. *The Arab–Israeli Conflict: Its History in Maps* (Weidenfeld and Nicolson, 1976).

Gilbert, M. *Jewish History Atlas* (Weidenfeld and Nicolson, 1976).

Golan, G. 'The Soviet Union and the P.L.O.', *Adelphi Papers 131* (International Institute of Strategic Studies, 1976).

Golan, M. *The Secret Conversations of Henry Kissinger* (Bantam Books, New York, 1976).

Guderian, H. *Panzer Leader* (Futura, 1974).

Halliday, F. *Arabia Without Sultans* (Pelican, 1975).

Hashavia, A. *History of the Six-Day War* (Ledory, Tel Aviv, 1969).

Heikal, M. *The Road to Ramadan* (Fontana, 1976).

Herzog, C. *The War of Atonement* (Weidenfeld and Nicolson, 1975).

Hobsbawm, E. J. *The Age of Revolution 1789–1848* (Mentor, 1962).

Horowitz, D. *From Yalta to Vietnam* (Penguin, 1967).

Hussein, King. *My 'War' with Israel* (Owen, 1969).

Hussein, M. *Class Conflict in Egypt, 1945–1970* (Monthly Review Press, New York, 1973).

Ismael, T. Y. *The Arab Left* (Syracuse University, 1976).

Jones, W. B. *The Lightning War* (Robert Hale, 1967).

Kent, M. *Oil & Empire* (Macmillan, 1976).

Khouri, F. J. *The Arab–Israeli Dilemma* (Syracuse University, 1976).

Khruschev, N. *Khruschev Remembers* (Sphere, 1971).

Kimche, D. and Bawley, D. *The Sandstorm* (Secker and Warburg, 1968).

Kurzman, D. *Genesis 1948* (New American Library, New York, 1972).

Lacqueur, W. *Confrontation* (Abacus, 1976).

Lacqueur, W. (ed.) *The Israel–Arab Reader* (Bantam, New York, 1976).

Lacqueur, W. *The Road to War 1967* (Weidenfeld and Nicolson, 1968).

Lorch, N. *The Edge of the Sword* (Putnam, New York, 1961).

Love, K. *Suez – the Twice Fought War* (Longman, 1970).

Luttwak, D. and Horowitz, D. *The Israeli Army* (Allen Lane, 1975).

Mansfield, P. *The British in Egypt* (Holt, Rinehart and Winston, New York, 1971).

Mansfield, P. *Nasser's Egypt* (Penguin, 1965).

Maull, H. 'Future Arab Options', *Adelphi Papers 114* (International Institute of Strategic Studies, 1975).

Meir, G. *My Life* (Weidenfeld and Nicolson, 1975).

Nutting, A. *The Arabs* (New American Library, New York, 1964).

O'Ballance, E. *The Arab–Israeli War 1948* (Faber and Faber, 1956).

O'Ballance, E. *The Sinai Campaign 1956* (Faber and Faber, 1959).

O'Ballance, E. *The War in the Yemen* (Faber and Faber, 1971).

O'Ballance, E. *The Third Arab–Israeli War* (Faber and Faber, 1972).

O'Ballance, E. *The Electronic War in the Middle East 1968–70* (Faber, 1974).

O'Ballance, E. *Arab Guerrilla Power 1967–72* (Faber, 1974).

Odell, P. *Oil and World Power* (Pelican, 1974).

Owen, R. (ed.) *Essays on the Crisis in Lebanon* (Ithaca Press, 1976).

Palit, D. K. *Return to Sinai: The Arab–Israeli War 1973* (Compton Russell, 1974).

Peres, S. *David's Sling – the Arming of Israel* (Weidenfeld and Nicolson, 1970).

Phillips, D. *Skyjack* (Harrap, 1973).

Rodinson, M. *Israel and the Arabs* (Pelican, 1968).

Rodinson, M. *Israel – a Colonial Settler State?* (Monad Press, 1973).

Safran, N. *From War to War* (Pegasus, New York, 1969).

Sampson, A. *The Seven Sisters* (Coronet, 1976).

Sharabi, H. 'The Arab–Israeli Conflict: The Next Phase', *Adelphi Papers 114* (International Institute of Strategic Studies, 1975).

Stephens, R. *Nasser* (Pelican, 1971).

Stetler, R. (ed.) *Palestine* (Ramparts, San Francisco, 1972).

Stockholm International Peace Research Institute, *The Arms Trade with the Third World* (Humanities Press, New York, 1971).

Stone, I. F. *The Haunted Fifties* (Merlin, 1964).

Strachey, J. *The End of Empire* (Gollancz, 1959).

Sunday Times 'Insight' Team, *The Yom Kippur War* (André Deutsch, 1975).

Thomson, D. *Europe Since Napoleon* (Pelican, 1966).

Teveth, S. *The Tanks of Tummaz* (Weidenfeld and Nicolson, 1968).

Tugendhat, C. *Oil – The Biggest Business* (Eyre & Spottiswoode, 1968).

Vital, D. *The Origins of Zionism* (O.U.P., 1975).

Whetten, L. L. *The Canal War* (M.I.T. Press, 1974).

Wilson, T. (ed.) *The Political Diaries of C. P. Scott 1911–1928* (Cornell University, New York, 1970).

Young, P. *The Israeli Campaign 1967* (William Kimber, 1967).

Magazines and other publications consulted include: *The Times*, the *Sunday Times*, the *Financial Times*, the *Guardian*, the *Economist*, *New Statesman*, the *Listener*, *New Left Review*, C.I.S. Publications (London), Merip Reports (Middle East Research and Information Project, Washington D.C.), documents from the P.L.O. and the Arab League; Jerusalem Papers on Peace Problems; and the annual surveys of the International Institute for Strategic Studies.

INDEX